GOD IS
BRAZILIAN

GOD IS
BRAZILIAN

CHARLES MILLER
THE MAN WHO BROUGHT FOOTBALL TO BRAZIL

JOSH LACEY

TEMPUS

First published 2005

Tempus Publishing Limited
The Mill, Brimscombe Port,
Stroud, Gloucestershire, GL5 2QG
www.tempus-publishing.com

British Library Cataloguing in Publication Data.
A catalogue record for this book is available from the British Library.

ISBN 0 7524 3414 4

Typesetting and origination by Tempus Publishing Limited
Printed and bound in Great Britain

Acknowledgements

Flying back from Brazil to Britain is no fun. The flight leaves late at night and, propelled into the future by the time difference, arrives midway through the following afternoon. Confined in that air-conditioned tube, fed on plastic food, trying to sleep, failing, you have several hours to think about the contrast between the sun-drenched place that you are leaving and the cold, grey, puritanical place that you are heading towards. When the flight is late, the baggage is delayed, and you know that your wife has been waiting for an hour and a half in Arrivals, you can't help hurrying through the customs hall, bad-tempered and jumpy. My blotchy skin, red eyes and expression of impatient fury must have made me look exactly like a frightened drug courier. 'Could I have a word, sir?' When the customs official tugged my elbow, I rolled my eyes and sighed. If nothing else had made him suspicious, that would have done. He asked me to put my bags on the table, and started rifling through them. 'Where have you been, sir?'

'Brazil.'

He nodded, and poked into the dark recesses of my bag. I could imagine the associations flicking through his mind: South America... Colombia... white powder... a nice drugs bust to end his shift and enliven his daily report. He said, 'And what was the purpose of your visit?'

'I've been doing some research.'

'About what?'

'Charles Miller.'

'Oh, yeah? Who's he?'

As I told him, the customs official slowly lost interest in my bag. He glanced inside, lifted a couple of items without really looking at them, held them in his hands and said, 'You're serious? From Scotland?' I gave him a potted history of Charlie Miller. He grinned and zipped up my bag, but wouldn't let me leave. Before I went anywhere, he wanted to know the answer to one question that had been bugging him ever since the last World Cup. 'So, why are they so bloody good at football? What have they got that we haven't?'

I would like to thank him, and all the other people who have shown an interest in this book. Many of them, like that customs official at Heathrow, gave me no more than a few words of encouragement or a reminder that this book was worth writing. Others provided a useful contact or an unexpected idea, an indispensable lead or a solution to some infuriating problem that had been blocking my progress. To all those people who helped me, sent me an e-mail, stopped to chat or simply pointed me in the right direction, I would like to express my gratitude. I was constantly astounded by the generosity of people in Britain, Brazil and, via letter or e-mail, all around the world, who freely gave me so much of their time. I would like to thank all of them for their help with ideas, material and inspiration. Without them, this book would not have been possible. Any errors of fact or interpretation are entirely my responsibility.

There are some people whom I would like to thank by name. Firstly, I am immensely grateful to Aidan Hamilton and John Mills, both of whom have already written about Charles Miller. They were always generous with information, and their passion for the subject was a great inspiration to me.

When I approached the families of the main participants in this story, all of them were hospitable and generous. I should particularly like to thank the members of the Miller family who helped me, especially Therezina Miller O'May Burt and her husband, Maurice Burt; Vera Miller; Stella Motta; Charles Miller Jnr; Luiz Fernando Miller Mello; and one of the few remaining members of the family in Britain, Mrs Ada Mobbs.

In Brazil, I should also like to thank the Rudge and del Picchia families. In Britain, I am grateful to Mr R. Fromm, the husband of the late Enid Fromm (née Ellaby).

I should also like to thank the following people who guided my attempts to uncover the life of Charles Miller in Britain and Brazil. Without them, I would have been lost. Gênese Andrade, David P.

Appleby, Alex Bellos, Leslie Bethell, James and Monica Birkinshaw, Guy Burton, Paul Catchpole, Geoffrey Crewe, John Cunningham, Clare Davidson, Maria Augusta Fonseca, Ross G. Forman, Robert Greenhill, Hilmar Hambloch, Scott Hamilton, Ulrich Hesse-Lichtenberger, Nigel and Darcy Hunter, Dave Juson, Margaret and Raymond Krinker, Fred Lane, Telê Porto Ancona Lopez, Jo and Derek Marcus, Oliver Marshall, Rory Miller, John Milton, Celia Moss, Stuart Nicol, Dr Robert Oakley, Ines de Oliveira, Ernesto Paglia, Raul Passarelli Jr, Kenneth Payne, Kate Pemberton, John Platt, Hester Plumridge, Harvey Sachs, Jessie Sklair, Barbara and Tassilo Siebert, Professor Goffredo da Silva Telles Jr, Flávia Toni, Robert Turner, Neil Williamson, Gibby Zobel.

I spent many happy hours in the London Library and the British Library, both at St Pancras and Colindale, and should like to thank the staff for their patience and assistance. I should also like to thank the staff of Glasgow University Library, the Public Records Office at Kew, the Biblioteca National in Rio de Janeiro, the Special Collections at University College London, Yale University Library and the Casa de Menotti del Picchia in Itapira. I should also like to thank the staff of the following institutions in São Paulo: the Clube Atlético São Paulo, the British Council Library, the Estação da Luz, the Biblioteca Mario de Andrade, the libraries at IEB and USP, the Centro Histórico at Mackenzie College and the Centro Pro Memoria at Club Athletico Paulistano.

I should also like to thank Neil Cassar at the Hampshire Football Association; Betty Hendry at the Watts Library in Greenock; Carol Morgan at the library of the Institution of Civil Engineers; Natasha Cole-Jones and Laura Taylor at the Lloyds TSB Group Archives; Paula Best, Archivist at the Wigmore Hall; Caroline Shaw at the Rothschild Archives; Tim Pearce and Christine Leighton at the Cheltonian Society, Cheltenham College; Cliff Davies at Wadham College, Oxford; Andrew Davis at the National Maritime Museum in Greenwich; Dirk Mansen at the HSV Museum in Hamburg; Elaine Camroux-Mclean at the Foreign & Commonwealth Office; Felipe Fortuna at the Brazilian Embassy in London.

In São Paulo, I am very grateful to Fernanda Gomes at the British Consulate; Nora D.M. Silva at Mackenzie College; Silvana Fontanelli at the Centro Pro Memoria do Club Athletico Paulistano; Philip

Hamer and Steve Wingrove at the British Chamber of Commerce; Romeu de Freitas at the archives of TV Cultura; Tim Butchard at the British Council; Rachid Benammar, headmaster of St Paul's School; the staff and residents of Stacey House; Rev. Roger Bird at St Paul's church.

I should also like to thank James Howarth, Holly Bennion and Rob Sharman at Tempus.

I shall not even try to name all the friends who have supported me in various ways, but I should particularly like to thank Chris Beauman, Eric Brown, Travis Elborough, Fergus Livingstone, Christine Kidney, Edward Platt and the Sklair family.

Finally, there are two people without whom I could not have written this book. The first is my wife, Andrea. The second is my godfather, Hugh Geddes. I would particularly like to thank him for the gift of some wonderful French wine, and apologise for what I did with it. He gave me three cases to educate my palate, and I sold them to pay for a flight to Brazil.

Football will not catch on here. It is like borrowed clothes that do not fit. For a foreign custom to establish itself in another country it must be in harmony with the people's way of life, and we already have the corn straw ball game.

Graciliano Ramos

*The sand of the desert is sodden red
Red with the wreck of a square that broke
The Gatling's jammed and the Colonel's dead,
And the regiment blind with dust and smoke.
The river of death has brimmed his banks,
And England's far and honour a name;
But the voice of a schoolboy rallies the ranks:
'Play up! play up! and play the game.'*

Vitai Lampada, Henry Newbolt

Introduction

The rich kids from Mackenzie College have been let out early. They're standing on the pavement, sucking a surreptitious cigarette, jostling and gossiping, waiting for their mums or dads or chauffeurs to whip them home. Some of them, the squares, the swots, proudly wear the school's uniform – a sweatshirt emblazoned with a big red capital M – and others hide their allegiance under a Benetton jumper or a black leather jacket. Massive cars with tinted windows jam the road, queuing to pause beside the group. A gleaming silver S-class Mercedes eases to a standstill. The passenger door swings open. A teenager pushes forwards, waves to her classmates, leaps inside and tosses her satchel onto the back seat. The door slams. With a snarl, the Mercedes rejoins the traffic, and its place is taken by a Toyota Land Cruiser. A rottweiler hangs out of the back window, blinking, slavering, his tail thumping when one of the boys emerges from the crowd and reaches for the door handle.

This is the old centre of São Paulo, the derelict heart of one of the most dangerous cities on the planet. That's what they'll tell you, anyway. Tourists are advised to leave cameras, jewellery and passports in their hotels. Doormen guard the entrance to every apartment block, scrutinising visitors through the boxed eye of a CCTV camera before easing aside the tall metal gates which divide residents from pedestrians, insiders from outsiders. Bulletproof windows are a standard extra offered on all but the cheapest cars. Residents swap horror stories. Some accept an occasional mugging as an additional urban tax. Others choose to insulate themselves. I know one wealthy woman who has always lived in São Paulo but has been robbed only twice in her life – once in Portobello Market, once on Park Lane. On her annual shopping trips to London, where she sheds her usual entourage, neglecting the precautions that she always takes at home, she comes into contact with the type of people who could usually get nowhere near her. Here in São Paulo, they wouldn't get within touching distance. In the sprawling suburbs of a city whose population is roaring towards twenty million, most of whom wallow in dismal poverty, the rich spend their lives cocooned behind high walls and toughened glass, protected from the streets by barbed wire, reinforced steel, underfed dogs and taut bodyguards with bulky shoulder holsters. Many of the middle class never even come into the centre of São Paulo. They recognise the city's oldest monuments only from pictures, and don't even know the names of these historic streets. It's too dangerous, they say. Too scary. Nothing will tempt them to desert their anodyne suburbs and hygienic shopping malls.

Walk for five minutes down the street from Mackenzie College, head through the Praça República, and you'll see why. Under the shadow of tall palms, lit by the jaundiced glow of flickering street-lamps, whores and drug addicts hiss at passers-by, reciting an endless list of promises and invitations. The homeless have pitched their tents on the pavement. A beggar gestures at the stumps of his legs, cauterised above the knees, and stretches out a bruised palm, begging for coins. Stallholders sell pirated tapes, cheap clothes, sugar cane, cigarettes, plastic lighters, counterfeit metro tickets. A child writhes in the gutter, both hands tucked down the front of his shorts, his eyes closed, his mind absent, frazzled by drugs.

The kids from Mackenzie College don't walk anywhere. They emerge from the school in a group and stick together while waiting for their rides. They don't wander. They don't even sneak down the street to the nearest bar, where a bunch of mechanics in blue dungarees are drinking beer. Nor do they glance across the road at the stolid entrance of the Protestant cemetery. If they did, they'd see me. I'm standing on the steps, doing nothing, watching them. But they don't look up – they have Prada bags to ogle, gossip to swap, scores to settle, and impatient parents to look out for.

There have never been many Protestants in São Paulo, and most of those who did live here took care to die elsewhere, but they were a sufficiently powerful minority to grab a prime slab of real estate to bury the incurable, the accident-prone and the stillborn. Alongside them lie those oldies who could not endure the long voyage home or the miserable weather that awaited them there. Just like the governors of Mackenzie College, the administrators of this cemetery, the prominent Paulista Protestants, have never seen any reason to move. Over the past few decades the local area may have lost its lustre, but these wide streets will be gentrified again one day. The rich will return, and pick up where they left off.

I turn around, walk up the stone staircase and pass through the tall black wrought-iron gates that protect the cemetery from intruders. Gravel crunches under my feet. A gardener kneels on one of the graves, pulling up weeds. As I pass, he lifts his eyes, and we nod to one another. Looking around, I notice a small army of uniformed gardeners and wardens, striding between the graves, polishing the headstones, keeping an eye on visitors, ejecting strays. For this intimate cemetery, smaller than a country churchyard, the number of attendants seems ludicrous. In Britain, one part-time gardener would do the same work as these eight professionals. I stroll into the most deserted corner of the graveyard, furthest from the gardeners, and try to forget them. It's a test. Can I convince myself that I am standing in a cemetery in Britain rather than Brazil? The light is different, of course, but I can pretend that the British summer sun occasionally glares with this harsh beauty. The polished marble, the gravel, the modest crosses, the cropped grass, the mottled stone – all of these could belong to a British churchyard. Looking at the gravestones, I see a succession of recognisably English and Scottish names. As in a cemetery in any British port, they are peppered with an occasional German or Scandinavian. Over there, I can see Hubert James Singleton Boyes, born in Swinton. Here is John Sutherland, originally from Aberdeen, now lying alongside his wife Maria and their three children, Christina, Elizabeth and Archibald. This stone is sacred to the memory of Hariett, beloved wife of F.C. Harrison, born in Nottingham, England, 1868. Beside her, I find Annie Harrison from Maidstone, and Kate Harrison, beloved daughter, born in Croydon, deeply regretted by all who knew her. A large tomb records the Rule family, the plaques beginning with Joseph Edward, born on 28 January 1845, and culminating with Anthony McCulloch MBE, who died on 2 December 2000. On the stones surrounding them, the names read like a roll call in a British classroom: Anderson, Andrews, Baring, Blackford, Campbell, Cotton, Crook, Dickinson, Dulley, Forster, Hall, Holland, Hunter, Lane, Lister, Neal, Nicol, Norris, Perman, Ralston, Scott, Singer, Skinner, Snape, Speers, Warner, White, Wilson, Wrigg. The repetition of these names might lull me into thinking that I really am walking through a country churchyard in England or Scotland, but one fact repeatedly nags at me, disrupting my pretence. Not the brash sunlight, nor the heat, nor the sound of roaring traffic and the helicopters buzzing overhead, but the empty plots scattered between the marble tombs. In Britain, these unused plots would be grassed over, neatly mown, patiently awaiting an owner. Here, they have been put to good use, and turned into miniature vegetable gardens. The fertile soil is covered with neat lines of tomato and rocket. Seed packets perched on sticks remind the gardener what he has planted and where. The tomato plants are tiny, not yet bearing any fruit, but the rocket looks excellent, pert and crunchy, and I'm tempted to snap off a couple of stalks to check the flavour. Grown in this compost, it must taste great. The bones of long-dead Protestants now make a generous contribution to someone's lunch. Perched among the seedlings, a white card is scrawled with a phone number and a message: *sepultura disponível*. This grave is available. Call now if you would like to make a reservation.

Down in the other corner, I find what I've come here to see. The Miller family plot has three heavy stone crosses and a succession of black marble rectangles inscribed with brass names and dates. Here is the sister who died before her second birthday. Here is the brother who never saw twenty. Here are the uncles, the cousins, the siblings who collapsed in this unfamiliar country, their foreign bodies worn down by heat and hard work and the strangeness of it all. And here is the man whom I have come to see. In the melancholy silence, I try to imagine what he was doing that day in June, a year ago, an hour before dawn. Did he stay right here, lying on his back? Or did he pad along the gravel to the gates and peer across the road to the cafe? From here, he wouldn't have been able to see the television screen, but he could have watched the cluster of mechanics in their blue dungarees, each of them clutching a beer in one hand, a coffee in the other, all of them united as they shouted encouragement at the players, their players, their heroes. From the expressions on their faces, their yells of joy or cries of horror, he would have been able to tell who was winning. When the game ended and the wrong side won, he turned his back on their delirious whooping.

That day, I was in London, sitting on the sofa with my wife, staring at the blurry screen of our small telly. My eyes hurt. We drank coffee. My wife was going to be late for work, but no-one in her office would mind. No-one would even notice. That day everyone would be late, not only in her office but throughout the country. Outside, the usual sounds of commuter traffic, squealing brakes and furious horns, had been replaced by unexpected noises – birdsong, a distant rumbling train, a child's voice. Later, I talked to a friend of mine who lives in Brazil. Not being a football fan, she hadn't bothered getting up at 3 a.m. to watch the game. Nevertheless, she was woken by the echoing shouts of despair or elation which greeted every goal. And they must have been bloody loud: she lives on the twenty-seventh floor of a tower block in the centre of São Paulo.

For two hours on that Friday morning, the streets were deserted in England and Brazil. Their populations clustered around TV sets, watching two teams kick a white ball around a grassy rectangle. This particular beautiful game was inconveniently timed for both of them – rush hour in Britain, pre-dawn in Brazil – having been planned for the convenience of spectators in Japan and Korea, but that didn't matter. Commuters missed their trains. Schools started late. In the absence of war, nations need a focus, a collective obsession that unites their citizens, and this was ours. For those of us who watched it in England, the match was a dreary disappointment. The English team wilted in the heat and crumbled under the Brazilian onslaught. After ninety minutes, eleven Englishmen stood on the pitch with slumped shoulders, weeping like children, wondering what had hit them. It can have been little consolation for Seaman, Beckham, Campbell or Ferdinand to remember that this particular sport had been introduced to Brazil by a British man who played for Southampton. But they probably didn't know. Not many people do. Charles Miller has been forgotten. A good proportion of Brazilians recognise his name, but even well-educated football fans can recite no more than a few inaccurate facts about his life. In Britain, no-one has a clue who he was, just as no-one knows why AC Milan isn't called AC Milano or Dynamo Moscow play in blue and white shirts.

Charles William Miller was born in Brazil but, like most of the sons of wealthier expatriates and Empire-builders, he went back home for his education. At the frail age of nine, he was put on a ship and sent to a boarding school in Britain. Ten years later, Charles sailed back to Brazil. On the long voyage, he practised his ball skills, dribbling from one end of the deck to the other. From his education, he had only learned one lesson that really mattered to him: the rules of football. His talent matched his enthusiasm. Having captained his school team, he played for the St Mary's Church of England Young Men's Association (now better known as Southampton FC) and the famous Corinthians. When the ship docked in Santos, Charles discovered to his horror that no-one knew how to play the beautiful game. The expatriate community retained many British customs – cricket on Sundays, afternoon tea at four, visiting cards on silver trays – but not football. Charles had found his mission. He summoned his friends, divided them into two teams and explained the rules.

A hundred and eight years later, England holds its breath while Ronaldinho lines up a free-kick. The ball soars, dips, slithers into the back of the net. Brazil leaps to its feet. In England, people put their hands over their eyes, then peek through their fingers to watch the replay. There it is again. There goes Seaman, wandering off his line. There goes the ball. And we've let those sneaky Brazilians grab another. A few minutes later, the scorer of that audacious goal gets himself sent off, but ten Brazilians seem to have no difficulty defending their lead against eleven Englishmen, and the game ends 2-1. Brazil heads towards the semi-final. England stands on the pitch, dazed, blinking, weepy. What would Charles Miller have thought? What would he have done if he had been there? Would he have hugged Rio Ferdinand and patted Beckham on the back? Would he have brushed away David Seaman's tears with a white silk hankie? No – he would have reminded them which shirt they were wearing, and why, and what it meant to wear those colours, to own that cap, to represent that country. I can see him now, hurrying back and forth across the pitch, going from player to player, whispering a few words of encouragement to each, telling them the words that had resounded throughout his own life: Play up! Play up! And play the game!

At the end of the nineteenth century, the British were everywhere. Wherever they went, they took their values. As Jan Morris writes,

'There were tastes and taboos so pungently British that the whole world knew them, and expected them to be honoured. *The Times*, the club, leaving the gentlemen to their cigars, the stiff upper lip, hunting halloos at midnight by tight young subalterns on guest nights, bacon and eggs, walking around the deck a hundred times each morning, cricket, *Abide With Me* – all these were imperial emblems, symptoms of Britishness, parodied and envied everywhere.' Britons amused themselves – and created their cohesive sense of identity – with famous and warmly remembered stories of pride, pluck and politeness. There were the two Englishmen whose paths crossed in some vast, barren desert, but neither even nodded to one another because they had not been formally introduced. There was the colonist who died of thirst on the banks of a river, unable to drink because he had no cup. These charming, idiotic and obviously untrue stories gave the world a keen sense of Britishness. And if someone failed to see the funny side, the Brits could always shout for help, and the world's biggest navy would come steaming down the coast.

The Victorians built an army of strong-chinned young chaps, tough-minded and broad-shouldered, ready to defend Britain and the Empire against the encroaching hordes. Wherever they went, these strapping young men took their games. Golf to America in the 1790s. Cricket to Barbados in 1806. Rugby to New Zealand in 1870. Football to Japan in 1874. And so on around the world. Although many of the players might have claimed that they were simply showing the natives a jolly good way to spend an afternoon, there is no doubt that many civil servants, administrators and theorists of the Empire understood exactly why games should be encouraged. Team sports instilled team ethics, displayed the importance of rules and regulations, and sublimated sexual desire. Manliness and muscle, self-reliance and independence, temperance and team spirit, fair play and patriotism – imperial games imposed imperial values. When these ideals came into contact with other cultures, strange things happened. The rules of soccer might have stayed the same in London and Lhasa, Birmingham and Buenos Aires, Dundee and Delhi, Southampton and São Paulo, but the players and spectators added their own innovations, instilling a sniff of their individual culture, sneaking under the skin of their rulers, using a feint, a move, a pass, which would never have occurred to their imperial overlords.

Brazil was not part of the British Empire, but British values, institutions, expertise and money permeated the country. Even São Paulo, a provincial little town of only 20,000 people, plopped in the middle of uninteresting farmland, had a strong British community that led a determinedly colonial existence. During the nineteenth century, South America had much stronger emotional, economic and cultural ties to Europe than to North America. The sophisticates of Rio de Janeiro or Buenos Aires would follow every change in artistic or cultural fashion in Paris, Berlin and London, but turn up their noses at anyone who chose to live in a hick town like New York or San Francisco. Likewise, the tight historical links between England and Portugal led directly to strong ties between Britain and Brazil. When the Portuguese Royal Family fled from Napoleon, they sailed from Lisbon to Rio under British escort. London banks supplied the capital that paid for Brazil's expansion, and the country's official bankers were the Rothschilds. British engineers built railways, ports and bridges, creating an infrastructure to facilitate Brazil's economic expansion, while British manufacturers exploited the Brazilian markets for their goods. This led to some ludicrous anomalies. If you were a Victorian visitor to Brazil, you probably would have returned to Britain with some nice souvenirs of your travels. A decorated knife, perhaps, or a frilly ethnic shawl. But you probably wouldn't have realised that both the knife and the shawl had been made in Scotland, and exported across the Atlantic to Brazil. While you wandered through the streets of São Paulo or Rio de Janeiro, admiring the local colour, you might have bought a bag of Brazil nuts to fend off hunger pangs. There can be nothing more Brazilian than Brazil nuts, can there? Maybe not, but any Brazil nuts eaten in São Paulo would have arrived in the city via Liverpool. Grown and harvested in Manaus (a city in the north of Brazil), they were transported across the Atlantic to Merseyside, cleaned, sorted and packaged in Liverpudlian factories, then sent back across the Atlantic to Santos (a port in the south of Brazil).

Along with cash, trade and railways, the British brought football. When Charles Miller sailed from Southampton in 1894, his luggage contained eight items that would change the course of Brazilian history: an air pump, two football shirts, a pair of football boots, a book of rules and two footballs. Now, hardly more than 100 years later, Brazil is the undisputed ruler of world football, winning the World Cup with infuriating regularity, producing an endless stream of players who make the rest of us look like lumbering loons. The spread of football from Britain to Brazil is a story with many ramifications, and acts as a neat riposte to anyone who is fearful of cultural imperialism. The English may have invented the rules of football, and the British may have carried the balls and the rule books in their imperial baggage, but Brazilians took to the game with unexpected skill and enthusiasm, and quickly remade it in their own image. A hundred years later, talents and skills are flowing back the other way. In Britain, just as all over Europe, home-grown players display the skills and techniques that they have learnt from their Brazilian colleagues. The gift is being repaid.

In 2002, having beaten England, the Brazilian team raced past Turkey in the semis, and faced Germany in the final. During slack moments in the game, TV cameras swept across the crowd crammed into the stadium, usually zooming in on the green and yellow bikinis bouncing on the terraces. At one moment, as the camera searched for lithe Brazilian babes, the picture picked out a long, slim banner waving among the fans. Whoever painted the banner had used English rather than Portuguese so the whole world would understand. In big bold capitals, they had painted three words on the white material: GOD IS BRAZILIAN.

Deus é brasileiro. It's a well-known phrase in Brazil, summing up something about the country, although perhaps no-one is quite sure exactly what. Nowadays, it would be impossible to say 'God is an Englishman' without sarcasm, but the inhabitants of Rio de Janeiro and São Paulo retain a quiet confidence that God really is Brazilian. If He came to earth, they feel sure, the Almighty would choose to live in Brazil. Who wouldn't? Take a stroll down the hot sand at Copacabana, and you might see Him, playing football on one of the impromptu pitches. He'll be barefoot, wearing shorts and a t-shirt, running as if He doesn't even notice the heat. He picks up a loose ball, dodges past one defender, then another, and fires an unstoppable shot at the goal.

Just like God, football is Brazilian. A hundred years ago, both of them might have been English, but there's no doubt where they live today. Charlie Miller can't be blamed for the deficiencies of the English football team, but he does bear the ultimate responsibility for the brilliance of the Brazilians. If Charlie Miller hadn't carried a couple of footballs across the Atlantic in 1894, Brazil might never have fallen in love with the game, and God might still be an Englishman.

One

For a journey through the jungle, there is no better implement than a tightly rolled umbrella. Before Daniel Makinson Fox sets sail for Brazil, this is the single piece of practical advice that he is offered by James Brunlees, his employer. Brunlees has a great deal of professional advice for him: the manifold advantages of hiring a British or German draughtsman rather than relying on locals; how to deal with a difficult client while retaining your composure in the tropical heat; the vital importance of keeping two copies of all notes, charts and details of expenses. Other than a strong handshake and a smile, Brunlees offers only one single sentence of personal advice. He strongly recommends the purchase of a well-built umbrella, preferably black.

On the slow voyage to South America, Fox sometimes retires to his cabin, removes the umbrella from his baggage, lays it on his bunk, and laughs at his own foolishness. James Brunlees is more than an employer to him – he has also been a teacher, a mentor, almost a father – but that is no reason to follow such a ludicrous piece of advice. What he should have done, Fox now realises, was purchase the umbrella, and leave it at his parents' house in Hull. Would Brunlees have discovered this act of deception? Of course not. They would be separated by a vast ocean, a month's voyage, 6,000 miles. For the next year, Fox would be his own man, supervised by no-one, plotting the route of a railway from Santos to São Paulo. His small act of personal betrayal would remain undetected. On his return to England, he could invent some picturesque tale to explain the umbrella's loss – a fight with a jaguar, perhaps, or a rainstorm that washed away half his possessions. As the ship leaves Southampton, passes the rainy shores of France, slides across the Bay of

Biscay and sails into the vast waters of the Atlantic, he is even tempted to toss the umbrella overboard. The skies are clear, the sun beats down on the deck, and he imagines hurling it like a javelin at one of the spouting whales, or a dolphin, or those flying fish that leap out of the water and hang for a moment alongside the ship, reminding Fox of the Scottish salmon that he knows so well.

Twenty days later, he arrives in Santos with the umbrella still occupying valuable space in his luggage. He hires a cook, two guides and several mules. Their small convoy leaves the coast and heads inland, following the course of the river. The ground is flat for a few miles, then shoots suddenly upwards at an abrupt angle, scrambling over scraggy rocks, engulfed by jungle. Foliage hides the sky. Creepers wriggle along the moist earth. The convoy makes slow progress. To his astonishment, Fox soon realises that Brunlees was right. Among all the luggage that he brought from England, nothing is more useful than that spindly umbrella. It protects him from the vicious midday sunlight. During the frequent rainstorms, his clothes stay dry. Hiking across streams, he has a rod to test the current and check for hidden holes in the riverbed. Struggling along overgrown paths, the umbrella acts as a walking stick, a scythe and even a weapon, slinging a snake from under his feet, skewering a succession of spiders, centipedes and giant ants. Ten times a day, he gives thanks for the strengths of British manufacture. A foreign-made umbrella would have buckled, crumpled, snapped and collapsed under the pressures of tropical life. He would have discarded it months ago, left it lying in the lush foliage, another unfamiliar species among the jungle's bewildering profusion. At night, they cut down trees to clear a space for their tents. They never need to use pegs: the ropes are tied to nearby trunks. Could there be a better demonstration of the jungle's astonishing density? Overhead, the foliage is so thick that the sun rarely penetrates. After three weeks, the small group of men emerges white-faced and wan, having hardly felt sunlight on their skin during the entire trek. They find themselves in a low valley. A light rain falls. Fog smothers the landscape. Seen through the mist, the distant trees could be spruce, ash or oak rather than palms, cacti and bananas. Fox raises his umbrella, opens his notebook and starts sketching a plan of the valley. Peering at the line of treetops through half-closed eyes, measuring proportions with his stubby pencil, he wonders whether he has ever really left England.

He works like this for eighteen months, walking every valley, clambering to the summit of every hill, plotting the landscape, discovering a route for the railway. On his infrequent meetings with other educated men – German merchants, cotton farmers from Texas, a Swiss botanist – he explains his scheme and endures their scorn. 'Your railway is a physical impossibility,' they say. 'The Portuguese could hardly even build a road from São Paulo to the coast. Have you seen the gradients? How can you even think of hauling a carriage up this slope? You English – you're mad! Brave, but mad.' Fox smiles, and invites them to come back in ten years to ride the railway. He will give them a free ticket, he promises.

Having walked the entire route from Santos to São Paulo three times, and paced several sections on twelve or fifteen separate occasions, he returns to the coast, and boards a ship bound for Southampton. The umbrella is packed carefully in his luggage. None of the spokes has snapped. The fabric has faded but never torn. Many compliments have been paid to that faithful umbrella, not least from the men who accompanied him. They stood disgruntled, soaked by the rain or scalded by the sun, while he remained dry and cool, shielded by his faithful umbrella. If he was not so busy, he might earn a nice living by importing well-made British umbrellas across the South Atlantic. But he has no time to think of commerce. He boards the ship and paces the deck, staring at Santos, wondering whether this will be his last sight of the port – its frilly palms, single-storey warehouses and distant mountains. Watching the figures on the dock, he has a sudden thought. He hurries to his trunk, removes the umbrella, runs down the quay and hands it to a fellow Englishman, the consul. They shake hands, and Fox promises to be back to pick it up.

São Paulo was founded by Jesuits on 25 January 1554 – by a neat and unlikely coincidence, the anniversary of St Paul's conversion. For the following few hundred years, the town remained a small, pleasant outpost in the jungles of southern Brazil, occasionally visited by travellers, rarely affected by events in the rest of the world. They had everything that a man could need: water, sunshine, good soil. If you throw a seed on the ground, they liked to say, a plant will grow. The temperate climate has no real winter, and two crops can be sown each year. Aided by slaves, the Paulistas led a languid life, only mildly jolted when their city became the province's capital. The honour belonged to Santos until a pirate from Ipswich, Thomas Cavendish, sacked the port, and the government decided to head inland, beyond the reach of greedy British buccaneers. Over the following few centuries, São Paulo owed a great deal of its wealth and influence to the British, so it is gratifying to remember that the city's first step towards prominence was the result of an Englishman's actions. To complement its new status, São Paulo gained a theatre, some newspapers and a few schools, but managed to avoid too much confrontation with the outside world. Paulistas preferred the quiet life. Their isolation surprised another Englishman, John Mawe, when he visited the city in 1808:

> Our appearance in S. Paulo caused considerable curiosity among all descriptions of people, who seemed by their manner never to have seen Englishmen before. The very children testified their astonishment, some by running away, others by counting our fingers, and exclaiming that we had the same number as they.

Richard Burton, explorer, translator and pornographer, detested São Paulo. Posted there as British consul, he claimed that the city possessed only one distinction: it was the dullest place that he had ever been. Throttled by boredom, he begged the British government to send him elsewhere, and shirked his duties to make long expeditions into the jungle. When the Foreign Office finally sent him to Africa, his wife Isabel was rather disappointed. She had enjoyed the placid pace of life in São Paulo, which was the first place that she and her husband had ever stopped for long enough to set up house together.

São Paulo's cosy existence was finally destroyed by a drug. Like all the best drugs, this one filled its followers with an implacable sense of their authority and brilliance. To their own intoxicated ears, their conversations suddenly sounded wittier than ever, laden with wisdom and wit and urbanity, while their hearts and egos swelled with a booming self-assurance, suitably befitting to their era of confident industrialisation. In the middle of the nineteenth century, the world's richest citizens craved huge supplies of this dark, powerful intoxication. Driven by addiction, they threw open their purses, offering to pay high prices to anyone who could supply sufficient stocks. Even for the idle citizens of São Paulo, suckled on laziness, the temptation of hard cash proved irresistible. They shook themselves awake, blinked away their introspection, dug their fields and started planting long rows of coffee bushes.

The rosy future of those farmers must have seemed assured. Throughout Europe and North America, the newly emergent bourgeoisie demanded caffeine. Of all the temperate regions on the planet, none could be better suited to coffee cultivation than the plains of southern Brazil. The landowners of São Paulo should have been laughing, but one impenetrable obstacle stood between them and unimaginable riches. Cross that obstacle, and they would be rich. But how?

São Paulo sits on a vast plateau, two and half thousand feet above sea level. The plateau itself is fairly flat, and stretches without much interruption all the way west to Paraguay and Argentina. But the route east isn't so straightforward. The plateau ends abruptly, and a sudden, precipitous line of cliffs named the Serra do Mar plunges down to the Atlantic Ocean. 'The depth of the valleys is tremendous, and the number of mountains, one above another, seems to leave no hope of reaching the end,' sighed a Jesuit priest, Vasconcellos, who ascended the route in the seventeenth century. 'The greater part of the way you have not to travel, but to get on with hands and feet, and by the roots of trees; and this among such crags and precipices that I confess my flesh trembled when I looked down.'

A string of shipping lines started running regular services along the Brazilian coast, continuing south to Argentina and Uruguay, returning north to New York or Southampton. Every year, the ships were larger and faster. Warehouses and offices sprouted along the docks in Santos. A swelling gang of labourers, lawyers and merchants lubricated the trade. But none of them could solve the most pressing problem: how could the Paulistas get their beans from the bush to the cup? However fast the farmers worked, sacks took a fortnight to cover the eighty miles from their farms to the docks at Santos.

A road zigzagged down the Serra do Mar. Every few days, a long line of mules left São Paulo and plodded along this slippery path, bound for Santos. Each miserable mule carried two heavy bags of coffee or two bulky bales of cotton to the coast, and returned laden with sacks of salt, flour and European consumer goods. The weight squeezed their ribs. Leather straps chewed into their skin. Worn down by labour, they wheezed and groaned, their hides covered with a battlefield of welts, bruises and bleeding scabs. They stumbled down the track, two or three hundred of them in single file. At the head of the convoy rode a white horse with a string of bells tied around its neck, a jangling guidance for those unpleasant afternoons when fog suddenly descended and smothered the landscape, reducing visibility to a few feet. In difficult weather, a mule would lose its footing and, unbalanced by the sacks strapped to its back, topple off the road, plunging several hundred feet to the rocks below, exploding on the wet stones in a splash of blood and coffee.

The narrow track offered few passing places, and ascending travellers who had the misfortune to meet a convoy simply had to scramble up the hillside and wait until the mules had passed. Regular bouts of heavy rainfall turned the road into a river, and occasional landslips added some extra excitement for unwary walkers. At night, the mules would be let loose to graze on the rocky hillside, while their guides and passengers huddled around a fire before sleeping in a flea-ridden bed or wind-torn tent. This dangerous path offered the only way for farmers to take their produce to the port, and thus reach international markets. To impatient Europeans, tapping their feet on the quay in Santos, the delays seemed unbearable. In the 1830s, a German merchant named Frederik Fromm came up with a plan to change all this: he acquired a franchise from the Brazilian government, allowing him to build a railway from Santos to São Paulo. Fromm wrote to Robert Stephenson in England, suggesting that, as the world's foremost railway engineer, he was the perfect candidate to construct it. Stephenson pored over the maps, scrawled some calculations, shook his head, and wrote a dismissive reply to the German, declaring that the vast investment needed to build the railway would cripple its profits for so many decades into the future that the whole enterprise was pointless. If Robert Stephenson couldn't do it, no-one could. Fromm gave up. The mules kept walking. Nothing changed until the 1850s, when Baron de Mauá intervened.

Baron de Mauá was born Irineu Evangelista de Sousa in 1813. The son of penniless parents, fatherless from the age of nine, he travelled to Rio as a teenager and set about earning a living. By luck or guile, he ended up in the warehouse of an English merchant, Richard Carruthers, a well-travelled trader from Carlisle, to whom he became a pupil, an adopted son and eventually an heir. Working with Carruthers every day from seven in the morning till ten at night, Mauá absorbed an English education – practical and financial rather than intellectual or athletic – and learnt English so well that it became his favoured language. Carruthers made him a partner in the firm, then retired to Carlisle and devoted the rest of his life to fishing in the river Eden.

In 1840, Mauá spent a year in England, and returned to Brazil ablaze with revolutionary passion, inspired by the vibrancy and power of a nation writhing in the throes of industrialisation. He became Brazil's most ingenious, energetic and innovative industrialist, involving himself in a vast range of schemes – supplying Rio with clean water, laying a transatlantic cable, draining swamps, constructing tramlines, illuminating cities and building railways. As any adoptive Briton must, he adored railways. Looking at the vast landscape of Brazil, he understood that his own country's immense economic potential would remain unfulfilled unless the disparate regions could be connected. Only trains could make those connections. Mauá was responsible for the first railway in Brazil, inaugurated in 1854, which ran for only ten miles. Invigorated by its success, he bought the Santos to São Paulo concession from Fromm's widow, raised an enormous loan in London, and, needing a reliable, well-respected engineer to survey the line, summoned James Brunlees.

Later in life, James Brunlees would diversify, even wasting several years on a ludicrous scheme to run a tunnel under the Channel from Dover to Calais, but his early career depended on railways. Having a busy British practice to run, he had no time to dilly-dally in Brazil, and plucked a young man from his office, a bright, ambitious boy named Daniel Makinson Fox. Aged twenty-six, Daniel Fox was already an enterprising engineer, armed with guts, a good eye and some useful experience of plotting railways in Morecambe Bay and Málaga. From the latter, he spoke a little Spanish, which qualified him perfectly to work in South America. Even if Spanish wasn't quite the language of Brazilians, Brunlees had complete confidence that Fox would manage to communicate with the natives. After all, one foreigner is much like another.

After eighteen months in the tropics, Fox returned to England. Brunlees tidied the young engineer's findings into a neat little booklet, and put him on a new job: building the pier at Southport, a bustling seaside resort on Merseyside. *A Report Upon the Proposed Line of the Railway from Santos to Jundiahy in the Province of São Paulo in the Empire of Brazil* was sent to Baron de Mauá in 1858, offering him a potential route, a list of costs and a timetable for construction.

The day that Southport Pier opened, Daniel Fox was not among the ranks of residents waving Union Jacks. He missed his chance to see the fireworks, cheer the marching bands and address the ceremonial banquet, because he was already aboard another Royal Mail steamer, heading for his next job. Mauá had approved the plans, London banks had arranged the first stage of the necessary massive loans and Fox was bound for Brazil again. This time, he was not the lowly and nervous prospector, dispatched by a busy boss to prepare plans. Just thirty, he had been promoted. As a reward for his excellent work in planning the railway, Fox would build it.

The locals soon christened the line with a nickname: 'a Inglesa' – the English. The British nature of the railway is evident in every detail of planning, construction and operation. Even the railway's official name betrayed its roots. Timetables, advertisements and accounts determinedly referred to the San Paulo Railway rather than the São Paulo Railway, and not one of them bothered translating the line into its Portuguese name, a Estrada de Ferro do São Paulo. This was a British enterprise, owned, built and administered by Britons.

The very design of the railway is emblematic of a confident imperial power at the height of its influence. Just as the Romans drove their roads directly across a landscape, refusing to deviate for piddling irritations like hills or ravines, so the SPR shoots up the mountainside. A more nervous engineer might have taken a long, slow route, tacking upwards in short, sideways bursts like a yacht sailing into the wind, but Daniel Fox had no such fears. He stood at the base of the mountain, saw his destination at the top, and drew a line between the two. His railway went straight up

Such an obstinate route obviously required an extraordinary design. Fox built four enormous wheels along the route of the line, one above the other on the mountainside. Each wheel used a thick steel cable to haul the train up the track. As the train reached one wheel, the cables swapped over, and the next wheel started turning. To reduce the load placed on these huge wheels, the weight of a descending train pulled up an ascending one. If the railway succeeded, it would be one of the greatest engineering feats that the world had ever seen.

Work started in 1860, and proceeded slowly. Navvies built iron bridges to traverse four rivers, and started cutting a swathe up the Serra do Mar. Due to the precarious slopes on which they worked, the engineers never used gunpowder. The mountains had to be reshaped with nothing fiercer than a pick or a shovel. They worked day and night, smoothing rocks, punching tunnels, subduing the landscape while engaged in a constant battle with the climate. Clouds of mosquitoes swarmed around their heads. Almost every afternoon, fog descended, soaking their clothes with dew. The rains came so frequently you might have supposed yourself in England, until the force of the water falling from the sky washed away your tools or your tent, soaking you through, and you remembered that only tropical weather is so brutal, so gargantuan, so determined to brush you off the land's back.

After four years, money started to run out. Fox wrote to London asking for cash, but the banks refused to advance another penny. In the end, the railway only proceeded because Mauá paid for the work out of his own pocket. A few years later, he came to regret this. The SPR's shareholders refused to reimburse him, and Baron de Mauá, Brazil's greatest industrialist, destabilised by bad debts, plunged into bankruptcy.

Locals started to grow sceptical that the SPR would ever run, and even foreign visitors had their doubts. When John Codman travelled a portion of the unfinished railway in the early 1860s, he grumbled about the discomfort and delay. The makeshift carriage juddered over every sleeper, hurling its passengers from side to side, and the train averaged only one and half miles per hour. He advised other travellers to stick to the mules. The indigenous population showed even less enthusiasm. Isabel Burton described the reaction of the local Indians, confronted for the first time by a locomotive:

> They looked upon the engine as a kind of malignant beetle, but at last they got less frightened, and all clambered upon it; but when it was time to start, and the driver gave the preliminary whistle, they sprang off like mad, and ran for their lives, nor could they be persuaded to mount again.

Local newspapers ran reports advising residents not to sleep on the line after a railwayman took his siesta on the ground, lying with his feet propped on the tracks. He slept through the roar of the approaching train, lost both legs, and died soon afterwards. His death stood as an example to fellow workers: don't doze on the job. Perhaps Fox invented the story *pour encourager les autres*. Sleepy workers caused him constant problems. With puritanical scorn, Fox fumed at the indolent habits of Brazilians. By the terms of their contract, the railwaymen had been banned from using slaves. Without much success, the British were trying to enforce an end to slavery in Brazil. In 1822, slaves formed half the population of Brazil; by 1888, on the eve of abolition, only one in twenty Brazilians was a slave. Arriving in the country midway through this process, Fox found an economy depressingly dependent on forced labour. Mauá himself despised slavery, an unusual attitude for a wealthy Brazilian, probably absorbed from his English education. However, Fox quickly discovered that even free Brazilians had little enthusiasm for work. In a lecture to the Institution of Civil Engineers, delivered on a visit to London, Fox explained:

> The native Brazilian has an indisposition to work, partly from the false pride engendered by slavery and partly from the indolence induced by the absence of incentives to work, when he can easily live in his simple way without it. Soon the solid advantages of work, in the shape of good wages regularly paid, induced numbers to leave their cabins and little plantations of bananas, beans, and Indian corn, always, however, to return home at the planting season.

In a country that had not yet abolished slavery, why would a free man dirty his hands with labour? This is one of the reasons that Brazil required such a huge influx of immigrants at the end of the nineteenth century, when slavery was finally declared illegal. Any self-respecting Brazilian – even one who had just been released from slavery – would refuse to work for a living. This aristocratic attitude infuriated Europeans and North Americans (and its remnants still do today). One British writer, travelling through Rio in the nineteenth century, described his own appalling behaviour: he carried his baggage through the streets! Nothing could have been more shocking to the locals. 'I well remember the gauntlet of eyes fixed upon me in blank amazement each time I landed from the *Petropolis* steamer, and walked bag in hand through the rank of greasy chapmen to the nearest tramway. Sometimes there was pity, but always the most profound astonishment at the menial tastes of one who seemed certainly quite as white and nearly as well-bred as themselves.' The same writer recalled a boy of fifteen from a poor family, who travelled with no more luggage than would fit in his pocket. Even so, the boy walked into town unencumbered. He was followed by a slave to carry his toothbrush. 'This occurred over and over again, and yet we are told labour is scarce in such a country!'

Eager to meet his deadline, Fox relied on local labour as little as possible. The station buildings might have been built from Brazilian bricks – even they crumbled too easily, according to Fox – but German and Portuguese masons did the work. Designers, managers and engineers sailed out from Britain, as did many of the skilled craftsmen. They brought a British aesthetic, creating a neat little railway which wouldn't look out of place in Surrey, Cumbria or Lanarkshire. Almost all the materials were imported from Britain too – not merely the complex machinery, the comfortable first-class compartments, the cattle trucks, horseboxes and prison vans, but even the wood and steel from which the railway was built. Boilers came from Cornwall, carriages from Manchester, and locomotives from the Avonside Engine Company. When the first trains started running, they burned high-grade coal shipped from Newcastle. Along with coal and carriages, all kinds of people flooded from Britain and Europe to southern Brazil, attracted by the possibilities offered by an efficient railway sneaking into virgin territory. Anyone with a scrap of forward thinking could see what would happen in the next few years. As the railway opened routes into the state of São Paulo, the economy would boom. Property prices, population and trade would inflate at an enticing rate. Canny families bought as much land as they could afford, and started businesses in anticipation of growing trade. The three Sharpe brothers, the SPR's major contractors, bought a large tract of land and built themselves a farm. When John Codman rode the railway, he slept in a hotel on the route run by an entrepreneurial German landlord and shared his supper with a Scottish doctor who had recently moved to the area.

A typical story is that of George Jeffery, an Englishman born in Bath in 1823. He emigrated to Canada, set up home in New Brunswick, and married there. He and his wife Hannah had a daughter, and seemed comfortably settled in Hopewell, a town with the curious distinction of having the world's highest tides. Then, George accepted an invitation from a friend, a sea captain, to take a trip on his steamer down the eastern coast of America. For an adventurous man, the opportunity must have been unmissable. The steamer would sail from top to bottom, north to south, Canada to Patagonia, and back again. When the ship sailed down the humid coast of southern Brazil and reached Santos, George walked down onto the quay to look around, and refused to walk back up. He had met a group of congenial Britons, whose work intrigued him, and abruptly decided that this was the very place that he wanted to live. The steamer continued to Patagonia without him. When it returned to Santos on its northward voyage, George handed a letter to the captain, asking him to deliver it in Canada. In the letter, George had given some instructions to his wife: sell the house, sell the land, pack what possessions you can and sell what you can't, then take the proceeds, our daughter and yourself to the nearest port, and get on a boat to Brazil.

Aided by his new friends, George Jeffery found a job on the railway. As the work moved inland, so did he, accompanied by his wife and an increasing brood. In the thick pages of a heavy Bible, still owned by his descendants, George recorded the birthplaces of his children. Almost every new station brought another child. When the track reached its conclusion, the family settled in São Paulo. It was a small, quiet town. Chickens ran along the dusty roads. Horses were tethered to posts outside the whitewashed houses. Farmers brought sacks of fresh produce down from the hills. Mules pulled rickety carriages through the streets. Living alongside the local Brazilian population, Jeffery found a few other immigrants – Germans, French, Italians – and a small group of fellow Britons, most of whom he already knew from the railway. He brought up his family there. Twenty years later, one of his sons, Walter James Jeffery, showed great aptitude for a curious new-fangled game imported from England.

In the 1860s, the men building the San Paulo Railway never played games. They had little time for relaxation. Severe financial penalties would be imposed if the railway missed its deadline. Daniel Fox forced his men to work through the night, illuminating their progress with torches. He was determined that this enterprise would follow its timetable, just as his trains, when they finally ran, would leave and arrive precisely at their appointed times. He had no intention of adapting his behaviour to local customs.

Fox achieved his aim. The rails were laid in 1866 and the line opened on 16 February 1867, ten months ahead of schedule, earning the contractors a bonus of £43,750. When the first train reached São Paulo, a reception committee waited – a large crowd, cheering and waving flags. They must have sensed that this gleaming black locomotive, whistling and gushing steam, would change their lives, but few of them can have been prepared for the immense disruptions that lay ahead.

Like a shot of caffeine, the railway jolted São Paulo out of its mid-afternoon snooze. Without the SPR, São Paulo might have remained a small, unimportant town in the hills, dwarfed by more important cities like Rio de Janeiro and Bahia (now called Salvador da Bahia, usually abbreviated to Salvador). When the railway was built, the population exploded and production boomed. Farmers flooded out of the city and fanned outwards across the plateau, partitioning the soil into estates, pushing the natives further towards the hinterlands. Advertisements in Britain, Italy, Spain and Portugal offered immigrants a taste of the promised land, and seduced millions of labourers into taking transatlantic passage. By the 1880s, Brazil was supplying most of the world's coffee, and the percentage increased every year. By 1900, half the coffee drunk by the world passed through the port of Santos. Money poured into the city and the state. The price of land shot up. Unimaginable riches sprouted in the wallets of those investors who had bought big estates at low prices – particularly the canny Britons who had known the route of the railway, and seen what land would become most valuable when trains started running. The small British community had always been influential. Now, they were also rich.

Daniel Fox could have returned to London in triumph, having built a railway that was heralded around the world as a majestic achievement, fêted in books and magazines, praised as one of the great wonders of the age. Instead, he chose to stay in Brazil with his wife and children, taking a job as the SPR's chief engineer and general manager. He also worked on other projects in the city, designing the waterworks and gasworks, consulting on other new railways, sitting as a director on the boards of several British-owned companies. He helped construct the British church, a little Protestant chapel predictably called St Paul's, which became a focus for the British community.

Few traces of Daniel Fox's presence remain in the city today. There is a commemorative tablet on the wall of the church. A street is named after him. One family keeps a large silver cup in their front room, standing proudly on a sideboard. This cup was presented to their ancestor by Fox. In flowing capitals engraved on its silver surface, the cup records one of the community's sporting events.

Challenge Cup for billiards
Won by Mr Miller
Presented by D.M. Fox Esq
San Paulo Railway Book Club.

The inscription gives no first name, and the family's descendants have no idea which of the Miller brothers won this cup. Four of them lived in Santos and São Paulo – Andrew, John, William and Peter. Tall, handsome Scotsmen, they were well-known in the British community. The visiting representative of the South American and General Steam Navigation Company, William Hadfield, records a meeting with Andrew Miller:

> We reached Santos early the following morning. The steamer was at once moored alongside an iron wharf, facing the Custom House, and Mr Miller, one of the railway officials, came on board with the unpleasant news that the railway was stopped, owing to heavy rains, which appeared to have prevailed here as at Rio. The town did not look very inviting under the influence of a hot sun, but Mr Miller kindly offered us rooms at the station, where he himself lived, and made us very comfortable.

The following morning the rains stopped, and they travelled on the railway with Daniel Fox and the Burtons. On arriving in São Paulo, they might have met Andrew's brother, John Miller, who worked as a merchant, earning a tidy commission on goods that he traded between Britain and Brazil.

The Millers were the sons of a Scottish shipowner. A regular service ran between Greenock – where their father's business was based – and Rio de Janeiro, carrying coal to Brazil and sugar back to Scotland. Although the boats took no paying passengers, the Millers must have used their connections to secure a passage to South America. They arrived in the early 1860s. By the end of the decade, they were putting down roots. In 1868, Andrew Miller married a Brazilian girl. Four years later, his brother John made a even better match. He married Charlotte Fox, the great-niece of John Rudge, thus directly linking the Millers to the Rudge clan, the largest, smartest, richest and longest-established British family in São Paulo and for miles around.

In 1808, John Rudge had arrived in Rio de Janeiro from England. The eldest of three brothers, he was born in Stroud, a leafy market town in Gloucestershire. Rudge is still a well-known name around Gloucester – John's brother lived and died within three miles of Stroud – but John himself decided that he needed wider pastures. Heading into the hinterland east of Rio, he bought a large plot of land near a little-known town called St Paul's. If he still owned the land today, he would be the wealthiest property magnate in South America. On his new land, John Rudge planted tea.

In any Brazilian cafe, signs offered 'chá da India' and 'chá Nacional' – tea imported from China and tea from Brazil. Much of the apparently foreign tea had actually been grown in São Paulo, sent to Rio, packed in boxes smothered with Chinese lettering, and sent back to gullible Paulistas as genuine Oriental tea. John Rudge advertised his own tea truthfully as the produce of Morumbi, the region covered by his plantations. He was a skilled planter. His tea tasted so refined that customs officials thought it must be Chinese rather than home-grown, and threatened to arrest him for illegally importing foreign produce.

John Rudge's influence literally crossed the heart of São Paulo, and still does. When a long bridge was built to draw the two halves of São Paulo together, residents named it after the salesman who sold his wares in the valley. The bridge has been rebuilt, but still bears the same name. The Viaduto do Chá – the Bridge of Tea – remains one of the few monuments in the vast city that all twenty million inhabitants would recognise, although no more than a handful of them know that it was named after an Englishman. Another large district bears the family's name – Rudge Ramos – and Morumbi, the site of John Rudge's tea plantations, has become one of the city's most fashionable areas. Rudge's mansion is now a glitzy restaurant. Although the family moved out of that house long ago, they remain a large, influential clan. They are thoroughly Brazilian, of course, and even the pronunciation of their name has lost all trace of its roots. If a man from Gloucestershire wished to ask after his distant relatives, he would have to say not 'Rudge' but 'hu-djeh,' putting a strong stress on the first syllable.

John Rudge achieved his prominence through a combination of luck, perseverance and cunning. He arrived in São Paulo before other investors, allowing him to buy the best land. He made his first fortune by growing tea while everyone else was chasing coffee. He eased his children into marriages with useful locals. Flush with success, he summoned other friends and relatives from Stroud. Among them were his niece, Harriet, and her husband, Henry Fox.

Harriet and Henry Fox settled in São Paulo and had six children: Henrietta, Anna, Wilhelmina, John, Charlotte and Isabel. For a genteel family in a foreign country, there can have been few greater disasters than this succession of women. Their one son popped into the world surrounded by five girls. Five daughters! Finding one suitable young man would be trouble enough – but five? How could a proud family possibly cling to respectability in a foreign country with five daughters?

Although the Foxes and the Rudges might have sniffed a hint of ill-breeding in John Miller, the neatly dressed, handsome twenty-eight-year-old possessed one indisputable advantage which made him a more suitable contender for Charlotte's hand than almost anyone within 1,000 miles. He was British. He wasn't English, unfortunately, but beggars can't be choosers. Charlotte was not merely one of the five daughters of a large family, but portly and quite plain. Her parents, Henry and Harriet, told her to choose between two possible futures. She could decide to spend the rest of her days living with them in their large house, darning socks, quarrelling with the servants and acting as godmother to her innumerable nephews and nieces. Or she could accept the attentions of this eager, roguish Scotsman.

On 2 March 1872, John Miller and Charlotte Fox were married in the British Consulate. It was late summer. The vicar, witnesses and guests must have been sweltering in their long coats and tight collars, wide hats and expansive dresses. Despite their red, sweaty faces, the bride and groom made a perfect couple. Who could imagine a better match than a daughter of São Paulo's best-connected English family and the son of a Glaswegian shipowner? Their union promised greatness.

Two

Behind the glittering promise of this new union between the Millers and the Foxes, there lurked just one small problem. John Miller's father was not a Glaswegian shipowner. He was a porter on the docks at Greenock.

People who emigrate to a new world are always looking for a new life, and usually trying to escape some aspect of their old life – the embarrassment of their birth, the mistakes of their youth, a foolish marriage, a criminal record, whatever burden hangs around their neck, preventing them from achieving the position in life that, they believe, is rightfully theirs. John Miller was no different. Arriving in Brazil, he reinvented himself, discarding his past and providing himself with a fresh history. He gave himself the father that he deserved: a wealthy patron who owned a fleet of those gleaming steamers that tracked up and down the Clyde. The truth was more humble. The elder Mr Miller only stepped inside the smart shipping offices on Greenock docks to collect his pay or accept a reprimand, and spent the remainder of his working week lugging heavy sacks up and down gangplanks from cargo hold to warehouse.

As John Miller adjusted to the comforts of married life in Brazil, he must have grown increasingly convinced that his secret was safe. If his new relations doubted the details of his identity, the Rudges and Foxes were unlikely to sniff around his background. None of them would be making the 6,000-mile trek from São Paulo to Glasgow. Even a letter would take a month to reach Britain and another month to return. And apart from time, expense and distance, one vital factor prevented anyone from investigating his past: in turn, he might have been tempted to investigate theirs. In a country populated by people who have reinvented their own identities, no-one asks awkward questions. Within a generation or two, quiet lies will have become accepted traditions. Today, it is amazing how many Brazilians claim descent from wealthy and aristocratic European families, and how few have any evidence to prove their heritage.

If his new relatives tried to test John Miller with a couple of underhand questions about shipping, he would never have been caught out. He knew every detail about boats, docks and the details of international cargoes. He spent his childhood watching ships, and his youth working among them. Having been born in a little village alongside the river Clyde at a time when Glasgow had the largest and most productive shipyards in the world, John devoted his first few years to sitting on the beach, watching windjammers and steamers heading towards the open seas. Perhaps these glistening vessels, their sails filling with wind, their crisp bows scything through the waves, their freights bound for every port on the planet, inspired John Miller with the desire for exploration.

Fairlie was – and is – a small, quiet village clinging to the coast, thirty miles from Glasgow by road, a couple of hours from the city's docks in a ferry. A few minutes walk to the north of Fairlie lies Largs, now a pretty town packed with ice cream parlours and pensioners. In the middle of the nineteenth century, when John Miller was born in Fairlie, smart prosperous Glaswegians came to Largs for their vacations, building themselves neat little villas by the beach. In the proud words of a contemporary pamphlet, Largs 'is now one of the most favourite retreats on the west coast for ruralising and bathing, the communication with Glasgow, and other large towns on this side of the country being rendered convenient and expeditious by means of steam-boats: during the season it is enlivened by the presence of a great number of visitors; and the general accommodation afforded by the abundance and superior style of the lodging-houses, together with the agreeable manner of the residents, fully entitles it to the extensive patronage it enjoys.'

While the bourgeoisie flocked to Largs to enjoy the invigorating breezes and plunge into the freezing waters, the peasantry stayed in Fairlie, tending sheep and weaving tweed. The weavers lived in a row of small thatched cottages set back from the sea. Here, John was born in

1844, the third son of Andrew and Elizabeth Miller. Their house still stands. Burnfoot House is now a smart family home overlooking the coast road. Alongside Burnfoot Lane, a gushing river runs to the sea – this is the burn from which the house and road take their name – but the sound of water is obliterated by passing traffic. Throughout the century, this compact white villa housed not one family, but six. Each had two rooms, one for sleeping and eating, the other for cooking. Andrew and Elizabeth must have felt fortunate that they shared their tiny home with only four children; upstairs, living in an equivalent flat, Andrew's brother and his wife had ten. All six families shared a single outside loo at the end of the garden. The burn supplied their water for drinking and washing. As the women kneeled on the grass and washed dirty linen in the running water, rats leaped over their hands. Life was harsh. They grew potatoes in the field behind the house and made a few pennies from weaving on the loom, but Fairlie offered few opportunities to an ambitious man. In the 1850s, Andrew and Elizabeth Miller escaped from the village and moved twenty miles up the coast to Greenock. Andrew's brother stayed behind, and brought up his ten children in Burnfoot House.

All the Millers shared some traits. The men were tall and handsome, the women short and fat. Neither sex was afraid to speak their mind or prepared to suffer fools. They were strong-minded, determined, outspoken and brave. Their nationality and religion moulded their character and outlook: they belonged to the Free Church of Scotland, later known as the Wee Free, a strict, evangelical sect which broke away from the Scottish Church, horrified by the liturgical laxity of that austere institution. The Millers possessed an energy, dynamism and creativity which allowed them to grab the economic opportunities offered by Victorian imperialism. If you travel to Singapore, for instance, you will find a street named Burnfoot Terrace. Two of the Millers made their fortune in the Far East, built themselves a mansion, and named the street after the cramped Scottish house in which they had been born. By moving from Fairlie to Greenock, Andrew and Elizabeth Miller made the first step of this leap to the wider world. Now, rather than watching the big ships sailing down the Firth of Clyde, John Miller could walk along the docks, see the ships being built and launched, and perhaps sneak aboard to peek at the cabins, the engines, the cargo holds. Exoticism spilled off the decks and wriggled into Greenock, inspiring its inhabitants with a lust for travel. Huge boats brought sugar from Brazil, rice from China, grain from Canada. Strolling along the docks, you would smell cinnamon, coffee and a thousand other lingering scents, some familiar, others unidentifiable, all of them prickling your nostrils with a sense of the world's vastness. In the pubs alongside the docks, sailors would pull up their sleeves to display writhing tattoos punctuated with incomprehensible symbols, and show off their foreign prizes. An emerald parrot, plucked from the jungle. A shivering monkey, shocked by the cold. Dirty postcards of dark women. Alongside their booty, every sailor had a hundred stories of terrifying storms, blissful landscapes, explosive sex, weird food, brain-frazzling drink and strange, strange, strange foreign habits.

By the beginning of the 1860s, the Millers had had nine children, only one of whom died as a baby. The survivors – three girls and five boys – lived in a tiny tenement on Lyndoch Street, sharing the house with eight other families. While Andrew found a job as a porter in the docks and his eldest son Robert worked as a blacksmith, the more entrepreneurial Millers grabbed the economic opportunities offered by the world's centre for shipbuilding. John became a clerk with a ship yard and Andrew headed directly for Brazil.

Few records have survived, and no-one knows how Andrew found a route across the Atlantic. Perhaps John used a contact in the boat yard who offered free passage in exchange for working as a cook or a deck hand. Perhaps Andrew blagged his way aboard a random ship and discovered to his surprise that he was bound for Santos. Perhaps he was recruited directly from Greenock to work on the San Paulo Railway. Crossing the equator and arriving in the steamy tropical splendours of southern Brazil, he must have written enthusiastic letters home, describing the opportunities offered by a new country, an unknown continent. Over the next few years, four of Andrew and Elizabeth Miller's children went to São Paulo, leaving only the three girls and Robert, the eldest, the blacksmith, the stay-at-home, enduring Glaswegian winters while his brothers sweltered under the Brazilian sun.

In 1869, Andrew Miller drowned in the Clyde. John dealt with his father's affairs. At that time, John was working as a merchant and commission agent, liaising between firms in Brazil and Scotland. In São Paulo, there was an eager market for any goods imported from Britain. As soon as a Brazilian family came into money, they bought French products – or, if unable to afford the real thing, British imitations of French sophistication. Cheese, biscuits, ham, mustard, booze, soap, perfume, ink, cutlery, porcelain, watches, pianos and even potatoes poured into São Paulo from British farms and factories. Copying the latest fashions, Brazilians carried umbrellas, despite the lack of rain. When the contradiction was pointed out to him, one dandy apparently twirled his umbrella and answered, 'Well, it may be raining in London.'

John Miller must have travelled often between the two countries, liaising with suppliers, and happened to be in Greenock when his father died. John witnessed his father's will, which is simple, short and curious. One fact stands out. Although Andrew Miller worked as a porter in Greenock's docks, he did own a tiny portion of a ship: a sixty-fourth of a little steamer called the *Acadia*, built on the Clyde in 1866. This paltry inheritance must have lingered in John's imagination, and inspired him with the idea of crafting his father into a shipowner.

Just as history has failed to record how Andrew obtained his share of the *Acadia*, so no-one knows what happened to it after his death. The money can't have been invested wisely, and the Miller women moved almost annually to smaller tenements in Greenock, sinking slowly down the social ladder. Deprived of their breadwinner, they fended for themselves, scraping a living however they could. They took in lodgers. They embroidered. They made dresses and curtains. They worked in the very few professions open to unmarried women clinging to respectability. This humiliating situation lasted for little more than a decade. By the 1880s, Elizabeth Miller no longer needed to work. She received regular sums from abroad, where her sons had found work, married well, and reinvented themselves as prosperous gentlemen.

Three

I n the middle of 1874, Britain and Brazil were physically joined for the first time. Between the two countries, a cable ran along the ocean's floor. It offered new and thrilling possibilities for communication between the Old World and the New. As soon as the cable was active, the Emperor of Brazil transmitted the following message:

> To Queen Victoria
>
> Electrical Communication between our countries is an event of most auspicious future for two peoples that maintain most friendly relations between them.
>
> I pray my Sister and Cousin to transmit my longing remembrances to all her family in England and Germany, not to delay them.
>
> Rio de Janeiro June 22d 1874
>
> D. Pedro II

No more than a day later, a message zipped back again. A week earlier, this exchange would have taken two months. Now, queens and emperors, merchants and bankers, poets and philosophers, parents and children could communicate within minutes.

> To the Emperor of Brazil
>
> I have received your message on my way back from Scotland. I learn with the greatest satisfaction that telegraphic communication has been established between our two countries, which, I trust, will cement still more firmly the friendly relations between them.

I have duly conveyed your friendly message to my family here and in Germany. Those in England unite with me in thanking you for your greeting, which they warmly return.

Victoria

Windsor Palace.

Six months after the inauguration of the cable between Britain and Brazil, Charlotte went into labour for the second time. Her and John Miller's first son, John Henry, had been born in 1872. Their second was born on 24 November 1874. They christened him Charles William, taking his first name from his mother and his second from his father's brother, also resident in São Paulo.

Before the end of the decade, John and Charlotte had two more children, but neither survived. Carlota lived only eighteen months and Adolph died just before his second birthday. Living in the tropics, the British community could not allow themselves to be sentimental. Their bodies wracked by heat, damp, insects and unfamiliar diseases, their lives threatened by the air, the food and the water, they forced themselves to be mentally and physically tough. A death or two occurred on every voyage from Southampton to Rio, and the body would be slid surreptitiously into the ocean. One of the railways in Brazil was said to have lost a workman for every sleeper under the tracks, and the route of the SPR must have been littered with impromptu graves.

Only three pictures remain of Charles Miller as a child, a painting and two photographs. In both photographs, Charles and John Henry are together, glaring into the camera with unnerving confidence. These children know that they have been born to rule the world. In the painting, Charles stands alone, dressed in gaudy Scottish splendour. He wears a kilt and a sporran. A tartan cloak is slung over his shoulder. This small oil painting now hangs in the hallway of his daughter-in-law's home in São Paulo. Painted when he was four years old, the portrait shows a small boy with bright eyes and an intense gaze. He looks strong and determined. The type of child who not only knows what he wants, but knows exactly how to get it. If the Millers of Burnfoot House saw this portrait, they would recognise the lad as one of their own. A feathery palm waves its fronds in the background, but the landscape lacks any picturesque tropical elements. No pineapples or marmosets dangle in the trees, and the dark, overcast sky promises heavy rain rather than sunshine. The artist seems to have painted a deliberately Scottish landscape – although, for the background, he has used palms rather than firs, probably because they were the only trees that he knew how to paint.

Despite the efforts of his father, determined to keep him Scottish, and his mother, always reminding him to be English, Charlie must have grown up in a state of cultural confusion. The British kept themselves to themselves, but they remained a small community in a vast country. They worked together on the railway, in the bank and at various mercantile companies, and they socialised together, but like the British anywhere in the world, they couldn't help becoming infected by the individual spirit of the country that they inhabited. When the children scurried into the kitchen to sneak some scraps from the larder, the cook would scold them in Portuguese. If the Miller boys wanted to understand the world around them – the coachman's flirtations with the maid, the old women in the market, the kids playing in the dusty street – they would have to learn to speak the local language. Brazil sneaked into the British side of the house too. Only the very wealthiest families could afford a European cook, and even they would have to depend on local ingredients. Charlotte might have taught the cook to make a few British dishes, but she, like her sons, had been born in Brazil, eating food that had been cooked by a Brazilian. Like her children, she walked a tightrope between the two communities, and even had two names, one for each language. Depending on the company, she would be called Charlotte or Carlota.

Brazilian smells, tastes, sounds and customs wriggled into the Miller household, and only the elder John would have been unnerved by them. Only he lusted after black pudding and porridge. To the rest of his family, nothing could be more normal than the huge bunch of bananas always hanging in the larder, a hundred tiny green fruits slowly ripening. Nothing would smell more wholesome than rice and beans, the daily diet of their servants. In the afternoons, John and Charles would hurry out of the house, carrying a few coins, and buy puddings from vendors in the street. A dolce de leite, sickly sweet, made from sugar and condensed milk. Some cocado with its rich taste of coconut. A spoonful of goiabada or marmelada, the stiff jams made from guavas and quinces.

Charles and John would have learned to behave like proper English gentlemen, speaking correctly, opening the door for a lady, discussing the weather, refraining from emotional outbursts. At the same time, like any energetic boys growing up in a small town, they would have made friends with the local kids, and picked up their culture and attitudes. From an early age, the brothers would have been fluent in both languages, English and Portuguese. Like their mother, they learnt the need to have two names, one for each culture. To the stiff-necked British, they were Charles and John Henry. Among the Brazilian kids in the street, they became João and Charlie. Like anyone who speaks two languages, or possesses two names, they would have changed not only their behaviour to suit their surroundings, but their posture, their language, their attitudes, even their thoughts.

Perhaps the best way to understand Miller's situation is through the character of another boy who lived between cultures. He was the only son of Kimball O'Hara, an Irish soldier who travelled to India with the British army. There, he married his colonel's maid. When the regiment returned to Ireland, Kimball O'Hara decided to stay in India with his wife and child. His wife soon succumbed to the climate and died of cholera. Left alone with the child, O'Hara took to drink, which made him unemployable, then opium, which killed him. The orphaned child was left in the custody of native women. His name was also Kimball O'Hara, but everyone knew him as Kim. He lived like an Indian, speaking the local language better than English, acquiring local customs. He learnt to dress, speak and even look like a native. He was indistinguishable from the other grubby, ragged kids in the bazaar. Kim travelled across India with a Tibetan lama, searching for enlightenment, until he made the mistake of allowing an Englishman to spot his true identity as a white European. Captured, scrubbed, domesticated, sent to school, Kim nevertheless refused to be anglicised, and continued to live between two cultures, owned by neither, comfortable in either – and thus perfect material for a spy, which is what he became, working for the British in the Great Game.

Perhaps Charlie Miller never read Rudyard Kipling's *Kim* – he doesn't seem to have been much of a reader – but he would have recognised something of his own predicament in the central character. Both Kim and Charlie were born in a foreign country of British parents, capable of passing as native in either community but fully belonging to neither. Although Kim was Irish and Charlie was Scottish, both of them could act the part of the English gentleman, adopting the accent, the swagger, the confidence of the ruling class, just as each of them could shake off their Englishness and act the role of a native. Such dislocation brings astonishing freedom. Like an actor, you can change your identity, showing different faces to different audiences, revealing your true character to no-one. But there is an obvious danger. If you always adapt your personality to the people around you, changing yourself as your company changes, you may lose all sense of who you really are.

One other fact about Kim's world view is important. Although he lives as an Indian among Indians, capable of hiding his Englishness behind an impenetrable disguise, he can never be equal to an Indian, because he has 'white blood' flowing through his veins. All but the most outrageously liberal nineteenth-century Britons believed that their blood differentiated them from other races, and that they were not merely different, but superior. Charles Miller would have shared this belief, just as he would have accepted the casual racism that nick-named the inhabitants of Brazil as wops and niggers. Such terms were rarely intended to be malevolent or even derogatory, but their use stemmed from a deep-rooted sense of superiority. The British saw the world's population as a pyramid with themselves at its apex. Beneath them, they would find fellow Europeans. Further down, the yellows and the browns. At the bottom, a vast mass of blacks, whom God had provided as labourers for the whites. In the words of one of Britain's greatest Victorian heroes, the explorer Sir Francis Younghusband:

> No European can mix with non-Christian races without feeling his moral superiority over them. He feels, from the first contact with them, that whatever may be their relative positions from an intellectual point of view, he is stronger morally then they are. And facts show that this feeling is a true one. It is not because we are any cleverer than the natives of India, because we have more brains or bigger heads then they have, that we rule India; but because we are stronger morally than they are. Our superiority over them is not due to mere sharpness of intellect, but to the higher moral nature to which we have attained in the development of the human race.

Brazilian society was founded on racial division. After the American civil war, Brazil found itself in the uncomfortable position of being one of the few countries in the world to rely on slavery. In 1871, parliament passed a law which brought about the first steps towards emancipation, stating that anyone born after that date could not be a slave. On the plantations, people remained enslaved, but their children would be born free. However, landowners still retained use of their newborn slave's labour until he or she was twenty-one.

Legal barriers between the races concealed a certain amount of confusion in everyday life. A small proportion of the population were white and wealthy; a diminishing proportion were black and enslaved; between the two, there was a mass of Brazilians whose precise status and skin colour was difficult to define. According to Gilberto Freyre, a Brazilian anthropologist who published his first book in 1933, the distinctive character of Brazil can be explained by the preference of Portuguese sailors for travelling without women. Arriving in Brazil, the Portuguese thrust themselves onto the local female population, and bred a new mixed nation, neither black nor white, neither American nor European, neither slave nor master, but always somewhere between these extremes.

Sensing the ease with which racial, sexual and social boundaries could be crossed in Brazil, the British imposed strict boundaries around their own community. They remained intensely conscious of the thin border between themselves and their neighbours, the need to keep the barrier intact, and the horrifying potential for moral and physical corruption. When the naturalist John Ball visited Brazil, he noticed that 'the children of European parents born in the country speedily acquire the indolent habits of the native population of Spanish or Portuguese origin.' After spending a few weeks in the country, he had no doubts as to the cause of this moral dissolution.

> Where mere existence is so enjoyable, where physical wants are so few and so easily supported, the chief stimulus to exertion is wanting, and the natural distaste for labour prevails over the hope of gain. A boy will prefer to pick up a few pence by collecting flowers, or roots, or butterflies in the forest near his home, to earning ten times as much by walking to a distance, especially if expected to carry a light weight.

Later in his travels, Ball describes hiring a German boy to guard his horse. Together, they walked into the dense jungle behind Rio de Janeiro. When the undergrowth grew too thick for the horse to negotiate, Ball continued alone, and spent the day collecting plant specimens. At dusk, he returned to find the horse alone and unguarded. The German boy had tied the bridle to a tree and wandered off, not bothering to wait for his pay, choosing to lose the money rather than spend a dull afternoon tending a horse. No child in Hamburg or Munich would behave in such a manner. The boy had been corrupted by his surroundings and shed his Teutonic values. Among Brazilians, he had learnt instead to privilege pleasure over work and profit.

This worrying moral lesson was reiterated by Daniel Fox in a lecture to fellow engineers in London, whom he warned that 'too often in Brazil the Englishman "loses his head" and by his unsteadiness and misconduct allows the despised native or foreigner, whom perhaps he has taught all he knows, to supplant him.' Fox must have made the same point to his friends and neighbours, and warned them to protect not only themselves, but their children. The young are more corruptible. Their values are still fluid. Their minds, like their muscles, are still growing, and have not yet found their true shape.

That was why every Briton abroad liked to send his sons back to the Old Country for their schooling. British identity was embedded by education, and vulnerable youngsters could only be protected from the corrosive influence of local customs by attending a British school. By the beginning of the twentieth century, the British had started their own school in São Paulo, but nothing so sophisticated existed in the 1880s. Many Anglo-Brazilians had to send their children to local schools, despite the obvious dangers of moral contamination, because expense and distance prevented them from doing otherwise. Since the voyage took three weeks, a child could hardly come home for the holidays, and he would have to be lodged with relatives when the school closed, or stay in the school itself, paying even more fees. None of these factors presented any problems for the Millers. They had money in the bank and family in Britain. In 1884, not even ten years old, Charles Miller was put on a boat bound for Southampton. When he returned, a decade later, he would have been branded by Britishness.

Four

On the voyage to England, Charlie is never bored or lonely. He travels in a group with his brother, his uncle and his cousin, and they have the run of the ship. The *Elbe* carries few passengers – the holds are filled with produce rather than people, carrying sacks of sugar and coffee to European markets – and the adults in first class fit around a single table in the dining-room. Charlie, Will and John Henry have a second table to themselves. Unsupervised, they tip back their chairs, tease the waiters and play with their food. John Henry is eleven, two years older than Charlie. Their cousin, William Fox Rule, is fifteen. Their guardian and temporary parent, Uncle Peter, won't even be thirty till next year. He leaves them alone and devotes his attention to a slim young German woman, travelling back from Buenos Aires to Hamburg. He walks the deck with her, playing court, pretending that he wishes to learn her language. He repeats after her a line of Goethe, a string of irregular verbs, a snatch of song from a new composer named Richard Wagner, some of whose works, she tells him, have already been performed in small concerts by the German communities in Brazil and Argentina.

To Charlie, Will and John Henry, the *Elbe* is a long, slim playground, packed with opportunities for mischief. The confinement accentuates their sense of freedom. They balance buckets on the top of doors, trying to hide their giggles as the steward hurries down the corridor with a tray of drinks. They beg scraps of bread from the white-aproned guardians of the galleys, sprint to the end of the boat, and flick crumbs over the bow, watching the seabirds swoop and scuffle. None of them has ever been further than 100 miles from São Paulo before, nor escaped the supervision of their parents, and they take every advantage of their new-found freedom. When the *Elbe* docks in Rio de Janeiro, Uncle Peter invites his German belle on a carriage tour of the city's sights, leaving the three boys to run riot through the streets, stealing bananas from the market, pulling the tails of well-groomed horses, begging some coins from a British merchant whose voice they over-hear, then splurging their wealth on an orgy of cocado, marmelada and dolce de leite, knowing that this is their last chance to eat Brazilian sweets for a long, long time. That night, back in their cabin, as the *Elbe* steams slowly northwards and the waves rock their beds from side to side, the three boys take turns to run for a porthole and empty their stomachs into the sea.

They stop for a few hours at Pernambuco. Small boats bob along-side. Eager hands hold up bananas, pineapples, coconuts and cashews, shouting the prices. Their voices are whipped away by the wind. Another boat carries a festival of colour and movement, animals and birds plucked from the jungle, coati, armadillos, green parrots, even a baby puma. Uncle Peter negotiates on behalf of his belle, yelling and gesturing to the boatmen, then hands some coins to a sailor, who clam-bers down to the boats, returning with a marmoset tucked under his arm. The tiny monkey wriggles desperately, trying to escape his grip, but can't get away. Its limbs are tied together with string.

The steward tells the German girl that she has made a mistake. Even if her new pet survives the journey to Hamburg, it will shiver to death in the winter. 'Marmosets, madam, are not designed for frost.' She flounces to her cabin, where she cuts the string, frees her marmoset's paws, decides that he is a boy, christens him Siegfried, and feeds him on a steady flow of bananas, nuts and fresh water.

Next day, a scream echoes through the ship. The marmoset has bitten his mistress, and fled. Passengers and crew mount a search around the ship, calling down corridors and into hatches – 'Siegfried! Siegfried!' – until one of the sailors feels a patch of wetness on his scalp, and looks upwards. High above the deck, the marmoset is hanging on a mast, legs open, peeing on him.

Throughout the rest of that sunny afternoon, Siegfried leaps from mast to mast, swinging on the rigging and taunting the upturned faces. He gibbers, gestures, shouts and spits, keeping them entertained with a steady flow of monkey obscenities. Even after nightfall, his furious cries are still audible over the crash of waves and whistling wind. Lying in their cabin, the three boys are lulled to sleep by the sounds. To them, the screeching of an angry marmoset is much more comforting and familiar than the groans of a large ship easing through the open sea. Next morning, Siegfried cannot be heard. The rigging is empty. Maybe he secreted himself somewhere aboard the ship. More likely, he was blown overboard by an unexpected gust of wind, and flung into the Atlantic. The *Elbe* steams onwards. The marmoset is forgotten, the memory of him hidden under a daily whirl of deck cricket, fancy-dress parties, a ritual ducking for every passenger who has never previously crossed the line. Day by day, the sea turns greyer, thicker clouds cover the sky, and the air is chillier. Rain sweeps across the decks. After three weeks, they dock in Southampton.

Peter leads his nephews and their cousin down the gangplank. For the first time in their lives, the three British boys step onto British soil. When they complain about the breeze and the rain, Uncle Peter laughs. 'You'd better get used to it.' They climb into a waiting cab. Their bags will follow. The cabbie flicks his whip and drives his horses along the dock. As they trot through the city, they stare in delight at the large houses, the elegant inhabitants. In comparison, São Paulo now seems to be a poor, filthy, rough, disagreeable city. Southampton is a beautiful place: wide clean macadam streets, grand old elm and horse-chestnut trees. The parks are laid with velvety turf. Gothic churches stand among ancient stone buildings, covered to their summits with ivy. After a half-hour ride through the elegant streets, they pass through a pair of tall head posts, clatter down a long, narrow drive, and reach a splendid country mansion, surrounded by woodland. A lush lawn runs down to a pond. The house itself is a pleasant Georgian villa, the white walls punctuated by stucco pillars and sedate windows, the symmetrical features unbalanced by a single tower perched on the right-hand side, overlooking the grounds, offering a view down to the city and the coast. This is Banister Court. It will be Charlie Miller's home for the next ten years.

Herbert Branston Gray, one of the late Victorian era's great headmasters, warned the parents of prospective pupils that 'any charlatan can set up a brass plate to advertise his establishment as "a Preparatory School for Young Gentlemen," and actually carry on a flourishing trade in boys' minds and bodies.' He tells the story of a maid and a butler who hired a large house, put a brass plate on their front door, employed a couple of scholars with some knowledge of Greek and Latin, and ran a profitable school for unwary, ambitious parents. Throughout the century, private schools boomed as the newly rich bourgeoisie attempted to imitate their aristocratic superiors and educate their sons. Daughters stayed unschooled for a few more decades. Unscrupulous operators saw the potential for easy profit. As Flint says in Rudyard Kipling's *Stalky & Co.*, 'we aren't a public school. We're a limited liability company payin' four per cent.' The education offered to Stalky might have been based on aristocratic values, but it was firmly anchored within the reach of a middle-class wallet. Many of the Spartan virtues taught by the public schools – the joys of cold showers, the necessity of sport – might be explained by a simple fact: they were cheap. The sons of aristocrats hunted, shot and fished; the sons of the professional classes played rugger and footer, simple games that required nothing pricier than a leather ball, some boots and a field.

In *Tono-Bungay*, H.G. Wells gives a succinct description of the class divisions in British schooling: 'The public schools that had come into existence with the brief glow of the Renascence had been taken possession of by the ruling classes; the lower classes were not supposed to stand in need of schools, and our middle stratum got the schools it deserved, private schools, schools any unqualified pretender was free to establish.' The great public schools had tradition, size and wealth, whereas the private schools were newer, smaller, entirely dependent on fees, and run as business concerns. These are slippery distinctions, of course. In his autobiography, Anthony Trollope found himself unable to find any real difference between public and private schools other than age and prestige: 'The only meaning or possible definition of a public school is, one the foundation of which was intended not for a parish or other district, but for all England. If mere success, and consequent size be held to confer a claim to that title, it is clear that there is no "private" school which would not become a "public school" tomorrow if the master and proprietor of it could command a sufficient amount of success.' In other words, an honest headmaster could start a small private school not merely for profit, but in the hope that his establishment would eventually join the hallowed panoply of Britain's great public schools, and his name would be celebrated alongside the founders of Harrow, Winchester and Eton.

One such man was the Reverend George Ellaby, a teacher employed at a small school in Shetland. When the school's owner, Arthur Anderson, co-founder of the Peninsular Steam Navigation Company – now better known as P&O – wanted to start a new educational establishment for the sons of his captains, he invited Ellaby to become headmaster. The school would be founded in Southampton, close to the port, so the captains could easily visit their sons. Fees would be halved for employees of the Peninsular Steam Navigation Company, thus ensuring a regular and eager clientele. Ellaby moved his wife and young family from Shetland to Southampton, rented a house in the city centre, bought twenty desks and started teaching. The school expanded so quickly that Ellaby soon needed larger premises, and moved out of town to a country mansion surrounded by fields, ponds and landscaped gardens. Banister Court had stood empty for the past eleven years, so the owner was delighted to find a tenant, and gave a low rent. Ellaby took a seven-year lease, and invested all his savings in repairs and renovations. A few months later, disaster struck. Arthur Anderson died. His successor lacked Anderson's paternalistic instincts, the Peninsular Steam Navigation Company lost interest in the school, and Ellaby found himself lumbered with an expensive lease, a large house and no savings. After long discussions with his wife, Ellaby decided to keep the school open, bearing the entire financial burden himself. By doing most of the teaching, he managed to keep Banister Court afloat with only thirty or forty pupils every year, although the stress and labour took a terrible toll on his health, and he grew frailer year by year.

Among his pupils was his own son, Christopher, who remembered his schooldays as riotous and violent. Regular fights with 'the town boys' were followed by aggressive battles with nature. 'A great deal of time was given to collecting birds' eggs, and to shooting birds with a catapult in order to have them stuffed. So skilful were some boys that they could hit a small bird at the top of a tree, and I was once with a boy who hit a policeman's helmet many hundred yards off in the London Road.' When Christopher was fifteen, his father died, worn down by single-handedly running the school. Friends and local citizens organised a fund to pay off the school's debts. Led by Canon Wilberforce, grandson of the abolitionist, godson of Queen Victoria, a fiery proponent of temperance and the vicar of St Mary's in Southampton, the fundraisers filled Mrs Ellaby's bank account with enough cash to repay the mortgage on Banister Court and hire a series of temporary masters until her eldest son could decide whether he wanted to run the family business. The fund even stretched to paying for Christopher's education and, between the ages of sixteen and twenty, he boarded at Cheltenham College.

Founded in 1841, Cheltenham could not have claimed to be one of the great public schools, lacking either prestige or history. Designed to educate the children of the middle class rather than the aristocracy, the school produced boys who either went to Oxford and Cambridge or directly into the Indian Civil Service. About twenty times the size of Banister Court, the school averaged 650 pupils, three-quarters of whom boarded. Among this mass of boys, Ellaby made a name for himself as exceptionally clever, winning both the English Essay Prize and the Iredell Prize two years running. However, he soon discovered that academic success meant little in a Victorian public school, and 'your position absolutely depended on your success in games. You were popular when your name appeared on the list of the chosen, and unpopular when it was omitted.' These sad words come from a letter of Ellaby's, written to the school's historian, in which he goes on to remember that 'life in the workroom was such as the average boy loves, plenty of play and noise, but not pleasing to the boy who loves reading. Knuckle-bones were the favourite missile; and they hurt. I never had a moment's peace until I got my Second XV Football colours.'

From Cheltenham, Christopher won a place at Wadham College, Oxford. Until the beginning of the 1890s, when C.B. Fry and his racy chums put the place on the map, Wadham was a minor, uninspiring college, famous only for being one of the dullest in Oxford, producing generation after generation of earnest middle-class men to become clergy or run the empire. As soon as he arrived, Ellaby put into practice what he had learned at Cheltenham. The key to social success was not books, but football. In an undistinguished college of fifty-five myopic students his skills shone, and he found himself appointed captain of the team. Despite his efforts on the pitch, he also managed to get a first in Greats, which inspired him to stay in Oxford for an extra year to try for a Fellowship at All Souls'. He failed. In 1884, he returned to Southampton, accepting his anointed place at the head of the family firm, and became headmaster of Banister Court. Lacking a wife, children, friends or other intellectual interests, and forced to support not only his mother and sisters but the whole weight of a family business, he hurled himself into the work. He was twenty-four. If anyone had told him that he would never have another job in his life, Christopher Ellaby would surely have turned and fled. He was not a natural schoolmaster. His love of football had been studiously acquired to avoid the kicks and punches of less intelligent boys. He would have been happy with a quiet, lonely room and a pile of dusty books. But he never grumbled. An idealistic young man and a dutiful son, he threw himself into running the school and making friends with the boys. 'I liked teaching, and I was fond of boys, and I was popular on account of my football and swimming.'

Apart from Ellaby himself, the school could afford only two other teachers: a mathematician with a decent degree from Cambridge and a 'raw country lad' who lacked education but possessed great skill at football 'until in a match he, unfortunately, broke his leg, and after that he was never really of much use'. Ellaby hired another young man as a replacement, Arthur Denning, an enthusiastic sportsman in his twenties. Educated at Corpus Christi, Cambridge, Denning had devoted much of his energy to leading the college's football team, then moved to Somerset, where he played for the county. After his arrival in Southampton, Denning threw himself into local football, playing for Banister Court, Hampshire and a local team named St Mary's. He even found time to do a little teaching.

A larger school would have possessed more diversity. Boys would have been subject to various influences – not only a wide range of other pupils, but their housemaster, the headmaster and many different teachers. At Banister Court, Christopher Ellaby fulfilled all these functions at once. Such a small school took its character from the headmaster, who seemed to be everywhere at once, pacing through the corridors at night, eavesdropping on conversations, watching the cricket, playing alongside his boys at football. Christopher Ellaby was Banister Court, and he intended to produce generation after generation of men moulded in his own image.

Among the intake in his first year he had three boys from Brazil. William Fox Rule and the Miller brothers constituted almost a tenth of the school. They were a family unit, a battalion within the army. Loneliness would have affected them less than the other boys who had been deprived of their families for the first time, but culture shock must have been more of a problem. By the day of his tenth birthday,

Charlie Miller had been living in his new home for almost four months, and he must have become accustomed to the cold, the dreary lessons, the draughty dormitories and the tasteless food. Victorian schools took Sparta as their model, not Athens or Rome. The boys lived in an atmosphere of hardship and brutality. Even in *Tom Brown's Schooldays*, a rosy idealisation of public school life, violence is never far away. Here is a description of Tom's first night at school. We find him huddled in his bed, tucked in the corner of a large, cold dormitory:

> A noise and steps are heard in the passage, the door opens, and in rush four or five great fifth-form boys, headed by Flashman in his glory.
>
> Tom and East slept in the farther corner of the room, and were not seen at first.
>
> 'Gone to ground, eh?' roared Flashman. 'Push 'em out then, boys; look under the beds.' And he pulled up the little white curtain of the one nearest him. 'Who-o-op!' he roared, pulling away at the leg of a small boy, who held on tight to the leg of the bed, and sang out lustily for mercy.
>
> 'Here, lend a hand, one of you, and help me pull out this young howling brute. Hold your tongue, sir, or I'll kill you.'
>
> 'Oh, please, Flashman, please, Walker, don't toss me! I'll fag for you. I'll do anything – only don't toss me.'
>
> 'You be hanged,' said Flashman, lugging the wretched boy along; ''twon't hurt you, – you! Come along, boys; here he is.'

Charlie Miller had celebrated his first nine birthdays in the bright sunlight of a Brazilian summer, feasting on pineapples. On his tenth birthday, he consoled himself with boiled potatoes and rice pudding, while trying to protect his small bones from the chill of a British winter and the fists of bigger boys. That night, he slept in a crowded dormitory, rain pattering against the windows, a strong breeze rattling the panes. Over the next few years, he could have been forgiven for sinking into gloom or retreating into his imagination. Instead, he devoted himself to football.

One of the boys had a famous father, Colonel Sir Charles Wilson RE KCB KCMG FRS, who graced the school with his presence year after year, distributing prizes and making a speech. Wilson had gained his string of abbreviations by being an heroic failure. He sailed up the

Nile to rescue General Gordon, and arrived a little too late. Nothing could be more guaranteed to stir British hearts. 'I have never met anyone who seemed to me to have more qualities of a really great man,' wrote Ellaby. 'He never spoke of his own exploits, but was quiet and modest in his manner, yet you felt that he would never permit an impertinence.' In his speech to the boys of Banister Court, Wilson explained that he did not like to give prizes for scholarship, but for 'excellence of conduct', rewarding punctuality rather than academic achievement. He gave one piece of advice for their adult lives: 'There was always room for those who wished to do their duty, and they would be sure to get on well if they set their duty above everything.'

Although Banister Court was a small, obscure school without any history or prestige, the values that Charlie Miller learnt there would have been those of the great institutions: honesty, bravery, duty and endurance; chivalry and self-sacrifice; respect for Queen and Country; belief in Christianity and Empire; obedience to those above you in the hierarchy and dominion over those below. Such a strong sense of what was right had an obvious and necessary corollary: a strong sense of what was wrong. Again, different headmasters and schools had particular dislikes, but the schools in general had no love for anyone who fell outside their system of beliefs. Cheats, liars and drunks could expect little sympathy. The working class had their place, and were expected to stay in it. Women and white foreigners were tolerated. Jews and Catholics could expect only ridicule. Blacks hardly qualified as human.

School values were imposed by a discipline and ideology borrowed from the military: a school song, a uniform, organised sports, ritual humiliations, bonding ceremonies. These basic values were enforced by violence. Break the rules, and your palm, spine or buttocks would be lashed six times with a cane. Physical strength and endurance acquired high value, and a love of luxury would be stamped out. There is the famous story of a public schoolboy who is found to have taken not just one bath in a week, but two. Two hot baths in a single week. He is summoned by his housemaster, who orders the boy to desist, explaining that such habits are 'the kind of thing that brought down the Roman Empire.'

Only the most naive commentator forgot the examples of previous empires, all of which had followed the same cycle – growth to a peak followed by decay to obliteration. That would not happen to the glorious British Empire, decided the Victorians, and built themselves an army of empire-builders and administrators, inculcated with imperial values. The ideal young imperialist was fit, sporty, proud, confident, determined and ready to rule the world. To this end, the schools' moral, sporting and scholastic lessons were designed to destroy individualism and promote collectivism. Boys worked as a unit, playing in teams, scorning idiosyncrasy and personal creativity. Exceptional boys would be tamed, levelled and forced to adapt to the group. A contemporary novel described the simple choice that boys would be offered: 'conform or be kicked.' It is a sad irony that Christopher Ellaby spent his schooling in despair at the narrowness and stupidity of a culture that prized athleticism above intellectual or emotional growth, then devoted his adult life to enforcing it. He might have tried to struggle, but he was too weak. After a few years, the boy who would have preferred to read rather than play football had become a headmaster who urged his boys to play football rather than read. His pupils went through the same transformation, as did other boys all around the playing fields and dormitories of late Victorian Britain. As A.C. Benson wrote in *The Upton Letters*, 'One sees arrive here every year a lot of brisk healthy boys, with fair intelligence, and quite disposed to work; and one sees at the other end depart a corresponding set of young gentlemen who know nothing, and can do nothing, and are profoundly cynical about all intellectual things.'

To produce a steady stream of strong-chinned chaps to build and run the Empire, Victorian education involved a deliberate dampening of intellect, imagination and empathy. If a man busies his intelligence with complex ideas, learning to examine every problem from a variety of angles, seeing all the different sides to an argument, he will be unable to act quickly in the heat of battle. If a man can empathise with other men and women, he will never govern them successfully. In larger schools, rebellion might have been possible, but in a small, enclosed, inward-looking school like Banister Court, any intellectual endeavours were doomed. Conform or be kicked. The young headmaster must also have felt his own pressure to conform – schoolboys come down heavily on anyone, pupil or teacher, who exhibits the slightest sign of unconventionality – and his own intellectual aspirations dwindled year by year. As Edmund Gosse wrote about his experiences at another school, 'The conventionality around me, the intellectual drought, gave me no opportunity of intellectual growth.' Twenty years later, when Christopher Ellaby did finally manage to find the time and energy to write a book, the resulting volume was not a scintillating critique of Virgil's *Eclogues* or a piercing interpretation of the *Iliad*. Instead, ironically, tragically, it was a guidebook to Pompeii, aimed at middlebrow middle-class British travellers on their first trip to Italy.

Due to his father's excellent relations with the Church, Ellaby managed to persuade the local clergy to educate their sons at Banister Court. Charlie knew two of them, Arthur and Harold, the sons of Rev. Gregory of St Michael's in Southampton and Rev. Davidson of St Mary's in Sholing. Apart from locals, other boys in his generation were mostly the sons of men living in the colonies or working on the ships that docked in Southampton. One contemporary of Charlie's came from Uruguay. Others had been born aboard steamers in the Red Sea and the Pacific. They were ordinary boys from middle-class families, comfortable without being wealthy, sensible rather than extraordinary, and seemed destined to grow into the backbone of Britain and the Empire.

As a child, you might have a sense of which of your contemporaries will succeed as adults and which will fail, but you are almost certainly wrong. There is no way that Charlie Miller would have known that many of his fellow pupils would distinguish themselves in later life, and a few of them would be famous throughout Britain, their names on the front page of every newspaper, their deeds discussed across bars and breakfast tables around the country. No-one would have been surprised if a small school had produced one famous son – the man who introduced football to Brazil, say – but Banister Court did much better than that, producing a babbling stream of celebrities. Of Charlie Miller's direct contemporaries, several pursued conventional upper-middle-class careers, becoming a bishop in Argentina, a colonel in the Canadian Army or a housemaster at a minor public school in Wiltshire. Others were less conventional. One caused a political scandal that nearly brought down Lloyd George's government. Another had the misfortune to be eaten by a lion while performing in Skegness Amusement Park.

Charlie Miller arrived a few years after the departure of the most famous Old Banisterian, a short, frail, nervous boy named Jellicoe who failed to distinguish himself at school, but later rose through the Navy's ranks to become Admiral of the Fleet at Jutland. As punishment for his incompetence at that battle, Jellicoe was appointed Governor-General of New Zealand, and forced to eke out his days on the wrong side of the planet. A few years after Jellicoe left the school, Wilfred Macartney arrived. Aged twelve, Macartney used to be excused classes at Banister Court to travel on the train to London and attend board meetings of his father's construction firm, where he ripped reports into shreds, chewed the paper to a pulp and made soggy balls that he hurled at the secretaries. Later, he rejected capitalism, wrote for the *Sunday Worker* and fought with the British battalion in the Spanish Civil War. He spent two spells in prison, nine months for smashing the window of a jewellers in Albemarle Street, followed by ten years for passing secret documents to the Russians. Finally, after his release from Brixton, he was deported to Moscow.

When Charlie Miller sat on his bed and looked around the dormitory for the first time, knowing that he would spend the next decade in this chilly, barren room, he would have spared no time worrying about the future careers of his fellow pupils. He had more immediate fears. The cold, for instance. The icy draught rattling the windows, the damp sheets of his uncomfortable bed and the freezing water that trickled out of the taps in the bathroom that he shared with twenty spindly boys in shorts and boiled shirts. Before absorbing any other lessons, he would have learnt to respect his fellow pupils. They held the key to his survival. When thirty boys are locked in a house together, hardly supervised, the weak sink fast. Even if the school lacked a bully like Flashman, emotional and physical brutality would have been everpresent. In this passage from Forster's *The Longest Journey*, Rickie tells his wife about his own memories of boarding school, which have been revived for him by the recent experience of starting work as a teacher:

'There was very little bullying at my school. There was simply the atmosphere of unkindness, which no discipline can dispel. It's not what people do to you, but what they mean, that hurts.'

'I don't understand.'

'Physical pain doesn't hurt – at least not what I call hurt – if a man hits you by accident or in play. But just a little tap, when you know it comes from hatred, is too terrible. Boys do hate each other: I remember it, and see it again. They can make strong isolated friendships, but of general good-fellowship they haven't a notion.'

After a night in the dormitory, listening to the moans and snores of other children, a boy spent the mornings bluffing his way through a Latin grammar. As Rickie learns to his despair, every schoolmaster's duty can be summed up in four phrases: 'Organize, systematize, fill up every moment, induce esprit de corps.' Rather than learning to think, boys were taught to remember. They learned Latin texts by rote. By the end of term, each pupil could spout line after line of Virgil. A few of them could even understand a little of what they were saying, but most might as well have been reciting a railway timetable. In their daily lessons, the masters taught discipline and obedience rather than creativity or individualism. Boys learnt little of practical value, leaving school with scarce knowledge of science, history, geography or any modern languages. The only lessons that they acquired with real skill were the rules of football and cricket.

Not a rich school, Banister Court lacked a gymnasium until the 1890s, and used the fields for sports. Running in foul weather toughens the spirit, Victorian schoolmasters liked to say, and the boys played football in rain, sleet and snow. That autumn in 1884, before Charlie, John Henry and William Fox Rule participated in their first game of football, they would have been taught the rules. Although they might have kicked a ball around the dusty streets of São Paulo, none of them had ever seen a game of soccer, played by the rules set down by the Football Association of England. This is not the place for a history of football – many other books will provide that – but a quick reminder of the sport's development might be useful. For thousands of years, all around the world, people have kicked and thrown spheres for fun and competition, but the British codified these games in the nineteenth century into specific sports, and modern football derives from their efforts. Just as elsewhere on the planet, early football in Britain was an unregulated game, played by two teams with tens, hundreds or even thousands on either side. A typical game would involve two villages, and all the men who lived in them. A ball would be placed midway between the two villages. Each side tried to get the ball into the other village. The ball might be kicked, carried or thrown. If your opponent had the ball, you could use any means to remove it from his grasp. Unsurprisingly, such games left a trail of bruises, broken limbs and the odd corpse. In the Middle Ages, the English had a frightening reputation throughout Europe as violent, drunken louts whose idea of a good time was breaking things and hurting people. Football suited them perfectly. As Philip Stubbes complained in *Anatomie of Abuses in the Realm of England*, written in 1583:

> As concerning football playing I protest unto you that it may rather be called a bloody and murthering practice than a fellowlye sport or pastime. For dooth not everyone lye in waight for his adversarie, seeking to over throwe him and picke him on his nose, though it be on hard stone, on ditch or dale, valley or hill, or whatever place soever it be he carethe not, so he have him downe.

At the beginning of the nineteenth century, a strict division could still be found in Britain between working-class and aristocratic sports. Hunting, angling and shooting belonged to the upper classes. Working-class games were rougher, tougher and much more chaotic. Throughout the century, under the influence of the public schools, games like football were adopted by the upper and middle classes and, as schools and universities began to play, rules and codes were imposed. In 1863, the Football Association was formed with the object of uniting the public schools, defining a single set of rules by which they could all play, thus allowing them to compete with one another. However, although the more modern schools were happy to join the Association, most of the grand, ancient schools preferred to continue playing by their own rules. Even among themselves, the FA's members could not agree whether a player should be allowed to pick up the ball with his hands. By 1871, the competing groups had agreed to separate into separate sports. One batch formed the Rugby Football Union, naming themselves after the school, while the others played the first Football Association competition, now better known as the FA Cup. The public schools and universities provided names for the two new games. Just as boys talked about 'brekker' rather than breakfast, so they changed Rugby Football into 'rugger' and whittled down Association Football to 'soccer'.

Like a virus, the new games spread across Britain, seeping out of the playing fields of Eton and Harrow, crossing the quads of Oxford and Cambridge, spilling into the streets of Manchester, Blackburn and Glasgow. In the war over ownership of football's rules, the Union and the Association won, defeating their divided opposition. Gradually, grudgingly, the great public schools accepted that they had lost their individual battles to retain their idiosyncratic games, and accepted one all-embracing set of rules. A few schools continued in isolation, playing games that no-one else understood, just as a few countries grumpily invented their own rules, refusing to accept those set down in England. A hundred years later, some of them still exist. At Winchester College, for instance, boys still play an archaic version of football, kicking and carrying the ball along a pitch enclosed by nets. While the rest of the world has moved on, these schoolboys in Hampshire are still stuck in the nineteenth century. In Australia and the USA, similarly idiosyncratic versions of football still survive, and indigenous teams continue playing football by rules that the rest of the world doesn't understand. Like genetic failures in the global struggle for sporting dominance, these wounded remnants of a previous struggle – American Football, Australian Rules, Winchester College Football – now simply serve to underline the fact that soccer has become the planet's most popular game.

Quickly, Victorian schools incorporated football into their educational programme. The ethical significance of games became expressed in everyday speech from the simplest proverbs – 'don't take your eye off the ball' – to proud moral maxims: 'that's just not cricket', 'keeping a straight bat', 'being a good sport' and 'the game of life.' Sport imposed a sense of collective identity. When their team played, the entire school trooped down to the field and watched. Young boys cheered on their elders. Spectator or player, everyone felt involved in the ritual. Of course, a few boys sneaked away to play in the woods or read a book, but they would be soundly thrashed for their lack of spirit.

Sports helped to safeguard the exclusively masculine atmosphere of schools. Sporting bodies such as the Football Association, the MCC and the Rugby Football Union excluded women from membership and forbade them from taking part in games. Scientific theories backed up this discrimination. Doctors affirmed that women's bodies would be irreparably damaged by playing physically draining sports. The female reproductive system could not cope with the strain imposed by a game of cricket.

Football was also extremely useful for exhausting the boys. A tired boy is less likely to vent his sexual frustration on a housemaid or fellow pupil. Every school had problems with sex – a maid who has to be bundled away before her bump grows too big, or a lithe, blue-eyed boy who discovers that the elder prefects are more than merely friendly – but regular cold baths and intensive exercise usually managed to keep the problem under control.

Some boys rebelled, cracked or crumbled. One of those was Harold Davidson, Charlie's contemporary, a short, thin boy, the son of a vicar who rode around Southampton's suburbs on a tricycle, lecturing his parishioners on the evils of drink. While Charlie organised football teams, Harold languished in the sickroom or the library, huddled over a book. A dreamy and imaginative child, he was unsuited to the vigorous atmosphere of Banister Court, and eventually managed to get himself transferred to a school in Croydon. Surprisingly, he seems to have missed his old school, and returned often, plotting artistic extravaganzas with his two closest friends, Arthur Gregory and Ernest Du Domaine. The school divided into two camps: conformists versus nonconformists, footballers versus poets, cricketers versus artists, hearties versus aesthetes. Ernest, Arthur and Harold stood on one side of the battle lines, and Charlie on the other.

In the summer of 1885, John and Carlota Miller came to live in Britain. A picturesque family legend explains why they decided to leave Brazil. At São Paulo railway station, says the legend, John damaged his back while helping two old ladies unload a coffin from the train. Suffering terrible pain and distrusting the local hospitals, he headed for home. The truth is more prosaic. Documents in Glasgow show that John intended to run his mercantile business from Scotland rather than Brazil. Two other members of the family performed the same reverse-emigration: John's brother William and Carlota's sister Anna Louise, the widow of Charles Dulley, a civil engineer in São Paulo. Together, the four of them lived in the centre of Glasgow for eighteen months, until John suddenly and unexpectedly died of an aortic aneurysm. The funeral was held six weeks before Charlie's twelfth birthday.

Having already lost a brother and a sister, Charlie cannot have been too shocked by the death of his father. If he was ever a sensitive child, he had buried his sensitivity under many layers. Privately, he may have mourned. Publicly, he thrust aside his finer feelings and devoted himself to action. He played cricket and football, throwing himself into vigorous communal activities. Soon, he was not only playing in the school's first elevens, but organising them too, arranging matches, choosing teams, inspiring his fellow pupils with competitive spirit.

A psychologist might draw a direct link between Charlie Miller's enthusiasm for the Spartan virtues of the football field and his youthful familiarity with death. Sport and violence are certainly never far apart, and they were particularly close for Victorian schoolboys. At Tom Brown's first game, he is warned by a fellow pupil, 'Why, there's been two collarbones broken this half, and a dozen fellows lamed.' In *The Longest Journey*, when Gerald is mortally wounded in a football game, no-one seems terribly surprised. He is laid on the floor of the cricket pavilion, inspected briefly by a doctor and a clergyman, then left to die in the arms of his fiancée. Only four years before Charlie arrived in Southampton, a young clerk named Stanley Ernest Gibbs had broken his back in a game of rugby, and died a few hours later. The city's mayor tried to have football banned from public land, but his proposals were gleefully ridiculed, and a local newspaper printed a list of supplementary rules, supposedly issuing from the mayor's office, which insisted that 'every player must wear garden slippers' and no-one, whatever their age, could play without written permission from their parents.

Attempts to mollycoddle players were greeted with similar ridicule by schoolmasters. Several public schools justified their refusal to join the Football Association because the FA wished to stop hacking – the practice that allowed a player who ventured into the other side's half to be kicked in the shins, tripped up and thrown to the ground. Those lily-livered rule-mongers in the FA wished to ban this practice, which had done so much to build the stamina and endurance of British boys. The schoolmasters were right to be worried. Professionalism was gradually sweeping violence out of the game. After all, if your livelihood depended on playing football, you didn't want your ankle broken by some idiot on the other side. His hack might mean weeks without a wage, and thus no food for your wife and kids. To the leisurely inhabitants of schools and universities, such materialism not only sounded ungentlemanly, but stank of cowardice. The odd scratch never hurt anyone, and the occasional mortality was a necessary consequence of living in a martial, imperial society. Death on the playing field and battlefield had to be tolerated. One of the greatest contemporary headmasters, Dr Temple of Rugby, was remembered for his admirable lack of sensitivity:

My father was one day watching a game by the Doctor's side, and, commenting on the scrimmage in which the boys seemed inextricably mixed up, and limbs seemed to have but an off-chance of emerging whole, my father said, 'Do you ever stop this sort of thing?' 'Never, short of manslaughter,' was Dr Temple's characteristic answer.

Temple a charmingly eccentric man. Obsessed by climbing trees, he forbade the boys from ascending any of the tall elms in the school's grounds, but only issued the edict after he himself had climbed every one of them. On a visit to Wellington College, Temple was taken to see a ancient, huge beech. 'Temple admired it very much, and, after looking at it for some time, cried out to Benson, "I can't resist the temptation – look out!" and before Benson could turn round, Temple had made a rush and a leap, and was scrambling up the bole of the tree.'

An enthusiastic athlete, Temple promised the boys that he could run, swim, leap or climb with any of them. 'Games were more to him than a mere joyous recreation; they were a potent factor in his hands for the moulding of human character.' In turn, the boys adored him. When Temple left Rugby to become Bishop of Exeter (and later Archbishop of Canterbury), the whole school mourned. Temple preached a final sermon in the school chapel. As the boys filed out, a master noticed 'one boy remained as if ill. On going to his help he found the tall, six-foot lad prostrate with uncontrollable sobs. He had never been taught by Temple, he was not in his house, he had probably never had six words with him in his life – and yet the sense of parting broke the schoolboy's reserve, and forced him to expose his emotion before his brethren.' For the well-bred Englishman, the death of a parent or a sibling might cause the stiff upper lip to quiver, but only the departure of your headmaster could bring forth tears.

When William Fox Rule returned to Brazil at the end of the 1880s, followed soon afterwards by John Henry, Charlie found himself alone at Banister Court. If he was lonely, he buried his feelings under even greater sporting achievement, making a name for himself not merely in the school but around Southampton. St Mary's gave him a place in a practice match, where he managed to outwit their captain and score a neat goal. If he had been older than sixteen, they might have offered him a place in the team. Meanwhile, as his own family slipped away, he found a surrogate in the Ellabys. One of Christopher's brothers, Frank, played alongside Charlie in that match for St Mary's, while Christopher himself took Charlie to meetings of the Hampshire

Football Association, showing him the duties and responsibilities of adulthood. Together, headmaster and boy walked to the Adelaide restaurant in Southampton or caught a train to the bicycle club in Bournemouth, and sat through long discussions, appointing a team for the county's games, arguing over the minutiae of new rules, deciding how to discipline a player for punching an opponent.

In the spring of 1892, Charlie received a telegram from home. Perhaps he was summoned into Christopher Ellaby's study, and told to prepare himself for bad news. A few words had been transmitted through the transatlantic cable running along the sea bed and carried by a boy from the office in Southampton. Telegrams were expensive, and his mother's words would have been carefully chosen. 'Take a seat', Ellaby would have said before starting to read. 'Something has happened to your brother.'

As a bright, bilingual teenager, John Henry Miller had had no diffi-culty finding a job in São Paulo. He entered the London and Brazilian Bank at the age of seventeen, working as a clerk. A photograph in the bank's staff book shows a neat, handsome youth with a sharp nose, small mouth and precise features. His manager described him as a very satisfactory employee who spoke excellent Portuguese. Promotion beckoned, but his progress was cut short by a bout of fever. A couple of months before his nineteenth birthday, John Henry took to his bed and died.

Brazil may have offered extraordinary economic opportunities to the Millers, but the climate did not agree with them. While Charlie was at school, his family had been succumbing to heat, disease, infection and exhaustion. That day in March, standing in Ellaby's study, listening to the curt words of a transatlantic cable, Charlie learnt that he had now lost not only his father, but his sister and both brothers. For him, the choice was simple. Surrender to grief or repress his emotions. Like the true English gentleman that he was learning to become, Charlie chose the stiff upper lip. If he mourned, he did so alone. His public face remained plucky, determined and bullishly competitive. A few days after learning of his brother's death, Charlie won a famous football match for Banister Court, skipping past his opponents with such verve and confi-dence that he was immediately asked to play for two different teams. One of them, St Mary's, was based in Southampton. The other, the Corinthians, drew its members from all over England.

Each of these two teams fought on different sides of the war that was tearing football apart, dividing footballers into amateurs and professionals, gentlemen and players, leisured aristocrats and paid workers. Today, the war is over. St Mary's has become Southampton Football Club, a multi-million-pound business, attracting tens of thousands of spectators every week, playing their games against the biggest clubs in England. The Corinthians have vanished, their name merged with another tiny antiquated team, their history continued by a group of businessmen who play in Surbiton. Nowadays, a young footballer offered the opportunity to play for one or other wouldn't even hesitate. For Charlie Miller, the choice was not so simple.

Five

On 19 April 1892, the Corinthians arrived in Southampton to play Hampshire. A man short, having travelled with only four of their five forwards, they asked to borrow one of the locals. Someone recommended a young schoolboy named Charlie Miller. That day, still only seventeen, he played alongside some of the finest footballers in the country – men like C.B. Fry, G.O. Smith and Charles Wreford-Brown (who is remembered today as the man who invented the word 'soccer'). During the game, Charlie impressed onlookers, players and journalists, one of whom wrote 'so well did he adapt himself to the style of the famous amateurs that he was one of the features of the match.' Another spectator, rather less generously, reported that 'little Miller, of Banister Court, who was substitute for G.L. Wilson, was by no means the worst player on the pitch.' The Corinthians played with their usual swagger, and won the game by a goal to nil.

There can be no doubt that Charlie Miller considered this match among the most important moments in his life. For ninety minutes, he played alongside legends, and acquitted himself with distinction. Years later, when Brazilian journalists arrived at his home with their notebooks, he always mentioned this particular game, just as he always took the trouble to express his preference for amateurism over professionalism. With a stern morality that would have impressed the Corinthians, he wagged his finger at the young hacks, and let them know that greedy, cash-guzzling professionals had destroyed the game that he loved so much. Money corrupted the sport. Players should love football, respect their opponent, behave on the pitch with honesty and honour, and play for pleasure rather than profit. These were the ideals that the Corinthians espoused, and Charlie Miller clung to the same ideals for the rest of his life.

Ironically, the Corinthians would not have allowed him to join their club. He could admire from afar, and even play as a substitute if they arrived a man short, but not cross the threshold into the team itself. Its hallowed hallways were opened only to men who had attended Oxford, Cambridge or one of the great public schools. The club had been founded in 1882 with fifty members, charging neither entry fee nor subscription, stating two reasons for its existence: firstly, to allow ex-public school men to indulge their love of football in more than the occasional old-boy match; secondly, to provide a better football team for England. In the previous nine years, Scotland had beaten England in eight of their annual matches. An Englishman named Nicholas Lane Jackson surveyed this appalling situation, and saw that the English needed a group of upstanding sportsmen who could form a solid team by playing regularly together. He called a meeting of his chums, and they formed themselves into the Corinthians, borrowing their name from a group of regency dandies and dilettantes. Perhaps Jackson and the club's founders never entirely understood the name's significance, which had originally referred to men like Beau Brummell, frivolous toffs who disdained bourgeois values, pledging their lives to frippery. Although self-consciously amateur and apparently devoted to aristocratic values, Jackson's Corinthians rarely allowed themselves to be flippant. However much they might have pretended not to care who won a match, they celebrated victories, sulked after defeats and played with ferocious competitiveness.

Two years after their founding, the Corinthians challenged Blackburn Rovers to a game. Blackburn had just proved themselves as the best soccer team in the country – and thus the world – by winning the FA Cup. In an embarrassingly one-sided game, the Corinthians knocked eight goals past these newly anointed, grubby-palmed champions, and let in none themselves. The honour of English gentlemen had been restored. After that, the England team started winning too. By 1886, the national team consisted of two players from Blackburn and nine Corinthians. Discussing etiquette for their games against the Scots, Jackson suggested that 'all players taking part for England in future international matches be presented with a white silk cap with embroidered red rose,' which is why players are now said to be 'capped' when they play for their country.

In sport and life, the Corinthians made strenuous efforts to be amateur. They played in cricket shirts and trousers. Shin pads were considered a weakness. During the first two decades of their history, they would permit themselves only friendly matches, although they did later enter the FA Cup. Their style was quick and aggressive, whipping constant passes across the pitch, relying on team effort rather than individual heroics. As G.O. Smith wrote in a little manual on the rules and tactics of football, 'The great object of forwards should be to work together with the precision of a machine, and that the individual credit of anyone should be subservient to the good of the side. A selfish player, however brilliant he may be, should never be allowed to remain in any team – he seeks for self-glorification rather than the victory of his side.' The ethics of these 'men of Corinth' can be summed up in their attitude to penalties. As far as they were concerned, a gentleman would never commit a deliberate foul on an opponent. So, if a penalty was awarded against the Corinthians, their goalkeeper would stand aside, lean languidly on the goalpost and watch the ball being kicked into his own net. If the Corinthians themselves won a penalty, their captain took a short run-up and gave the ball a jolly good whack, chipping it over the crossbar.

Of the men whom Charlie Miller played alongside on that sunny spring day in 1892, one forward and one full-back epitomise the Corinthian spirit and its contradictions. Gilbert Oswald Smith was a slim, meek, intellectual youth, crippled by asthma and modesty, whose personality underwent a bewildering change as soon as he pulled on his boots, strapped up his garters and stepped onto a football pitch. There, he transformed into 'a terror to every great back and goalkeeper in England.' For twenty years he played for his team and his country, first studying at Oxford, then working as a teacher at a prep school. In their history of association football, Alfred Gibson and William Pickford eulogised Smith, describing him as an exemplar of greatness in the English game. 'He knew that football is a manly game, calling for qualities of pluck, grit and endurance, and when he got hurt – as all men do – he never whined or grumbled. He took his courage in both hands, and never funked the biggest back that ever bore down on him. If not exactly a sprinter few men could run faster with the ball at their toe, and one wondered where he acquired the power that sent the ball whizzing into the net like a shot from a gun. To see him walk quietly on to the field with his hands in his pockets, and watch the fine lines of an intellectual face, one wondered why the student ventured into the arena of football. But watch him on the ball with opposing professionals – maybe the best in the land – in full cry after him, and you saw a veritable king among athletes.'

Smith had a rival to the Corinthian crown in Charles Burgess Fry, a fellow student at Oxford. Compatriots on the playing field, their personal styles could not have been more different. Over the next few decades, Fry would not only play football and cricket for England, but equal the world long-jump record, tour Hollywood, write a self-aggrandising autobiography and receive an invitation to be King of Albania. He accepted, but the duplicitous Albanians changed their minds. Unlike the modest, gentlemanly G.O. Smith, Fry was a bully, a braggart and a brute, often strongly criticised for his aggression. Playing for Oxford against London Caledonians, for instance, not only did he call one of the opposing players a 'pig' but prefaced the word with an adjective that the *Scotsman* declined to print in its report. In later life, describing his youthful exploits, he was also a liar, exaggerating charismatic episodes in his autobiography, ignoring humiliations, and – could a sportsman commit a worse sin? – fiddling with his cricket scores. In the 1930s, he acquired a passionate devotion to Hitler. Fry saw in fascism the opportunity to impose public school ideals on an entire population. He admired the Nazis' prioritising of the fit over the weak, the physical over the intellectual, the masculine over the feminine and discipline over creativity. In his autobiography, Fry even claimed that the greatest Corinthians fitted a particular physical type – tall, blonde, fair-skinned, blue-eyed and Nordic – but this seems to have been a blatant projection of his own Aryan sympathies. If you look at a photo of the Corinthians, you'll see immediately that they look a varied bunch. All of them are white, of course, but they are tall and short, broad-shouldered and slim, blonde and dark. Their faces have only one common feature: an expression of effortless superiority.

When Fry and Smith played in Southampton, both of them were only nineteen, and their divergent futures lay ahead, distant and unknowable. The modest schoolmaster, prepping posh little boys for

Eton, and the Nazi sympathiser, roaring his approval for Hitler and Oswald Mosley – that day, they were just two fresh-faced, handsome youths, strolling onto the muddy field, dazzling the crowd with their footballing skills. To an onlooker, or a schoolboy unexpectedly summoned to play alongside them, they must have looked like Greek Gods, natural aristocrats, true English gentlemen.

During the 1890s, footballing honours in Southampton belonged to two teams. One of them, a smart little team named Freemantle, faded over the course of the decade, and has since vanished. The other has prospered. St Mary's, better known as the Saints, has evolved into Southampton Football Club. The St Mary's team photograph for the 1892/93 season shows a group of strapping young gentlemen with moustaches, staring earnestly into the camera. Slightly to one side sits a small, uncomfortable man, arms crossed awkwardly over his knees. He looks different to the others: no moustache, less confidence, and... it's difficult to say exactly what, but something is missing. For some reason, Charles Miller looks as if he doesn't entirely belong with the team. Perhaps, in Britain, he felt foreign, different, tainted by his Brazilian upbringing – just as, in Brazil, he would symbolise everything that was British. Or perhaps his youth was a barrier between him and the other moustachioed gents in the team. They were teachers, engineers, doctors, working men with families, whereas he was just a skinny teenager, shorter, lighter and much younger than his fellows. They called him Nipper. It's a slightly patronising nickname, perhaps, but affectionate. For this slim boy to earn a place in the first team of St Mary's, which was quickly becoming one of the most successful for miles around, he must have been a startlingly good footballer.

Like Fulham, Aston Villa and Bolton Wanderers, St Mary's owed its existence to a group of god-fearing young men who praised the Lord in the pews while punishing their bodies on a football field. More properly known as the St Mary's Church of England Young Men's Association, the team was formed at a meeting chaired by Rev. Arthur Baron Sole in November 1885. The assembled players immediately invited Canon Wilberforce, Rector of St Mary's, to serve as their president. Rev. Sole and Canon Wilberforce enthusiastically encouraged their team, allowing them to practice on church grounds and immortalising their exploits in the parish magazine, which advertised their 'true British manly spirit' and encouraged parishioners to watch the games. 'All connected with the club are believers in muscular Christianity, and think that the advantage of strong developed limbs, a supple frame and a quick eye cannot be overestimated.' By the 1880s, the idea of muscular Christianity had become so familiar and widespread that it was simultaneously an accepted tenet of Victorian society and something of a joke. The peculiar phrase had originated in a review of Charles Kingsley's *Two Years Ago*, published in 1857. 'We all know by this time what is the task that Mr Kingsley has made specially his own – it is that of spreading the knowledge and fostering the love of a muscular Christianity. His ideal is a man who fears God and can walk a thousand miles in a thousand hours – who, in the language which Mr Kingsley has made popular, breathes God's free air on God's rich earth, and at the same time can hit a woodcock, doctor a horse and twist a poker around his fingers.' Sophisticates and intellectuals mocked such silly, simplistic ideals, but the public adored them, seeing these god-fearing poker-twisters as the proper guardians of Queen Victoria and her glorious Dominions. As James Cotton Minchin wrote, 'If asked what our muscular Christianity has done, we point to the British Empire. Our Empire would never have been built up by a nation of idealists and logicians.' Limp-wristed intellectuals could stay at home with their slippers and books, while the poker-twisters roamed the frontiers, pacifying the barbarian hordes.

Muscular Christians made fine footballers too. In 1887, football enthusiasts in Portsmouth, Bournemouth, Cowes, Winchester and Southampton founded the Hampshire Football Association and started two annual tournaments for local teams, the Junior and the Senior. St Mary's won the Junior Cup three years running, then moved into the Senior competition, and won that too. By the end of the decade, the team had grown so successful that they played in specially commissioned shirts. Canon Wilberforce resigned as president, and the post passed to a local doctor, Russell Bencraft. Wilberforce's enthusiasm for temperance, and his frantic attempts to close every pub in Southampton, had never made him popular with the players, particularly since the team had starting selecting members for their sporting ability rather than spiritual purity. Freed from their religious obligations, the Saints stopped practising in the grounds of St Mary's, discussed changing their name to Southampton FC, and took their first wary steps into the debate that was currently splintering English football into rival factions: the bitter division between amateurs and professionals. The situation is perfectly summarised by the football entry in the 1891 edition of *Whitaker's Almanack*:

Every year football, under both codes, the Association and the Rugby, seems to increase in popularity, and our national winter game has now quite as many adherents as its summer equivalent, cricket. It cannot be said, however, that this wide-spread favouritism has improved the game as a pastime pure and simple. Football is now, especially in the great Lancashire and Midland centres of the dribbling code, a commercial undertaking employing a large amount of capital and giving large profits, and under competent and experienced managers good players are imported from Scotland and distant parts into the towns where these powerful professional clubs are found for them and regular wages of £6 to £10 a week guaranteed whilst the men are at the disposal of the club or company running the team which can command big gates when playing another leading eleven in the district. This sort of thing is scarcely conducive to a healthy spirit of fair play and rivalry. It encourages betting, makes winning a match an absolute necessity of the business by fair means if possible, but when hard pressed rules are not too strictly observed, and, indeed, modern Association football has entirely changed in the past few years, not in every instance for the better. The play is perhaps more scientific, but the public school man is very rarely to be found in the crack teams, and hence the status of the game, from a social point of view, has decidedly suffered.

Opponents of professionalism had several objections. Here are a few:

Professional players indulged in sharp practice such as time-wasting or deliberately fouling an opponent.

Professionalism would encourage not only gambling, but cheating and fixing of matches.

Professionalism would lead to the collapse of smaller, poorer clubs.

If clubs could buy the best players from any source, local talent would suffer.

The game would be ruled by the rich, who would use their cash to buy the best players and dominate the leagues.

Football would become a business like any other.

The country's young men would grow flabby from choosing to watch sports rather than compete.

Ironically, although many of these objections might have seemed implausible at the time, even ludicrous, all of them have reached their complete fulfilment today.

The Saints never suffered any doubt over their allegiance in this battle, and defiantly displayed their future ambitions by playing a friendly against the Woolwich Arsenal, who had recently been banned from the London FA for paying players. Such behaviour had turned Arsenal into a pariah for amateurs, but a magnet for professionals. Players flocked to the club and teams organised a series of friendly matches to show their support, delivering deliberate snubs to the London FA. By inviting Arsenal to play a friendly in Southampton, St Mary's turned their back on amateurism. They had not yet officially paid a player, although locals heard rumours of underhand profession-alism. One player was said to have been brought down from the Midlands and, in exchange for joining the team, found a lucrative job at the Ordnance Survey. Even if this wasn't true, it could only be a matter of time before the Saints hired their first professional player. Divorced from their religious roots, drawing their team from engi-neers, teachers, clerks and other bourgeois trades, the Saints embraced a no-nonsense, materialist attitude to life and sport. They had no sympathy with dilettantes or toffs, and justified their callous material-ism by their unnerving ability to win everything in sight – a streak of success that finally came to an end in April 1892, when they lost the Hampshire Six-a-side Championship for the first time in four years. Their nemesis: a short, tricky player named Charlie Miller.

In the tournament, Charlie played alongside grown men like Arthur Denning and Leslie Gay, a Cambridge student who would later wear an England shirt. School sides could include not only masters, but anyone who fulfilled the 'residence' law, living within three miles. However, when Dr Russell Bencraft needed an extra player for St Mary's, he issued an invitation to only one member of this illustrious Banister Court six. He picked Charlie Miller. His trust in the young, skinny schoolboy was vindicated when the Saints played a team from the Aldershot Barracks, and Charlie scored once in a 3-1 victory.

Later that year, Charlie played alongside a professional for the first time, although he probably never knew it. St Mary's hired Jack Dollin, paying him a pound a week and finding him a job, but kept the deal secret. They had been stung once already, two years previously, during their first appearance in the FA Cup competition. Having beaten Bristol in the first round, they gathered 4,000 spectators for their second-round game against Reading, and won 7-0, aided by a pair of soldiers named MacMillan and Fleming. After the match, the official in charge of the Reading team asked the St Mary's secretary, Mr Hendon, if he might borrow a little cash from the day's takings. Mr Hendon handed over some coins. The Reading official hurried down to the telegraph office and used the money to send a telegram to the Football Association, complaining that the game had been played under illegal conditions. As soldiers from the 93rd Highlanders, Fleming and McMillan did not fulfil residency rules. After an enquiry, the Saints were disqualified. Scarred by that experience, they took great care to obey every rule, however arcane, and hid their accelerating professionalism behind a veil of amateurism.

In the spring, Stoke visited Southampton, the first English League club to play St Mary's. On the left wing, Charlie had to tussle with Tom Clare, who played for England. Stoke won 8-0, but the match was exceptionally well-attended, and St Mary's earned a small fortune from the gate. The directors suddenly realised how such lucrative spectacles would allow the club to leapfrog Freemantle and grow into Southampton's biggest team. By the 1893/94 season, they could no longer hide their lust for professionalism, and openly paraded a pair of signings, Henry Offer from Woolwich Arsenal and William Angus from Ardwick (now better known as Manchester City). Eight thousand spectators watched the final for the 1893/94 Hampshire Cup between Saints and Freemantle. One newspaper report estimated that one in three men from Southampton attended the game. Charlie Miller was probably there too, but he would have been watching from the stands rather than playing on the pitch. When professional footballers attracted such huge crowds, the services of local schoolboys were no longer required.

Even if St Mary's had no use for him, Hampshire did, and Charlie played regularly for his county, terrorising opponents in every match. Against Sussex, he scored once in a 3-0 victory, and twice in the game against Bucks & Berks. In the spring of 1893, the Corinthians visited Southampton again in the midst of a national tour. Only ten years after their foundation, cracks had already appeared in the Corinthian pose. Their refusal to train crippled their efforts against the increasingly professionalized outfits of the Football League, and they had just been beaten solidly by Liverpool and Aston Villa. Against Hampshire, they had no such problems, and won 4-0, untroubled by the skills of Charlie Miller, who played for his county rather for than his heroes and shot twice over the bar.

Throughout his last two years at Banister Court, Charlie captained the school's first team, winning a string of plaudits for his skill and commitment. Playing the local grammar school, for instance, he scored two of his team's sixteen goals. Christopher Ellaby's eloquent match reports capture the dedication and enthusiasm of both the players and the supporters, urging their side onwards through the rain and snow, never faltering, never doubting themselves, never giving up. In a game against the King's Royal Rifles from the Aldershot Barracks, one footballer 'met with an accident: he slipped, and his mouth struck the heel of one of the Banister Court player's boots rather forcibly, two of his front teeth being knocked out. Nothing daunted, he returned to the fray with redoubled energy,' and almost immediately assisted a teammate in scoring the winning goal.

Determined to lead rather than merely play, Charlie worked as secretary for both football and cricket in the school, developing his organisational skills, learning to take his place in the hierarchy. Having regularly attended meetings of the Hampshire FA with Ellaby for several years, he managed to get himself onto one of the executive committees, and showed an enthusiastic interest in the legislative side of football. The committee met every few weeks to decide disputes, interpret rules, appoint referees, suspend players for violent conduct or the use of offensive language, and, most importantly of all, draw names out of a hat to compete in local tournaments.

The Hampshire FA did not have the authority to legislate in the war between professionals and amateurs – such weighty matters were decided in London – but the committee's opposing groups allied themselves with each side of the battle. Dr Russell Bencraft represented those who lent towards professionalism, gathering support from the bigger clubs, Freemantle and St Mary's. Opposite them, on the amateur side, the smaller, weaker clubs assembled under the leadership of Christopher Ellaby. Year after year, the Hampshire FA held its annual general meeting, and elected its president for the following season. Year after year, Ellaby put himself forward, and so did Bencraft. Charlie Miller promoted his headmaster, but never succeeded in rallying sufficient votes. Support flowed towards the professionals. Year after year, Ellaby lost, and Bencraft was elected president.

Charlie Miller was nineteen, preparing to leave school, and approaching the moment when he would have to make a choice. Would he stay in Britain or return to Brazil? After a decade away, the country of his birth must have seemed unimaginably distant. Most of the Miller clan had succumbed to the climate. His mother still lived there, but his father, sister, brothers and uncles had died. His Portuguese had faded. Even the country itself had changed dramatically. On 13 May 1888, slavery was finally abolished. Largely as a result of the disruptions caused by aggrieved landowners, suddenly deprived of their enslaved labourers, the Brazilian parliament suffered a series of crises which culminated in a peaceful military coup. On 15 November 1889, the army asked the emperor to abdicate. Blinking and surprised, unsure quite what had happened to him or why, Dom Pedro II boarded a ship in Rio, and sailed across the Atlantic to spend his exile in Paris. Almost overnight, Brazil had been transformed into a modern republic of free citizens, governed by a president rather than an emperor. The rippling ramifications of these two changes – the abolition of slavery and the creation of the republic – had not settled by the early 1890s, and the country still suffered continual conflicts and upheavals. Little revolutions prickled the cities with rioting and gunfire. The future looked precarious. In London, bankers glanced uneasily across the ocean, and decided to begin a gradual withdrawal, worrying that their investments would be wiped out by a sudden violent change of government.

In Southampton, no-one knew whether Charlie was staying or going. Rumours circulated that he would be joining Freemantle. Competing whispers suggested that he was returning to Brazil or even heading for Buenos Aires. Had he chosen to stay, his skills could probably have secured him a job as a professional footballer. More likely, via an array of well-placed friends, he might have found a respectable job in an office or a bank, and continued playing as an amateur. He could even have arranged for his mother to join him in the peace and serenity of the Hampshire countryside. She would be safer there than in Brazil.

Throughout the winter of 1893 and the spring of 1894, his enjoyment of the football season would have been spoiled by news from Rio and São Paulo. If he wanted an excuse to stay in Britain, he would have found it in the reports carried in every newspaper, describing the violent revolution sweeping across southern Brazil. First, secessionists in Rio Grande do Sul provoked violent retaliation from the government. Next, a naval revolt in Rio de Janeiro blockaded the city. Foreigners had not yet been advised to flee, but their position looked precarious, and any official would have counselled Charlie to stay in Southampton. As the *Rio News* reported in September 1893, 'The British consul sent out a timely warning yesterday to all British houses in regard to the threatened bombardment, advising them to close their doors.' The revolution had begun as a naval mutiny and, that autumn, spread outwards from Rio, infecting cities up and down the coast. Ports were bombarded. Ships were unable to unload their cargoes, so trade came to a halt. Earlier in the conflict, battles had been fought with gentlemanly regard for protocol. 'At 4 p.m. a brief interval ensued to permit the sailing of the Royal Mail steamer *Tagus* and to give the combatants time to dine.' As the casualties stacked up, such niceties had to be neglected. Even the British could no longer remain oblivious to the inconveniences of living in a war zone. When the revolution started, the British cricket team had continued their match in Niteroi during a bombardment, ignoring the shells whistling overhead, but their attitude changed when a member of their community died. 'Firing was reopened soon after midday, and one of its first victims was Mr Henry T. Watmough, a London and Brazilian Bank clerk, who was struck by a piece of shell in the Leao do Ouro hotel, Rua da Candelaria, where he had been taking his lunch.' The tragic tale of Henry Watmough had an additional twist: he had arrived from Britain a year previously in a quartet of ambitious clerks, each of them determined to make his fortune in the tropics. Within weeks, all of them caught yellow fever. Three died, leaving only Henry. He survived a few more months before his skull was shattered by a piece of shrapnel. No wonder the Foreign Office advised even the most adventurous Briton against emigration to Brazil.

Those plucky Britons who managed to survive disease and gunfire had one more enemy to fight: the thieving dissidents. Revolutionary forces regularly stole supplies from the British, capturing barges packed with coal from the Brazilian Coal Company, who immediately complained to the Foreign Office. With worrying lack of urgency, the Foreign Office in London replied by telegram, promising to investigate, and did nothing.

Insulated by rural seclusion, São Paulo was protected from the war itself, but the citizens found themselves overrun by evacuees. 'There has been an exodus from Santos to the interior of São Paulo. It is stated that the São Paulo railway trains have carried as many as 800 passengers a day.' Hotels charged vastly inflated rates, capitalising on the flood of refugees. Trade halted. 'Large deposits of coal have been shipped from Santos to the interior of the state of São Paulo. The Santos people were apparently afraid the revolutionists would capture it.' As the days grew longer and hotter, the city's water tanks dried up. Food grew scarce. Stocks dwindled. Beggars filled the streets. Starving armadillos were seen rummaging in the cemeteries and feasting on recent corpses.

The British tried to continue with their normal lives. The Santos and São Paulo cricket clubs played one another. William Fox Rule captained the São Paulo Athletic Club side, and led them to victory. However, this display of British pluck began to look less brave than foolish. In October, British and American consulates advised their citizens to leave. The Brazilian government declared martial law, allowing itself the right to expel all foreigners from the country and confiscate their property, while threatening to prevent any additional foreigners from arriving. Only certain classes of foreign nationals would be excluded from this edict: any man married to a Brazilian woman, any widower with Brazilian children, and anyone who owned real estate in the country. None of these applied to Charlie Miller.

Perhaps he didn't care. Perhaps he didn't worry about the future. While Brazil tore itself apart, Charlie devoted his attention to football. He played several times a week, scoring goal after goal for Banister Court, and regularly representing the county. Newspaper reports of the games always mention his skill and speed. The *Southern Referee*, describing a game against Dorset played before a crowd of 1,500, suggested that Miller's new-found role as centre forward had made him the lynchpin of the team's attack. 'The Dorset defence was of the stone-wall order, and time after time broke up the prettily planned combination of the Freemantle wing and Miller's tricky play.'

Later that spring, the Corinthians visited Hampshire once more. This time, they played in Bournemouth rather than Southampton. Special trains – and cheap away-day tickets – brought spectators from surrounding towns. The match was the last day of an exhausting week-long tour, starting on Monday in Sunderland, whose team were the current League champions. After losing 3-1 there, the Corinthians played every afternoon throughout that week, travelling to Bournemouth via Derby, Gloucester and Taunton. If Hampshire were ever going to beat the Corinthians, this was their chance. A crowd of 1,600 filled the stands, and saw the game start well for Hampshire. Dorkin, one of the professionals from St Mary's, shocked the 'men of Corinth' with his pace, but shot straight into the arms of Leslie Gay. Fighting back, the Corinthians scored once, and once again. At that point, just as Hampshire seemed to have lost control of the game, Charlie Miller came to life. 'Several times the little Banister Court boy tricked Harrison. On the first occasion he deftly passed to Stewart, who put in a long shot, and George took the ball as it came across and whipped it into the net. Within a minute, Miller again got possession, and Stewart sent in a stinging shot. Gay got at it, and with a big effort, twisted it out of its course, but Dorkin, who came up with a rush, finished by dashing it into the net, and so equalised.' At half-time, the score stood at a respectable two-all. After the interval, things didn't go so well. The Corinthians scored four more times, Hampshire managed a single consolation, and the game ended 6-3. As the players stood on the pitch at the end of the game, William Pickford picked up the ball and handed it to Charlie Miller, a small gesture of gratitude for all his hard work.

After that final game against his heroes, Charlie played twice more for St Mary's, competing in the semi-final and final of Hampshire CCC Charity Cup. Charlie earned another medal for his collection. His final football season as a schoolboy had ended triumphantly. He was nearly twenty, and had nothing more to learn at Banister Court. This would have been an appropriate moment to deflate his footballs, pack his trunk and sail home to Brazil, where his mother was waiting. Instead, he stayed in Southampton, delaying his departure again and again. There was always one more game to play. At the end of term, he competed in the school tennis tournament, winning the doubles with Arthur Denning. He played cricket regularly for the school. Having scored a century, he features in a list of 'notable batting performances' in the Hampshire County Cricket Club's annals. He even got a game for the MCC when they arrived from London with only ten men.

By the end of that long, hot summer, Charlie had made a definite decision about his future. He was going to stay in Britain. Why? How? To do what? No-one knows. Charlie Miller did not indulge himself with expressions of personal emotion, wrote no passionate letters, and kept his own counsel. If a love affair kept him in Southampton, or a job, or fear, he left no record of it. The idea of returning to São Paulo must have been much harder at the age of twenty, surrounded by friends and familiar things, than the compulsory journey to Britain ten years previously. He had made a nest of friends and contacts in Southampton, much stronger than the depleted clan who awaited him in Brazil. Perhaps he simply felt no urge to leave the country that had become his home, the family that had virtually adopted him, and the man who had been as generous, supportive and influential as any father. That August, for whatever reason, Charlie made a definite commitment to Britain. Although he had not pledged his future to Freemantle or any other football team, he put himself forward for election to the Hampshire Football Association. This was a serious post, entailing onerous duties and important obligations to the county's footballers, and not a job that a responsible man would seek if he was planning to emigrate.

On the first day of September, the FA announced the results of their secret ballot. 'In Southampton Division, A.C. Knight and H.B. Johns (St Mary's), and Dr Cooper and E.M. Wood (Freemantle) are elected, C. Miller (Banister Court) failing to secure a place.' The votes had split down party lines. The two biggest teams in Southampton, St Mary's and Freemantle, took two seats each. Charlie Miller, representing no constituency but himself, and with no allies except Christopher Ellaby, found himself marginalised. A month later, he left Britain.

On 5 October 1894, Banister Court held its annual prize-giving ceremony, attended by parents, local worthies, and the vicars of every church within ten miles. One of the prizes went to Charlie Miller, but he was not present to receive it. That afternoon, as Christopher Ellaby gave his annual lecture, parents hid their yawns and straight-backed boys stepped forward to collect their prizes, Charlie was standing on the deck of a steel-hulled steamer, leaning against the rail, feeling the sea breeze on his face and watching the coast of England slip away from him. The night before, Ellaby must have presented Charlie with his prize in a private ceremony. Prizes at the school were always leather-bound books, embossed with the gilt arms and logo of Banister Court. On the first page, Ellaby had written a brief dedication, thanking Charles Miller for his hard work as secretary of the school's football and cricket clubs. The book itself was an appropriate gift for someone leaving England: *The Natural History of Selbourne*, an elegiac evocation of rural life and landscape, written in the 1780s, just as the first whiffs of industrialisation had floated across the countryside. Selbourne is a little village, nestling in the midst of a magical landscape, only a few miles inland from Southampton. Anywhere in the world, an emigrant might use this book as an *aide-mémoire*, a reminder of the country that he had left behind and the values that he carried with him. A man could open the stiff leather covers of his school prize, pore over the crinkly pages and, word by word, phrase by phrase, find himself transported back to the pre-industrial beauty of an English Arcadia.

The long voyage might have seemed like a good opportunity for some light reading, but Charlie's copy of *The Natural History of Selbourne* has survived the intervening decades, slotted into family book shelves, and shows few signs of ever having been opened. Judging by its pristine pages, Charlie treasured the book for sentimental and symbolic reasons, but never bothered reading it. If he ever wanted to read aboard the *Magdelena*, he preferred another book – a slim volume, printed on cheap paper, bound between flimsy blue covers, and bearing the name of William Pickford on its title page. Secretary of the Hampshire Football Association and a famous footballer in his own right, Pickford was even better known as an administrator, legislator and referee. Every year, the Hampshire FA printed a little booklet, describing the county's teams, laying out the fixtures for the following season, setting down a full list of the rules of Association Football and giving William Pickford's tips for referees.

Just as a missionary packs his trunk with Bibles, preparing to proselytise among the heathen hordes, so Charlie Miller took the tools of football, the objects that would allow him to play the game wherever he went, whatever he found, whoever his team or opponents might be. Alongside the rule book, he had a sturdy pair of boots, an air pump, two shirts – one from Banister Court and a second from St Mary's – and two leather footballs, deflated and laid flat. One of the balls was the gift from Pickford, handed to Charlie after his last game for Hampshire.

Although Charlie had been gone for only a few hours, his presence was missed already at Banister Court. Ellaby's eloquent description of the day, written for the school magazine, concludes by asking his readers to remember one vital fact: if the owners, administrators and teachers of Banister Court produced boys who merely passed exams and won prizes, they would consider themselves failures.

They hoped to form men of firm and reliant character, and such a man he ventured to say would be found in one who had just left. Charles Miller was not only a splendid player, but he managed the business in connection with the school games down to the very day before he sailed. He had also taken an interest in the management of county football. It was efficiency such as this, and what was far better, the unselfishness and industry that it implied, that made a man deserve success in life.

Six

Within a few days, he knows the face of every passenger in first class, and many of the crew too, the waiters and stewards who serve in the dining room, the officers who eat with them, the sailors with sooty faces, the engineers with oily hands. They recognise him too. They know him as the slim, short, fit young man who treats the deck as a training ground. Soon he has a nickname. They call him 'the player'. Every morning, he walks briskly ten times round the boat, the breeze ruffling his hair, the spray showering him with a light coating of salty water. Once his walk is done, he brings a leather ball onto the deck, and practises for hours, using the boat as his opponent, learning to combat its tilting deck, the unpredictable gusts of wind, the sudden lurches which send his football flying in unlikely directions. If he can persuade a couple of the other men to join him, they improvise a pitch, using a funnel as one post and a blanket for the other, taking turns to stand in goal. In the afternoon, a few more men might join in, so they stow the football and play cricket at the stern, trying not to hit any sixes. When the other men tire of the game, they wander away to gamble or drink or flirt with the few women on the boat, competing for the young and pretty ones. Alone, Charlie continues practising, his eyes fixed on the ball, his face coated with a sheen of sweat.

For the first day or two, those smart passengers travelling first class stay in their cabins, sheltering from the swell, nursing their queasy stomachs. As the *Magdelena* eases past Cherbourg and headed across the Bay of Biscay, even the spacious first-class apartments grow stuffy. The heat tempts them onto deck. They introduce themselves, and discuss the political situation in Montevideo, the best place to buy shoes in Buenos Aires, a scandal in Bahia. Several of the passengers have met on previous voyages. Others are earnest bankers heading to South America for the first time, who settle into deckchairs every afternoon for a diligent study of Spanish irregular verbs or Portuguese vocabulary. Soon, the heat lulls them, their books droop and they snooze, waking at dusk with sunburnt faces.

The ship pauses in Lisbon to pick up passengers and supplies. He hurries ashore, and takes the opportunity to practise a few sentences in Portuguese, seeing what he can remember after a decade of speaking nothing but English. He wanders through the streets, staring at the cakes and snacks in shop windows, many of which he remembers from his childhood, the shapes, the ingredients, even the tastes, but he can't recall a single name, and decides not to go through the pantomime of pointing. In the market, he tries to haggle with an old woman. She laughs at him, and snatches the glittering coin from his palm, passing him three oranges in return. When he pierces the skin, the sudden rising scent, the succulence of a freshly picked orange, sends him stumbling back into the past, overwhelmed by memories.

Back on the boat, they have their full complement. One hundred and eighteen crew, thirty-eight first class passengers, a hundred and sixty-four in second, three hundred and fifty-five travelling steerage. The separate classes do not mingle. Nor do the different nationalities, even in first. He chats to the British and Americans, wishes a good morning to the Germans, Portuguese and Brazilians, nods to anyone in second, and occasionally peers down on the muddled multitude in steerage, who remain permanently confined to the lower deck. Like animals, the passengers in steerage are fed from buckets, lowered into their quarters on a rope. A bucket of rice, a bucket of beans. At night, their songs permeate the rest of the boat, and the sound of their dancing lasts long after the first-class entertainments have ended. One of his new friends, a ruddy farmer heading for his father's estate in the Pampas, admits that he can't help feeling envious, hearing the music, gazing down on the women in their loose dresses, and tries to winkle a similar confession out of Charlie, a shared longing to swap their starched tablecloths and silver cutlery for a night of peasantry abandon. Charlie laughs, shakes his head, suggests a game of cards, changes the subject. Even if he felt the same, he could not admit it, not to a man whom he had only just met.

By the evening that they reach Madeira, the weather has lost all hint of northern chill. Long sunny days are followed by balmy nights. A shout of 'whale!' and all the passengers rush to the side of the boat. Clinging to the rail, they peer across the ocean, following the pointing fingers. The smooth, black back of a whale slides through the waves, punctuating its passage with tall spouts of seawater, impromptu fountains. They pass the huge peak of Tenerife. Fishing boats bob around them. A shoal of thirty dolphins accompanies the *Magdelena* for a mile or two, scything through the water, leaping into the air, putting on a show. At Cape Verde, passengers line the deck, and toss coins into the water. Local boys dive to fetch the glittering treasure from the clear water. Wags on board wrap copper coins in silver paper, and jeer when the shining black boys disapprovingly shake their heads. At ten o'clock on Sunday morning, cruising through the empty ocean, the passengers and crew gather on deck, dressed in their finest clothes. The captain preaches a brief sermon, and the congregation sings a couple of hymns.

St Vincent is an island with only three trees, so they say, where the inhabitants take turns to sit in the shade. He strides through the dusty streets. Naked children run after him, holding out their hands, chattering and bickering, giggling when he pleads ignorance of their language. He wanders into a church, and sees a service conducted by black priests. That shocks him more than anything – the thought that black men could walk through the church, backs straight, heads held high, acting like archbishops. Leaving St Vincent, they travel for five days without seeing land – the longest stretch on the voyage – but they are never bored, having found ways to occupy themselves. An early morning bath in salt water. After breakfast, a brief walk around the deck, stopping to peer down at the passengers in steerage. Among the poor, dirty, huddled masses, a few deaths will occur, but the mourning and burial will be conducted so surreptitiously that the other passengers will never realise that anything untoward has happened. During the morning, he jogs around the deck, and practises football. The first-class passengers eat together at lunch and dinner, and gather in the middle of the afternoon to learn the result of the sweepstake on the distance travelled that day. At night, four sailors carry the piano onto the deck, and the passengers gather, the young standing, the old in deckchairs, each of them taking turns to read a poem, sing a song, play a tune or recite a ditty. A late-night promenade is highly recommended. In the blackness, no sign of humanity can be seen. Not a light. No hint of land. The stars are indescribable. The ship leaves a vast phosphorescent wake, fizzing and bubbling through the waves, stretching towards the shadowy horizon.

Two days are devoted to athletics. The older women act as judges, the younger ones as mascots. The bursar has a roster of races, restricting entry to men over sixty, or boys between eight and fifteen, or unmarried girls. He sets rules for the three-legged race, the sack race, the egg-and-spoon race, the tug of war. Charlie wins the sprint (bow to stern) and the marathon (twenty times around the boat). That night, after dinner, prizes are distributed at a solemn ceremony. The elderly judge summons the victors to the captain's table, and hands out ribbons and trinkets.

The heat becomes unbearable. When the sun has been shining for a few hours, the deck is too hot to touch with bare feet. Railings scald skin. At night, the cabins are sultry and stifling. The British mutter. The Portuguese moan. The Germans huddle over their textbooks, memorising new words. A family of second-class passengers, unable to bear the choking stuffiness, driven half-mad, disobey instructions and open the porthole in their cabin. They sleep more comfortably, finally able to breathe. Around two or three in the morning, a flying fish leaps through the window and lands on the bed. Woken by the frantic flapping, the woman shrieks for help. Her husband yells. The children holler. Attracted by the screams, their neighbours come running. Hearing the screams, assuming that the boat is sinking, passengers rattle door handles and shout, waking their friends, warning the crew, rushing through the corridors. Within minutes, a riot has engulfed the lower decks. Desperate passengers struggle to reach the lifeboats, shoving one another aside. Next morning, the British smile to one another over their tea and toast. As they could have guessed, all the families involved were Portuguese and Brazilian, hot-blooded, undisciplined, not to be trusted.

At midday, the sun is directly overhead, and they stroll around the deck without their shadows, liberated from the person who has dogged their footsteps on every other day of their lives. Charlie has crossed the line already, so he has to suffer none of those tricks and games which are used to taunt equatorial virgins. On this smart boat, no-one will be tarred, feathered or tossed overboard, but Charlie plays a few mild gags on his fellow passengers, making some apple-pie beds, fixing a taut hair across a telescope and trying to persuade gullible onlookers that they are staring through the lens at the equator itself.

A mesh of black dots like swarming flies, which resolves into a flock of seabirds, is the signal that they are approaching land again. Their first sight of Brazil is not Brazil, but a blip in the ocean, Fernando de Noronha, 200 miles from the coast, used as a prison. Brazil dislikes the finality of execution, and confines its murderers to this island rather than hanging or beheading them. Charles Darwin spent a few hours here in 1832, but he was one of the last foreigners to visit. Since then, the Brazilian government has banned curious eyes. From the boat, the passengers peer at the island, hoping to see a raft bobbing on the waves, an escaping prisoner. A day later, they moor in Pernambuco, and little boats sail out, laden with fruit. Sixpence for three pineapples. Tuppence for a melon. Oranges are ten a penny. He goes ashore with some of his new friends. In the market, one of the Englishwomen is offered a naked black baby. 'Two shilling,' suggests the mother in halting English. 'Good price, two shilling. You want?' At other stalls, men sell monkeys, toucans, raccoons. Green parrots cost five shillings, and marmosets are ninepence apiece. The city's smells arouse long-forgotten memories – the rich stench of garlic, the decaying piles of rubbish, the hot pavements, the cloying scent of freshly sliced mangoes. At 4 p.m., a single shot from the *Magdelena* announces the signal for sailing. The blue peter has been hoisted. Passengers hurry back to the ship carrying their loot – bags of oranges, ornate crucifixes, pretty watercolours of the town.

They sail south, skirting the coast, passing mountain ranges and pimply lighthouses. He finds a patch of shade and practises all day, hour after hour, preparing for his arrival, determined to be picked immediately for the English football team in São Paulo. On the approach to Rio, people line the deck, straining their eyes, trying to spot the Sugar Loaf Mountain. Twenty times he is told the story of the Englishman who climbed it, only to discover on his return that no-one believed what he had done, so clambered up again and planted a Union Flag on the summit. When the authorities objected to this imperialist gesture, he had to climb a third time and bring it down. In Rio, they moor overnight, disembark most of the passengers, pick up a couple more, then continue south to Santos.

Standing on the deck, preparing himself for his homecoming, he tries to convince himself that he recognises this landscape, but nothing looks familiar – not the long range of mountains, shrouded in haze; not the beaches; not the frilly fronded palms; not even the wide bay of Santos, guarded by a long, low island. The *Magdelena* progresses along the docks, slowing, her engines groaning, churning the mud, easing past endless shabby warehouses. White storks perch on wooden posts. The smell of coffee wafts across the water. She nudges the dock, drifts back. Ropes are thrown. A swell of water foams against the hull. Clanking hawsers. Shrieking chains. Rushing feet. Farewells. He turns one last time, waves to his fellow passengers, nods to a couple of the crew, and trots down the gangplank towards the shore.

The history of Brazilian football starts at this instant. Pelé, Socrates, Ronaldo – they can trace their lineage from the dust that stirs as Charles Miller's boot scuffs against the dock at Santos. So say the footballing authorities in Brazil, and they date their game from this day, this instant, that cloud of dust. The first game might have been a better starting point, or the formation of the first league, but historians of the game chose Charlie Miller's arrival as the moment of their birth. At the end of the twentieth century, when Brazilians celebrated the centenary of their football, they partied on this date, a hundred years to the day since Charles Miller walked down a gangplank, carrying a football under each arm.

So it saddens me to report that at this moment in the life of Charlie Miller, we come to an event that is not only the most famous single action that he ever performed, and the act for which he is remembered, but the most awkward and embarrassing incident in his life for any biographer to describe.

Charlie Miller was a shy, quiet man who did not like to broadcast his emotions to the wider world. He kept his own counsel. In the latter part of his life, he gave some interviews to journalists, who always commented on his politeness, his good nature, his humility, his bashful refusal to brag, his ironic belittling of his own achievements, that ineffable quality of Englishness that clung to him, even after so many decades of living in Brazil. A true gentleman, they liked to say of him. A true English gentleman. Even in these interviews, some of which filled columns of newsprint, he managed to shield his personality, allowing little of himself to leak into the public arena, confining his comments to some stories about the introduction of football and some criticisms of professionalism. Among the few personal details that he did divulge, he told the story of his arrival in Brazil, and this quaint, quotable anecdote has become inextricably linked with the legend of Charles Miller, footballer, Englishman, pioneer of the Brazilian game. He talked to a journalist in the 1920s, a man who worked for *O Imparcial* in Rio de Janeiro. *O Imparcial* was running a series on the early history of Brazilian football, and their journalists interviewed several of the main participants. In the piece, the writer describes speaking directly to Charles Miller – although he doesn't say whether they spoke by phone or in person – and gives a short biography, which culminates in a delightful anecdote. The relevant section is worth quoting in Portuguese and English.

No cáes de Santos, solmne, como se fosse para uma missa, meu pae esperava que en desembarcasse com o clássico canudo do diploma. Mas, eis que, salto-lhe a frente com duas holas de futebol, uma em cada mão...
O velho, surpreso, indaga:
— Que é isto, Charles?
— O meu diploma, responda.
— Como?
— Yes! Your son has graduated in football...
Temperamento alegre, o velho riu-se do bluff. Estava salva a patria...

That is precisely how the story appeared in *O Imparcial* on 21 October 1927. If any Brazilian readers missed what was said, the headline translates the punch line into Portuguese, preparing readers for the meat of the story. 'Meu pae, bachalelerei-me em futebol!'

On the quay at Santos, solemn, as if he were at a funeral, my father was waiting for me to disembark holding my degree certificate. But in fact I appeared in front of him with two footballs, one in each hand... The old man, surprised, enquired:
— What is this, Charles?
— My degree, I replied.
— What?
— Yes! Your son has graduated in football...
The old man, in good spirits, laughed. I was off the hook...

This captivating anecdote, which seems to encapsulate so much about Charlie Miller's character and actions, has appeared in almost everything that has been written about him, both during his lifetime and in the decades since his death. In biographical sketches and newspaper interviews, books about football and guides to Brazil, this story is told again and again. Not merely is it a great tale, but the pluck and jollity of young Charles Miller seem to epitomise a lost era of innocence, a time in which people played football for love rather than money. His boyish passion for the sport, and his disdain for worldly achievements, are the attitudes that we feel should motivate footballers, even if most of them seem to be driven by little more than a lust for fat pay packets, big houses and silicon-assisted girlfriends.

If only things were so simple. If only gentlemen always told the truth. If only money was the sole reason that people cheat in sport, distort their biographies or rewrite history. As you will have noticed, Charlie Miller's description of his arrival at Santos has one small problem at its heart. You did? You spotted the flaw? You would have been forgiven for missing it. Generations of writers and commentators failed to notice anything amiss. But you are more astute than them. You have paid attention. You know very well that, on the day Charlie Miller walked down that gangplank and set foot on Brazilian soil, his father had already been lying in a Glaswegian grave for eight years.

Perhaps the newspaper made a mistake. Perhaps the journalist conducted the interview over a crackly phone line, and misinterpreted a vital word. Perhaps he lied. Perhaps he invented the entire interview or interviewed the wrong person or, inspired by a bottle of wine at lunchtime, added a few details. Perhaps Charles Miller found himself confused, or hungover, or had a migraine on the day of the interview. Many Brazilians have a cavalier attitude to the past – a good story is better than a dull truth – and perhaps Charlie decided to repay them with a touch of the same. Or perhaps he wanted to tease an irritating journalist, not expecting his little joke to acquire such a surprising momentum.

These are excuses. The basic fact is this: Charlie lied. He made a deliberate attempt to promote his version of events and create his own myth. It worked, and his invention, his history, his myth, is now celebrated as the birth of Brazilian football, remembered with fireworks and dancing in the street. The obvious question is, why should he have behaved in this reprehensible way? Why had he shattered the ideals to which he had always aspired? Why was he so ungentlemanly?

The answer is simple and sad. The interview in 1927 happened to coincide with an appalling moment in his life. Things had gone badly wrong. He had been attacked and humiliated. Having spent decades building a life for himself, the basis of his happiness had been stolen from him, and that theft plunged him into isolation and depression. If he consoled himself by showing off a little, puffing up his own importance and turning dreary reality into a good tale, who can blame him? The details will have to wait for another chapter, thirty years later in his life, when he was middle-aged, bitter and burdened with cares. For now, we shall have to restrain ourselves, remain in 1894, and imagine Charlie Miller as a spruce, confident, energetic lad of nineteen, wearing his best clothes, wanting to make a good impression. He strolls down that gangplank, taking care not to walk too fast, not wishing to seem impatient or over-emotional. He wanders from the *Magdelena* to the shore, where a small group of figures await him, peering into the sunshine and waving white handkerchiefs. Some of them he half-recognises, and others he has never seen before, and one of them, down there, a squat figure in a black dress, standing in the midst of the group, he knows immediately. He can't help himself – he starts hurrying down the gangplank, his soles rapping on the wood, and breaks into a run, and sprints towards his mother.

Charlie was lucky that the boat stopped at Santos. Only a couple of years earlier, the port had been closed to shipping. The town had a population of about 20,000, a tenth of whom had been culled by an epidemic of yellow fever. Trade stopped. Ships skipped Santos, cruising straight down to the next port on the coast. Shipowners had a dread of infectious diseases, which would disrupt their schedules, blockade their boats and destroy their business. If a single case was found on board, a steamer would be quarantined for weeks or months, forbidden from disembarking any passengers. Threatened by the presence of disease, captains usually chose to avoid a port rather than risk quarantine. Santos had suffered particularly badly. People still remembered the British ship whose entire crew died of yellow fever. Another crew sailed from Southampton. When they boarded the boat, the fever infected them too, and every sailor died. After that, the most successful of the British coffee traders, the Johnston family, built accommodation on the island that lies between Santos and the sea. Their sailors would hand control of their ship to a skeleton crew from the mainland, disembark onto the island, and wait there until their cargo had been loaded or unloaded.

Having gathered their prodigal son and loaded his luggage into a carriage, the Millers rode the railway back to São Paulo as quickly as possible, not wanting to waste an extra second in the unwholesome atmosphere of Santos. On the train, his cousins cooed over Charlie, and laughed at his stammering attempts to speak Portuguese with the porters and the guard. He could remember only a few words, and construct no more than a handful of hopelessly ungrammatical sentences, but his accent remained perfectly Paulista. In a few weeks, they promised him, he would be speaking like a native, and no-one would know that he had been away. As the train rattled across a bridge, they taught him the words for hello and goodbye, please and thank you, yes and no. One of his cousin put her hand on his knee, and asked him if he remembered the two most important words in Brazil, *amanhã* and *paciência*. He shook his head. She smiled. *Amanhã* means tomorrow, she told him, which is when you can expect whatever you wanted today. *Paciência* means patience. The more you have, the happier you will be. Welcome home, Charlie. Welcome to Brazil.

Later, when the children dozed or crouched against the side of the carriage, peering at the passing jungle, his mother gave him an inventory of deaths and births, marriages and engagements, achievements and disasters, telling Charlie what had changed in the past ten years. Just as the lives of family and neighbours had been disrupted by sudden deaths and unlikely marriages, so had the country undergone a succession of upheavals. The emperor had been banished to Paris, and died there. The country had become a republic, ruled by a president. Most importantly, perhaps, slavery had been abolished. Already, immigrants filled the quays at Santos and the streets of São Paulo, looking for work on the coffee plantations, filling the gaps left by newly liberated slaves. As the train lifted into the hills, pulled by the thick steel cable, the sea breezes slackened, and the temperature rose, filling the carriage with a fierce heat unlike anything that Charlie had remembered. He mopped his forehead, sipped water, and wondered whether he would survive the Brazilian summer. Did he grow up in this? Could anyone survive a whole season of this? And, most importantly, how on earth do they have the energy to play football?

The answer to that was simple. They didn't. When he arrived in São Paulo, and sought out his cousin and schoolmate, William Fox Rule, now an established member of the British community in the city, Charlie discovered that not a single person played football. The game was unknown, not just among the British, but in the city, the state, even the country. Throughout the vast land mass of Brazil, you would not find a football. They had no copies of the rules, no boots, no shirts, no pitch, no goals. William Fox Rule and his pals smiled at Charlie's horror. Confronted by his barrage of questions, they explained that Brazil had quite enough games already – cricket, cycling, polo, athletics – much more suited to the climate than football. When Charlie insisted that no other game could equal soccer and expressed his determination to start a team, they laughed. Go ahead, they said. You're welcome to try. But the tropical climate is wrong for football, they told him. In this heat, grass can't grow, and no-one will have the strength to run. The ground is solid, so the ball will bounce too high, and you'll break a leg when you fall over. If you want to play football, then play football. But it'll never catch on.

So he waited. Throughout that long, hot summer, as Christopher Ellaby and Arthur Denning were enduring sleet and snow on the pitches of Southampton, Charlie Miller donned his whites and strolled onto the baked earth of a tropical cricket pitch. When he arrived, his cousins, led by William Fox Rule, had interrogated him, demanding to know if he played cricket. Charlie nodded, shrugged his shoulders. A modest man, not liking to boast, he admitted to batting a little, and bowling a plausible spinner. He could usually make a decent catch, he confessed, then let slip the fact that he had played a game for the MCC, dropping those three initials into conversation as if they meant nothing to him. His cousins demanded to hear the full story. When they learnt that he had actually played a full game for the Marylebone Cricket Club, they laughed and clapped their hands, promising him a permanent place on the SPAC team. At first, he didn't know what they were talking about – spack? spack? what do you mean, spack? – but he soon learned that the São Paulo Athletic Club was the centre for the British community's social life, and one of the few places in South America where you could find a proper cup of tea.

In 1875, one of the São Paulo newspapers had drawn the attention of its readers to a peculiar foreign ritual which was being performed under their very noses. *'Realiza-se amanhã no campo Rua Mauá (Estação) uma partida de cricket, esporte inglês, entre paulistas e cariocas.'* In other words, a group of men from São Paulo (the Paulistas) had played cricket against a team from Rio de Janeiro (the Cariocas). This was the first recorded game in the city. Over a decade later, in 1888, the British in São Paulo decided to create a formal sports club. They christened themselves the São Paulo Athletic Club, immediately elided to SPAC. The acronym is pronounced 'spack' by English-speakers and 'spacky' by Brazilians, who can never resist adding an extra twirl to the hard end of a word. Within a few months, the secretary of SPAC had arranged games with British cricketers in Rio and Santos, and a team even visited from the British community in Argentina. Very appropriately, a rainstorm started on the day that the visitors arrived from Buenos Aires, and continued for the twelve days of their stay, washing out the ground. Not a single ball was bowled.

With institutions such as SPAC, the British built rigid barriers between themselves and the locals. The rigid lines of a cricket crease, the whitewashed edges of a football pitch, the wrought-iron gates and high walls of a sports club – with these barriers, Britons immunised themselves. In São Paulo, they had opened a Protestant graveyard in 1858 and built a British church in the 1870s. The year that Charlie returned to the city, the British opened the Hospital Samaritano, sharing the cost with the local Germans and French, hiring a Swedish doctor and Swiss nurses. Without their own clubs, societies, churches, hospitals and schools, the British risked tarnishing their values and ideals by contact with local culture. In his guide to Brazil, published in the 1860s, William Scully warned innocent young Britons against the potential dangers of that licentious country.

> A great want in Brazil is the out-door games, the debating clubs, the cheap concerts, the lectures, the periodicals, and all the various appliances which the European at home has at his command, to strengthen and improve both mind and body, and which would be of incalculable service to the youth of both sexes, in this delicious but enervating climate; and thus it is that the situation of the young Englishmen, sent out as clerks to the many English mercantile houses in Brazil, becomes most deplorable. Placed by their employees in a house with one or two negroes to attend them, and rigidly shut out from the society of their

compatriots, by that snobbishness of English intercourse abroad (nowhere greater than in Brazil) which makes the tinker of the kettle dread contaminating association with the tinker of saucepans, these, in many cases, gentlemanly young men, too often take refuge from the dreary monotony of their existence, and from their feelings of isolation in a foreign land, in all the excitement of immorality and dissipation.

Knowing Brazil, and understanding the Britons who chose to live there, Scully understood the easy availability of 'delicious' temptations. The heat, the sensuality, the half-naked native women, the flash of a breast, the touch of a thigh, the sweet scent of pineapples and papaya – taunted by such temptations, even the most upright Englishmen might be tempted to wander from the path of righteousness. Keep your eye on the ball, sir! Play a straight bat!

Members of Charlie Miller's extended family started and administered the São Paulo Athletic Club. His father's brother, Peter, was a founder member, as was another uncle, Percy Lupton, and a cousin, William Fox Rule. They played their first games of cricket on a large tract of land owned by Charles Dulley, a wealthy American who, having married into the Fox/Rudge clan, also happened to be another of Charlie's uncles. Via the astute marriage that his father had made, Charlie gained entrance to the pick of the British community in São Paulo. A small, wealthy, inter-connected group, they looked after their own, and quickly found him a couple of jobs, first helping out in the storeroom of the São Paulo Railway, then working in Percy Lupton's import-export business.

Day by day, Charlie saw more of the city where he had been born, and realised how much the place had changed. The coffee boom was gathering pace – by 1900, the port of Santos would provide half the coffee drunk by the world – and cash flooded into São Paulo, an unexpected booty that transformed every aspect of life in the city. No-one was immune to the power of coffee. The price of beans determined what Paulistas ate and wore, how they felt and what they did. When the price rose, as throughout the 1880s and the first half of the 1890s, the place buzzed. Residents swept aside the little town's provincial atmosphere and filled their nights with a riot of opera, theatre, art and high fashion. Ruddy-faced farmers wiped the soil from their hands and attached their finest fillies to sparkling new carriages. Lawyers started art collections. Bankers bought beautiful young brides. Paulistas swaggered through the streets, showing off their new-found sophistication. Following the boom, a bust would come – they all knew that – but no-one bothered thinking further than five minutes into the future. Some wit invented a phrase so apposite that it whipped around the city in an instant, dropping from everyone's lips. *O café dá para tudo*. Coffee provides for everything.

Over those feverish years, Paulistas talked of the 'green wave' sweeping across their landscape as thousands upon thousands of coffee trees were planted by ambitious farmers. New roads formed a grid across the city. Houses struggled towards the sky. Familiar landmarks vanished. After a ten-year absence, Charlie had to relearn the geography of his home town. Ponds had been filled, and woodlands razed. Hundreds of new houses had been built. The peasants huddled in huts, while local merchants invested their unexpected wealth in elegant mansions. There was even talk of building a system of electric lights to illuminate the streets at night, and replacing the mule-drawn trams with steam engines. The Viaduto do Chá was rebuilt, and a beautiful new bridge crossed the centre of the city. John Rudge had died, but his legacy continued.

When Charlie was born, 25,000 people lived in São Paulo. Heading for Banister Court, he had left a town of almost 40,000. Returning, he found himself in a city of 192,000. A village had swollen into a metropolis. In comparison to Southampton, of course, the city still looked primitive and provincial – but how could you possibly compare one of Queen Victoria's greatest ports with a secluded farming town in the middle of nowhere?

During that period of extraordinary growth – 40,000 to 190,000 in ten years – the size of the British population in São Paulo remained static. Whereas they had once been a powerful force in the city, their influence dwindled, simply due to lack of numbers. The British were also restricted to one segment of society, managerial and middle class, whereas most of the recent immigrants to Brazil had been labourers. The abolition of slavery, coinciding with a boom in coffee-drinking in Europe and North America, had radically altered the population of the region. Just as the railways had depended on British and German labourers to build tricky sections of track, so the farms needed willing bodies to replace the slaves who had been freed. Boats plied the Atlantic, ferrying families to South America, returning to Europe packed with sacks of coffee. Italy supplied such vast numbers of immigrants that Italian landowners began to panic: their crops mouldered, unpicked, as the workforce deserted the land. Some Italian steamers brought a couple of thousand people in a single trip, cramming them into a boat intended to fit no more than 500. Villages in Tuscany shed their populations. One steamer brought every inhabitant of Carpignano, a village near Lucca, whose inhabitants had simply walked away, taking their possessions and leaving their houses to the ghosts. In Britain, the government issued regular and repeated warnings against emigrating to Brazil. Horror stories appeared in newspapers, describing the miseries suffered by the few working-class Britons who emigrated to Brazil. Ignored by their fellow countrymen, abused by farmers, tortured by the climate, a few stray, hungry Englishmen could usually be found on the steps of the consulate in Rio or Santos, begging for coins. Kind-hearted consuls tried to make arrangements with the captains of British ships, persuading them to deliver these failed emigrants back to Southampton or Liverpool.

Over the following few decades, given the choice between Brazil or other, more familiar colonies such as Canada and New Zealand, energetic Britons rarely chose to head for South America. As their numbers dropped and their influence faded, those Britons who stayed in Brazil had to make a choice between isolation and assimilation. This was not a choice that they wished to make. Vocal Anglo-Brazilians hectored their banks, bosses and government, demanding more investment. They drew attention to their successes. The San Paulo Railway, for instance, could not be faulted. Mile by mile, the SPR was the most profitable railway in South America, and one of the busiest in the world. With a little more energy and cash, the whole of Brazil could be covered with such monuments to British pluck and gumption. One of the SPR's directors, Walter Wright, published a little pamphlet called *A Few Facts about Brazil by a Twenty Years' Resident in That Country*, drawing his countrymen's attention to the raw and thrilling potential awaiting them in South America.

Brazil, owing to its immense size, variety of climate, and richness of soil, is the finest country in the world; and, if the fates had decreed that it should have fallen into the hands of the English instead of the Portuguese, it would at this time be also the greatest country in the world; but as the fates did not so decree, and the enterprise of the descendants of Portugal is not equal to that of the sons of Albion, the country is still in its infancy, but it is a fine and promising child, and bids fair to become a colossus!

At the end of the year, a cholera epidemic struck São Paulo. The state government imposed a strict quarantine, stopping the movement of most goods. Travellers had to carry a 'sanitation passport' if they wished to enter the city. At Luz station, porters splashed disinfectant over letters and newspapers.

Charlie Miller couldn't have been happier. Without forms to fill or goods to pack, offices shut early, releasing a flood of bored young men onto the hot streets. Not liking to waste a sunny afternoon, the British played a lot of cricket. Charlie became a regular member of the SPAC team. Striding across the crease or waiting in the slips, he took stock of his fellows, memorising their names, observing their agility and their strength, mentally measuring their potential. Christmas passed. Then New Year. The sun lost its brutal heat. Summer faded into autumn. When the cricket season ended, Charlie picked twenty-two of his new friends, and invited them to join him. He had a neat little game that they might like to see.

Seven

'We'll meet on Sunday. Game starts at four. The sun is low in the sky by then, and the heat won't kill us. Wear togs that don't mind a bit of dirt and dust. Bring a decent pair of boots.' Wherever he goes, whenever he meets an Englishman or a Scotsman under the age of forty, he tells them about the game, inviting them to join his congregation. Almost everyone promises to be there. Charlie is gleeful, thrilled by the prospect of his impending triumph. He won't just have sufficient players to mount a full match – he will have cheering spectators along the lines of the pitch, and he himself will be free to referee the game.

Charlie is a brusque little man. The British community may have accepted him as one of their own, but haven't yet decided whether they actually like him. When that Sunday comes round, most of the chaps manage to find previously forgotten prior appointments. A family lunch, a trip to Santos, an unexpected meeting with a colleague. To Charlie's distress, he has to cross almost every name from the list. At the appointed hour, twelve men assemble at the Luz station, and two of them have only come to express their apologies in person. 'I'm sorry, old man, but Head Office wants this report pronto. Have a good game.' They shake hands, wink at the others, turn to go. 'Oh, Miller? Let me give you a word of advice. Drink plenty of water. Didn't you hear what happened in Buenos Aires? Some chaps tried to organise a game of footer, and one of them died. This bloody climate, you know?' Charlie nods and smiles, trying to conceal his irritation. When those two have gone, he counts the remainder. Ten plus himself makes eleven. That's enough. Decent fellows, these ten. They'll play an honest game. He knows them all, and has played cricket with or against most of them over the past few months. They work for the British firms based in São Paulo – the railway, the bank, the gas company – and are young, feckless, unmarried, red-faced and jolly. Some were born in Brazil, just like himself, and learnt Portuguese from the cook and the maid. Others arrived a few months ago, and still struggle to remember a single word of the local lingo. Although Charlie can't yet think of these ten chaps as his friends, all of them are the type of men whom he could imagine befriending. Walking through the city, they bump into a clerk who works for the Bank of London, and persuade him to join them. They stroll down to a patch of rough ground on the corner of Rua Santa Rosa and Rua do Gasometro. Mules are grazing on the grass. A couple of the men drive the animals away, and the others stand around, chatting, smoking, staring at the sky. Someone tries to sneak away, claiming a suddenly remembered rendezvous, but Charlie persuades him to stay. Men fidget and chatter. Discontent rumbles. They start pestering him with questions.

'Miller? Look here, Miller. You call this a pitch?'

'What if I break my bloody leg?'

'Are we allowed to carry the ball or not?'

'Miller? Miller! What is this game?'

'Where's the ball, then?'

'Here's the ball,' says Charlie, holding up a flap of sewn leather. 'We've just got to fill it.'

'Fill it? With what?'

'With air,' says Charlie.

They gather in a circle and watch, hardly pretending to hide their giggles, as Charlie kneels over the leather sock with an air pump. When the ball is taut, he bounces it on the ground, and looks at the other men. 'Good. I'll be one captain. Who wants to be another?'

With eleven men, they can divide into two teams, and play a quick game of nearly six-a-side. Charlie plays for the team with only five. They use one of the balls given to Charlie by William Pickford, so many thousand miles away, on that afternoon when the Corinthians came to Hampshire. Charlie tucks the ball under his arm and, yet again, slowly, concealing his impatience, answering every question as if he hasn't heard it before, explains the rules. Then he puts the ball on the ground, waits until everyone has taken their positions, and kicks off. Although they are playing late in the afternoon, the sun beats down on their skulls. The heat is unbearable. Damp patches swell across their neat white shirts. They have been playing for fifteen or twenty minutes when Paddy Walsh clutches his heart. He turns slowly on the spot, and shouts, 'I say, chaps! I say!' As soon as they are all looking at him, he shouts again, 'That's it for me! Goodnight, chaps! I'm a goner!' His eyes roll. He keels over, collapses, and lies face down in the grass. The other men run towards him, yelling. Someone shouts for a doctor in English, then in Portuguese. They reach the prone figure, and stand around him. No-one is quite sure what to do. Charlie takes control. He kneels on the earth, puts both hands on Paddy's shoulders, and turns him over, revealing a huge grin. Paddy sits up, pushing Charlie aside, and laughs until tears pour down his scarlet face.

'That wasn't funny,' says one of the men.

'You're a damn fool,' says another.

Tommy takes the opportunity to grab the ball in his fists, run down to the opposite end of the field, and throw it between the goalposts. A cheer goes up. Charlie puts his head in his hands, and dreams of a muddy field in Hampshire.

They play for another twenty languid minutes, then stroll over to the shade of a large tree, and lie on the grass. There, the men take turns to quiz Charlie about football in England. He tells them about William Pickford, and the Football League, and the Corinthians. From the rapt expressions of his listeners, Charlie knows that the game has captured their imaginations. He has made ten converts. Even Paddy Walsh promises to return for the next game. The seeds have been sown. Charlie asks them to tell their friends, their brothers, their fellows in the British firms. Spread the word, he says. A fortnight from today, we shall play again. A proper game. Eleven men on either side, and a full thirty minutes for each half.

His name is Mr Chillingworth, and he stands by the fireplace, preaching to his fellow Britons. Like them, he is drunk. Like them, he is adrift in a strange South American country, thousands of miles from home, surrounded by a population that he cannot understand and who do not understand him. He lifts his glass, raises his voice and calls for silence. When his fellow Britons are finally quiet, this is what he says.

'I've been thinking, that's what I've been doing. Now let's review the situation. Here we stand, a colony of English gentlemen: here we are, don't you know, far from our homes and country and all that sort of thing. What says the poet? I daresay some of you fellows remember the passage. But what for, I ask! What, gentlemen, is the object of our being here? That's just what I'm going to tell you, don't you know. We are here, gentlemen, to infuse a little of our Anglo-Saxon energy, and all that sort of thing, into this dilapidated old tin-pot of a nation.'

Mr Chillingworth is a character in W.H. Hudson's semi-autobiographical novel, *The Purple Land*, and his speech would have sounded familiar to Charlie Miller and the men who lived alongside him in São Paulo. They were milder, perhaps, then the wild Englishmen who saluted Mr Chillingworth with rum, fired their revolvers into the air, and sang a resounding rendition of *Rule Britannia*. The men who lived in São Paulo were more staid. They were engineers and bankers rather than ranchers or farmers. They did not have revolvers strapped to their waists or dust on their boots. But their values were the same, and they knew that this dilapidated old tin-pot of a nation would fall to pieces without their energy, expertise and cash.

They had a good life, Charlie Miller and his fellow young Britons. Blessed with a little wealth and a lot of confidence, they took their fill of the sun, the beer, the girls. In 1895, the gossip column of the *Rio News* reported a night out enjoyed by a couple of devil-may-care Britons 'who broke a few things to prove that their enthusiasm was genuine.' In one restaurant, they ran up a bill of 107 milreis, which consisted of 6 milreis for food, 15 for breakages and 86 for wine. The columnist commented that 'there is something genuine about a dinner like that' and reminded his readers that 'no one but a thorough Britisher could meet its requirements'.

One member of the British community told me how a typical weekend might go for the young British men in São Paulo. He was decades younger than Charlie Miller, of course, having grown up in the city during the 1940s rather than 1890s, but their lives wouldn't have been much different. They worked hard all week. Around lunchtime on Saturday, he and his friends met at the British club, and secreted themselves in the billiards room. In the middle of the afternoon, a tray of tea arrived, and perhaps some sandwiches. Later, they would head upstairs to the men's bar for a few drinks. On one of these afternoons, my informant told me, he saw an old man sitting at the bar, drinking a whisky and soda. Another lad nudged him. 'Do you know who that is? The old gent there. Yes, that one. He's Charles Miller. That's right, Charlie Miller. You know what he did, don't you?' After two or three beers, they left SPAC and headed into the city. Driving along the placid roads of São Paulo, they might play a few tricks on the innocent residents – leaping out of their cars, perhaps, and staging a fake fight in the middle of the road, yelling at one another in an incomprehensible mixture of English and Portuguese, pretending not to notice the staid Paulistas on the pavement staring at them with open mouths. In those days, Brazil was a quiet, polite, Catholic country, where people dressed smartly, spoke quietly, and kept themselves to themselves. Stifling their laughter, the young Scots and Englishmen bounded back into their cars and drove to a club, swaggering up to the bar as if they owned the place. They were clerks, junior managers or technicians, but they still wore suits of impregnable superiority. With their salaries paid in pounds, they were richer than all but the most well-heeled Brazilians. They went to the smartest clubs in town. When the bars shut, or the singers at the clubs started to sound monotonous, they would drive down to the brothels for another beer, and eye up the girls who paraded before them. None of the chaps actually took advantage of the services on offer. Being well-brought up young gentlemen, they paid for their beers, winked at the girls, and headed for home. That's their story, anyway.

Every Sunday morning, Charlie Miller goes to church. The congregation of St Paul's has swelled over the previous few years as the British community has become more cohesive. The church, the club, the railway, the bank – these are the places where they meet every day, distinguishing themselves from the natives, retaining the distinction between Them and Us. The vicar stands at the head of his congregation, and leads the singing. They have a small piano rather than an organ, and no choir, but their enthusiasm compensates for any lack of skill or technique. British voices belt out the familiar hymns, and British eyelids droop during the sermon, and British snores echo from the pews at the back. At the end of the service, the vicar stands in the doorway and shakes hands with his departing parishioners. Opposite him, another man is shaking the same hands, slapping the same backs, having a quiet word with some of the chaps. Each of them preaches a different creed. Whereas the vicar is calm and chatty, the man opposite him shines with religious zeal. Charlie pulls men from the crowd and reminds them of their duty, their task, the vital hours that lie ahead.

They stroll through the city, twenty of them, dressed in their Sunday best. A few rush home to change. Others have brought their cricket whites to church, and will change behind a tree before the game. They return to the same patch of scrubby grass where they played before. Once again, before even filling the ball with air, they have to drive the mules from the ground. Somehow, without a word being spoken, the atmosphere has changed since their first game. No-one giggles. No-one pesters Charlie with idiotic questions. They work briskly and efficiently, placing a jacket in each corner of the pitch, pushing bamboo sticks into the ground to serve as goalposts. A few local kids stop to watch. The footballers ignore them, and kneel on the grass to tie up their boots. They have a full complement of players, eleven on each side. The teams have been decided already. The Gasworks will take on the San Paulo Railway. Although Charlie is employed by neither, he plays for the railway, since he has a family connection to the SPR. He captains the team too, and plays at centre forward. They have no referee, so Charlie takes that role too. No-one questions his impartiality. They know that he wouldn't cheat.

Charlie places the ball in the centre of the pitch. There is a moment of stillness and silence. No-one moves or talks. Even the local kids stop chatting and watch in rigid silence, wondering what will happen next, unsure how this strange foreign ritual is going to proceed. Charlie kicks the ball with the side of his foot, knocking it to Walter, who boots it. Behind the goal, the kids watch in amazement as twenty men charge towards them, chasing a leather ball. Someone goes flying. A vicious tackle leaves another man on the floor, grasping his ankle. Charlie has the ball. He weaves past one full-back, then another. He bears down on the goal – and three of the local boys sprint towards him, waving their arms. One of the kids reaches the ball before Charlie, and boots it up to the other end of the pitch.

Charlie stops the game. He has a few stern words with the boys, wagging his finger, explaining that the pitch has boundaries that must not be crossed. The boys giggle at his unsteady grasp of Portuguese, but their smiles fade as a few more of the men gather round. The black kids are barefoot. Rags cover their skinny limbs. They are no match for twenty-two beefy red-faced men in cricket whites and strong boots. 'We promise,' say the kids, suddenly nervous, unsure how these bizarre foreigners are going to react. 'We promise, we'll keep off the field. We'll leave you alone. Just one question, sir. What do you call this game?'

'Football,' says Charlie, using the English word, since no equivalent exists in Portuguese. 'This is football played by the Association Rules.' The boys nod, although they have no idea what he's talking about.

The men jog back onto the pitch. Charlie starts the game again with a drop ball. The local boys stand behind the goal, cheering when Charlie dribbles halfway down the pitch and chips the ball over the 'keeper. The teams break for a fifteen-minute interval, then swap sides and start again. At the end of the game, the Railway has won comfortably. Final score: 4-2. As the British walk off the pitch, they slap one another on the back. 'What a fine game,' they mutter, and shout across the field to Charlie, who is kneeling on the ground, letting the air out of the ball. 'Miller! I say, Miller! Nice little game, old man! When do we play again?'

The British stroll back into town, not bothering to remove the bamboo goalposts, which stay there, standing upright in the earth. None of the Britons takes any notice of the scrawny black boys who have been watching. As the foreigners walk away, the local kids saunter around the pitch, inspecting the bamboo poles, discussing what they have seen. One of them shouts and waves. He has found a discarded newspaper in the grass, and rolled it into a tight ball. He kicks it along the ground. The others run forward. A vicious tackle is followed by shouts of fury. One boy writhes on the ground while the others charge after the ball. They tussle. The ball breaks free. With an impatient swagger, the slimmest boy nutmegs one of his friends, shrugs off another, sprints towards the goal and fires a clean shot between the posts.

Eight

That day, Sunday 14 April 1895, is remembered as the first football match in Brazil. It wasn't quite that. Before the San Paulo Railway beat the Gasworks 4-2, Charlie himself had already played a couple of games on the soil of São Paulo. Even before that, a few games of football had been played in other parts of the country, although none of them had been well-organised, and any decent referee would have been appalled by their lax interpretations of the rules.

From the early 1880s, British ships usually carried a football or two, deflated and tucked in a locker. Sailors rarely played on deck – how many captains would stop their ships to retrieve a ball that had been kicked overboard? – but they would inflate the ball in every port. While native porters dealt with the cargo, the sailors devoted their shore leave to drinking, whoring and playing football. British sailors almost certainly played a few games when they moored in ports along the Brazilian coast. In Buenos Aires, British sailors had played football as early as the 1840s. In Chile, Valparaiso Football Club was founded in 1889. In Uruguay, the Central Uruguayan Railway Cricket Club was founded in 1891 to play cricket in the summer and football in the winter. The first game between the teams of two South American countries was played in 1889, and took place in Argentina, where the Montevideo Cricket Club brought eleven footballers to challenge the Buenos Aires Cricket Club. The players from both teams were British, and the home side won 3-0. Two years later, the same city hosted South America's first league, consisting of five teams: Old Caledonians, Saint Andrew's, Buenos Aires al Rosario Railway, Belgrano FC and Buenos

Aires FC. As you could guess from the names of the teams, most of the players were Scotsmen.

In Brazil, things had proceeded more slowly, mostly due to the climate. The British merchants, engineers and bankers could have played football, but the heat flummoxed them and they stuck to cricket. Apart from passing sailors, the first people to play football were probably a few Brazilian schoolboys in Itu, a small town in the hills behind São Paulo, who had played some rudimentary games after their Jesuit schoolmasters visited Europe to pick up tips on modern educational techniques. Having watched the games played at Harrow, the Jesuits returned to Brazil with a leather ball, and tried to convince their pupils to see the joys of football. They had little success – and seemed to have forgotten most of the rules on the long sea voyage – but their schoolboys certainly played a game with a ball using their feet. So, the game played on 14 April 1895 was not the first football match in Brazil. But it was certainly the first game of soccer. The copy of Association Rules that Charlie carried in his trunk distinguished this game from any other method of kicking a ball around a field. Men had played games on Brazilian soil with a ball made from straw or run across a Brazilian beach after a satisfyingly spherical coconut shell, but they had never played soccer until Charlie Miller arrived from Southampton with a pump, a pair of boots, a leather ball and a book of rules.

Apart from these necessary accoutrements for a decent game of soccer, Charlie brought one more thing from Southampton. Without it, he would be as anonymous today as all the British sailors who kicked a ball along the quays in Santos or the Jesuit schoolmasters who encouraged their pupils to imitate Harrovians. Alongside the pump, boots, balls and book of rules, Charlie brought passion. There are many men who play football, watch football and talk about football, but their lives are dominated by other, bigger infatuations like work and sex. Charlie had only one passion. He never cared much about money. Unless he had very secret vices, sex played no part in his life until his thirties, when his footballing career had just about ended. No, a single passion dominated his days and nights. He had only one true love. And, like most devotees, he could not understand why anybody else might not feel the same way.

Nine

Students marched in the street, shouting anti-British slogans. Children chanted crude ditties about Gladstone and Queen Victoria. Men stood on chairs and delivered angry speeches, denouncing British imperialism. At night, someone threw a stone at the Victoria Stores, the only British-owned shop in the city, and smashed a hole in the big glass window. Then they tore down the portrait of Victoria that hung outside, and desecrated her image with black paint. Talk turned to war, and men warned their wives that they might be called to enlist. The British responded with calm smiles. They talked of Gordon in Khartoum and Clive in Calcutta. They called for another glass of lemonade, and discussed the prospects for rain. But when the servants had retreated to the kitchen, or the clerk had hurried down the street with a message, the British gathered round the newspaper, and read the reports of riots and speeches, and wondered when their own windows would be smashed.

Charlie was exhausted. His first full year as an adult resident of São Paulo had been eventful. He had already witnessed an attempted coup and an outbreak of bubonic plague, not to mention the usual deaths from cholera, yellow fever and knives drawn in a bar brawl. He was being worked hard by one of his uncles, Percy Lupton, who ran an import-export company, dealing in any British products that might be wanted in Brazil or anything Brazilian that could possibly be wanted in Britain. In a business directory, Lupton is listed as an importer of machinery, drugs, cotton, iron, steel, coal, zinc, copper, mineral water and wine. His company is also advertised as a 'commission agent', meaning that he is willing to transport anything for a percentage.

Family connections had secured the job for Charlie, but not an easy life, and he spent every day hunched over order books, checking figures and feeling the sweat dribble down the back of his shirt. Their office did not even possess a fan, and the heat was ferocious, reaching almost a hundred degrees Fahrenheit in the run-up to Christmas. Charlie couldn't wait for Christmas Eve, when Percy Lupton would lock the office and the whole family headed down to the seaside for the festive break. A few more days, and they would be loading their suitcases onto the train. In the office, they talked about little except cricket and the best beaches to be found near Santos. Then a short letter appeared in the *Diário Popular*, and the British realised that they weren't going to have a peaceful Christmas.

> In view of the rash and usurping proceedings of the British government towards the government of my country, I declare that from this day forward I decline the friendship which up to this date I have had with some Englishmen. I declare further that my establishment called 'Sereia Paulista,' as before, is open to receive any foreigner with courtesy – except the English, who belong to a country at present directed by an unscrupulous government.
>
> Long live Brazil!
>
> — Augusto Pedro de Oliveira.

Most readers in São Paulo recognised the writer's name. He was a well-known figure in the city. He ran a public baths known as the Sereia Paulista (the Paulista Mermaid) where people gathered to discuss business and exchange gossip. At another time of year, his letter might have been less incendiary, but he had picked his moment precisely, using the weather to his own advantage. It was the end of December, and summer had really arrived. Tempers were short. Scuffles broke out in the streets. Sullen men needed little incentive to become rioting mobs, intent on looting and lynching.

They should boycott Augusto Pedro de Oliveira, suggested one of the British. Then he might appreciate how much he owed to Britain. He should be banned from travelling on the San Paulo Railway, suggested another, or prevented from buying any more bottles of the whisky that he loved so much. But the jokes fooled no-one. Every night, the British placed wooden boards over their windows. Every morning, they scoured the newspapers, hoping that their government would have backed down and reached a compromise with Brazil.

The cause of this aggravation was a small lump in the middle of the Atlantic Ocean. Seagulls paused on the rock, and crabs scuttled along the shore, but not a single human lived there. Six hundred miles from the coast of Brazil, possessing neither natural resources nor vegetation, the tiny island of Trindade was no use to anyone. A passing British ship had placed a Union Flag on the rock, and claimed it for the Queen. Hearing of this, Brazilian politicians spluttered in horror, grabbed their maps, located the island, and declared it a valuable outpost of Brazilian soil. Neither side was willing to back down. Politicians sent angry cables under the Atlantic. Newspapers carried furious editorials. Students took to the streets, waving placards and chanting slogans. As the situation dragged on, the British started to feel the first twinges of panic. What would happen if the two countries found themselves unable to agree? Wars had been fought on more trivial pretexts. What if some unscrupulous politician saw this issue as an opportunity to make his name or a gung-ho Admiral sent the Royal Navy to mount an invasion? And if war did break out, what would happen to the British in Brazil? Would they find themselves stripped of their assets and thrown out of their homes? In Rio, Bahia, Pernambuco, Santos and São Paulo, the British residents barricaded their windows, locked their doors, and prayed that, before some hot-heated Latin decided to declare war on all the citizens of Queen Victoria, the damned lump of rock would sink under the waves and disappear.

A few months earlier, at the end of April 1895, Charlie and his twenty-one red-faced friends played another game of football on the same pitch as the first, watched by rowdy boys and curious passers-by. The atmosphere was not conducive to good football. Cheers or groans followed every move. They played there once more before deciding that they needed some privacy. They had no wish to be pestered by beggars as they strapped up their boots or jeered by idle boys when they missed an open goal. Charlie used his family connections to make contact with the Dulley family, and ask permission to use their grounds. SPAC already played cricket on the Dulley estate, so Charlie knew the place well. That long field deserves to be remembered by Brazilians. The focus for British and American socialising in the last decades of the nineteenth century, the grass was worn down by men playing cricket, baseball, golf and rugby. None of these games had been played before in São Paulo, and few of them had been seen anywhere in Brazil.

A message came back from the Dulleys: they would be happy to host Charlie and his friends. The following Sunday, the twenty-two gathered inside the estate, protected from the curious by high walls, and played a cracking game of football. For the first time since he arrived in Brazil, Charlie could almost convince himself that he was back in England. Two goals had been built from wooden posts. The boundaries had been marked with whitewash. A small group of pale women sat in deckchairs under the shade of a large tree, reading and sewing, taking no notice of the game. At half-time, two black servants walked down to the field from the house. One carried a tray of tall glasses, and the other held a jug of orange juice in each hand, the chunks of ice clinking as she walked.

Football was a success, and so was Charlie Miller. Only a few months after his return, he was an indispensable part of the British community. He played tennis, rugby and cricket. He knew everyone, and played every game that the community organised. When 'The Banks' took on 'The World' in a tennis tournament, Charlie played for the World. When the 'Whites' played the 'Niggers' at cricket, Charlie played for the Niggers. This didn't, of course, mean that he played alongside blacks, nor even Brazilians. The annual 'Whites versus Niggers' fixture was confined entirely to members of the British community. To quality for the Whites, you had to have been born in Britain. Anyone born in South America played for the Niggers.

In October, the club held their annual sports day on the Dulley estate. Events included the high jump, long jump, 100-yard race, three-legged race, wheelbarrow race, sack race and the egg-and-spoon race. Charlie Miller came second in the competition to see who could throw a cricket ball furthest, and won the sack race in a dead heat with his cousin, William Fox Rule. Prizes were presented by Mrs Lupton, the wife of Charlie's employer. The Italian brass band played all afternoon, and multi-coloured bunting fluttered from the trees. After the prizes had been presented, all the British and their guests gathered for a resounding rendition of *God Save the Queen*. In the stillness of the early evening, their voices carried a long way, bounding over the high walls, penetrating nearby streets, trickling through shuttered windows.

★

They have different names for the island. The British say Trinidad, and the Portuguese say Trindade. Each of them claims to have discovered it, but a Spanish navigator named João de Nova seems to have been the first man who actually took any notice of the lump, sailing past in 1501 and keeping careful notes of his observations. A couple of centuries later, Edmund Halley set foot on Trindade, where he 'saw many green turtles in the sea, but by reason of the great surf, could catch none.' Best-remembered today for attaching his name to a periodic comet, Halley had been appointed commander of a British ship by William III and entrusted with two missions: to investigate the longitude problem that was currently occupying so many scientific minds and to 'attempt the discovery of what land lies to the south of the western ocean.' Halley left Portsmouth in the cutely named *Paramore Pink* and sailed across the Atlantic. Stopping at Trindade to pick up fresh water, he 'went ashore and put some goats and hogs on the island for breed, as also a pair of guinea hens I carried from St Helena. And I took possession of the island in His Majesty's name.' He planted a flag in the rock, then left the goats, hogs and chickens to their fate.

The hogs and chickens must have died within weeks, but the goats lived on the island for the following few decades, breeding generation unto generation, receiving few visitors. They shared their kingdom with crabs, cockroaches, the odd rat and thousands of seabirds. Occasional British and Portuguese ships moored to fill their casks with water. Sailors sometimes tried to catch some fresh turtle meat or even grab a goat, but they rarely had much success. In his autobiographical novel, *Frank Mildmay*, Frederick Marryat gives a vivid description of the island's desolation and loneliness. 'Thousands and thousands of trees covered the valley, each of them about thirty feet high; but every tree was dead, and extended its leafless boughs to another – a forest of desolation, as if nature had at some particular moment ceased to vege-tate! There was no underwood or grass. On the lowest of the dead boughs, the gannets, and other sea-birds, had built their nests, in numbers uncountable. Their tameness, as Cowper says, "was shocking to me." So unaccustomed did they seem to man that the mothers brooding over their young only opened their beaks, in a menacing atti-tude, at us as we passed by them.'

Legends claimed that Spanish sailors had stolen every scrap of gold from the cathedral at Lima, and hidden a vast store of treasure chests on

Trindade, but no-one had ever managed to find a single piece of eight. Undeterred, a few optimistic prospectors arrived with shovels. Almost all of them fled quickly, empty-handed and windswept. One or two stayed behind, twisted under a rock or stretched out on the pebbles, their bones picked clean by the gannets and boobies. Uninterrupted by anything except a few wrecks, which littered the beaches with splintered wood, the goats continued their peaceful existence scarcely disturbed until the end of the nineteenth century, when they suddenly found their quiet lump of rock claimed by three different rulers – a King, a Queen and a president.

The trouble started with a man named James Aloysius Harden-Hickey, an American, a journalist, a novelist, a fantasist and one of the finest swordsmen in France. Born in San Francisco to Irish parents, he was taken to France at the age of ten, and educated in Paris. There, he won fame and friends for his skill with a sword, married a Countess, had two children and acquired the title of Baron, although no-one seemed quite sure how he had actually done this. Perhaps the French had bestowed it upon him. More likely, he had simply liked the sound of Baron Harden-Hickey, and decided to take the title himself. Being both imaginative and penniless, he exchanged his sword for a pen, and began writing novels. Over the next four years, he had eleven published, although none was successful. So he changed tack, and started a newspaper. His journalism caused nothing but trouble. He was sued on forty-two different occasions, fined hundreds of thousands of francs, and forced to defend his honour in a succession of duels. When his paper collapsed, Baron Harden-Hickey abandoned his wife and children, and fled to London. A few days in that city gave him a lifelong hatred of the English. As soon as he could find a berth, he boarded a boat, and sailed across the Atlantic, searching for adventure. In the middle of the ocean, hundreds of miles from any inhabited land, they stopped alongside a lump of rock. In rougher waters, no ship would come close to this jagged island, but the sea happened to be perfectly calm. A boat was lowered. Sailors rowed ashore. Harden-Hickey went with them, sprang onto the island, and claimed it as his own. Years later, he recalled raising a home-made flag on the beach, and perhaps he did. From Trindade, Harden-Hickey continued down the coast of South America, then joined another boat bound for Japan. He paused for a year in India, dabbling in mysticism, and visited Tibet to study in a Buddhist monastery. Returning to Paris, he met an American heiress, and married her. They settled in New York, their domestic bliss ruffled only by her father's refusal to fund the happy couple. Harden-Hickey should support himself, said the old man.

To Harden-Hickey, that seemed most unfair. For several months, he did nothing, hoping his father-in-law would see sense. Finally, he fell back on the trade that he knew best – being a hack – but he wrote much more fluently in French than English, and no-one offered him the editorship that he considered rightfully his. The experience must have depressed him, because he then published not a swashbuckling novel like his previous efforts, but a manual devoted to self-destruction. *The Aesthetics of Suicide* listed 139 ways to kill yourself. Like Harden-Hickey's other titles, it flopped.

One bright spring morning, every newspaper in New York City received a lengthy letter from 'the King of Trinidad'. In florid prose, peppered with French phrases, the letter announced that His Majesty King James I presently resided in New York City, and would be willing to welcome some selected visitors from the press. To the representatives of a few privileged newspapers, he would grant interviews and provide a full description of his kingdom. Always looking for column-filling funnies, editors despatched reporters to interview the king. Knowing the market, Harden-Hickey gave them exactly what they wanted. He flew the flag – a yellow triangle on a red background – and unrolled crinkly maps of the island. Sympathetic journalists received Trindadian titles in return for scribbling down the King's plans. He would soon be returning to his kingdom, he told them, and invited plucky American adventurers to join him. On the shores of his tropical paradise, they would make their fortunes by gathering guano and farming turtles for eggs, shells and meat.

Harden-Hickey sent cables to the President of Brazil, the Queen of England and all the heads of state in Europe, announcing his presence at the Grande Chancellerie de la Principauté de Trinidad, 217 West 36th Street, New York City. He invited them to visit. Not one replied. His Majesty didn't care. He hired a schooner to carry emigrants to the island, commissioned a crown from a local jeweller and issued hundreds of postage stamps, which were swiftly snapped up by philatelists. If his timing had been better, then James, Baron Harden-Hickey, the first King of Trinidad, would have remained nothing more than a filler in the funny pages of the New York papers, and his claim to the island might have gone unchallenged. Maybe he would even have gathered a gallant band of treasure-hunters and turtle-eaters, and set up a colony. Unfortunately for him, larger matters intervened. In 1893, Brazil passed a law which allowed the state to compulsorily purchase any telegraph cables laid along the Brazilian coast. The owners of the major cable, a British company, protested to their own government. The cable stretched down the coast to Argentina, linking London and Buenos Aires. Laying a replacement would be complicated and expensive. Could Her Majesty's Government do anything to stop those damned Brazilians? Civil servants peered at maps and consulted books of international law, then shook their heads. If Brazil insisted on nationalising the cables, then the cables would be nationalised. Finally, someone in the Foreign Office had a bright idea. Why not route a new cable from Europe to Argentina via the uninhabited island of Trindade? More civil servants consulted more old books, and discovered that no-one seemed to know who owned the island, mainly because no-one had ever particularly wanted it. Both the British and Portuguese had made vague claims, and Halley's looked as good as anyone's. A coded cable was despatched to the consul in Rio de Janeiro, who passed the instructions to the captain of the *Barracouta*, a British warship moored in the harbour.

Five days later, the *Barracouta* anchored in the choppy seas off Trindade. A boat was lowered. Sailors rowed ashore. Curious sharks swam alongside. The sailors leaped onto the beach, tied up their boat, and explored the island. In his report to the Admiralty, the captain of the *Barracouta* reported that he saw abundant stocks of firewood and innumerable crabs, but no signs of human habitation. Under his supervision, the sailors raised a white ensign and deposited a glass bottle, firmly stoppered, under a rock. The captain had stuffed a sheet of paper inside the bottle, a signed proclamation claiming this island as Her Majesty's possession. They rammed a shaft of wood in the rock, marking the bottle's position. Nearby, on a large flat rock facing the sea, they daubed six letters in bright white paint, spelling the word RECORD.

For a long time, no-one realised that the British had taken possession of Trindade. The Foreign Office didn't bother telling anyone. The island had no visitors. Only the turtles, the goats and the gulls saw the white painted sign. Months later, in the middle of a long, aggressive description of the Brazilian government's financial incompetence, a London newspaper carried a brief paragraph about the island, and Brazil realised that a chunk of the motherland had been chiselled off. Politicians frothed. Students rioted. British sailors in Brazilian ports were forbidden from venturing ashore. British residents of Brazilian cities kept their voices down, barricaded their windows and stayed in their homes after dark. The *Cidade do Rio* thundered to its readers, 'Our country has spoken. No, she has not spoken: she has wept; wept because she has been betrayed, degraded, deceived, robbed.' Another newspaper described the Trindade affair as 'the greatest affront which has ever been offered to Brazilian sovereignty.' Belasario de Souza leaped to his feet in the Brazilian Chamber of Deputies, and shouted, 'Never shall the banner of a foreign nation wave over Brazilian soil! We are a people of fourteen million Brazilians; our own struggles have cost us much blood, but we may still have some to shed in defence of our honour and our dignity; we must be worthy of our past history and of America!'

Behind the scenes, the two governments tried to reach an agreement, but the Brazilians found themselves backed into a corner by their own rhetoric. Their enflamed population would never forgive them if they retreated. Not even arbitration would do. Only two choices remained: either the British must surrender all claims to Trindade or they must fight for it! With both sides unwilling to back down, war looked inevitable – a war that neither government wished to fight, nor saw any way to avoid. A few months earlier, only four or five people in Brazil could have pointed to Trindade on a map. Now, the island had become a sacred part of the motherland, worth a million gallons of blood. Mobs marched through the streets, screaming their hatred of British imperialism. Parliamentarians roared with fury, and ministers promised action. 'When all diplomatic means have been exhausted,' one of them swore to his fellow deputies, 'this people, obeying the irresistible calls of patriotism, will rise and tear away the paws of the British lion from this piece of territory which is sacred to Brazil.' Some dull souls pointed out an awkward fact. Brazil had a tiny army, a smaller navy, and no spare cash to assemble anything bigger. How could they possibly wage war against Britain? Ministers brushed aside these silly objections. National prestige demanded a military reconquest of the island, so the country would build a modern army and navy. The government would gladly allot a huge budget for ships, rations and weapons. Cynics asked: where was the government going find all this money? They would borrow it, of course. And where would they borrow it from? The same source that the Brazilian government secured all its loans: the banks in London. The cynics chuckled and shook their heads. Would a British bank really be happy to fund military operations against a British possession?

Of course they would, replied the British bankers. You will have the money within a week, sir. Sign on the dotted line.

Now the British in Brazil had a stronger reason to keep themselves apart from the natives – not merely preservation of their culture and values, but preservation of their lives and property. At any minute, they worried, a gang of students might switch from rowdiness to violence. A political activist might decide to seek glory through assassination. Right now, wild-eyed men were probably preparing home-made bombs or waiting in alleyways, sharpening their knives, awaiting unwary Englishmen.

Brazil had always been a dangerous place for the British. As Charles knew only too well, northern Europeans coped badly with the climate, and died from diseases that would merely inconvenience a local. The remedies were rarely better than the diseases themselves. The British Consul in Santos had his own favourite cure for yellow fever, which he revealed to William Kennedy:

Castor oil.
Pump out the stomach.
Lime juice and rum.
Weak tea.
No food for a fortnight.
After black vomit, serve out arsenic on the fourth day, with coffee enema.

If patients managed to survive such treatment, other dangers lurked in the jungle. Everyone in São Paulo knew the story of a tall, broad-shouldered Scotsman named Templeton, who had been supervising operations on the new line to Santos. He quarrelled with an Italian workman, lost his temper and threw a punch, knocking the man to the ground. A few days later, Templeton was eating lunch in a village near the line, sharing his meal with another engineer, when the aggrieved

Italian arrived with several friends, determined to receive an apology. Templeton told him to get lost. The Italian drew a revolver. Templeton tried to grab him. They tussled. As the men fought with hands and knives, one of the village women ran for help. When she returned with reinforcements, they discovered six bodies stretched out on the ground. Templeton's corpse had nine separate knife wounds.

But these were the dangers that you might expect in any strange foreign country. The fuss over Trindade was quite different. Editors, ministers, students, the owner of the Paulista Mermaid – why did they feel the need to turn so brutally against the British? What had the British ever done to them? Confronted by this outpouring of bile and fury, the British felt justifiably aggrieved. They had provided Brazil with a constant stream of capital and expertise. They had played an integral part in creating the country's army, navy, industry and transport system. They had grabbed Brazil by the scruff of the neck, and jerked her into the modern world, forcing her to abolish slavery, teaching her to build railways, helping her to make trade links with everyone from the Belgians to the Chinese. In return, they had been rewarded with respect rather than love, and even the respect seemed to be grudging rather than grateful. Their business acumen and obsession with punctuality earned them admiration and ridicule in equal quantities. Brazilians still say 'para Inglêz ver' (for the English to see) an idiom that has come to signify a façade that is produced simply to delude an inspector. Doing a deal, the British would not be satisfied unless they saw the correct legal documents, so neat pieces of paper were produced solely to keep them happy. The British themselves liked to think that their efficiency and honesty gave them a special place in Brazilian hearts. As Charles W. Domville-Fife wrote in his guide to the country: 'In many parts of South America, a native, when he wishes to impress you with his trustworthiness and good intentions, will place his hand upon his heart and exclaim with final assurance, "On the word of an Englishman".'

Perhaps this was true. However, not everyone felt such respect for Britannia and her domination of the waves, tracks and markets. Not everyone believed that the British had forcibly ended the Brazilian slave trade for philanthropic reasons. Some said that Britons couldn't care less about the welfare of a few blacks, and simply wished to stop unfair competition. Others suggested that Queen Victoria had been hoping to enlarge the market for cheap imported goods. As early as the

1860s, Brazilian writers were protesting about the dominance of British capitalism. Here is J.F.K. da Costa Rubim:

> For a trifle, they buy our cotton, our sugar, our wood, the hides of our cattle and an immensity of objects that constitute a veritable fount of riches, for a trifle, that is exchanged for a small portion of cloth, that any other nation would furnish us at a more reasonable rate. They force all our produce to be sent to London, and after passing it through their factories, return it here to sell under the title of English manufacture, by virtue of which we do nothing more than buy very dear that which we have sold them very cheaply.

In São Paulo, nothing exemplified British-Brazilian attitudes more succinctly than the railway. Paulistas relied on British trucks and tracks for their wealth, but this reliance caused resentment rather than gratitude. From the early 1890s, bankers, farmers and merchants started complaining about the power of the San Paulo Railway. Although other operators ran tracks along the valleys of the interior, offering transport to hundreds of coffee plantations, all of them had to link with the SPR to reach the coast. A single line went from São Paulo to Santos, and the managers ran only a few trains each day, allowing them to exploit their monopoly to its full worth. The coffee barons petitioned parliament. Why should the British be allowed to run a monopoly? Why shouldn't a Brazilian railway work the same route? Why should a foreign company own the most profitable railway in the whole of South America, and retain all its profits for themselves? In response, the British gestured at all the other railways in Brazil. With a few British-owned exceptions, they were a mess. Construction and ownership remained entirely in private hands, so the industry lacked any centralised planning. Competing railways refused to communicate with one another. At one moment, seven different gauges were being used on networks throughout the country. For every line like the SPR that aided expansion and brought huge profits to investors, another line would be speeding directly into the jungle, heading for a town that seemed to have been randomly plucked on a map. Arriving at their obscure destination, the railwaymen discovered not only that no-one could possibly have any desire to go there, but also that nothing was produced there that anyone would ever want to bring back.

By the end of the century, only half the railways in Brazil were making an annual profit, and none of them came anywhere close to matching the success of the SPR. Mile for mile, the San Paulo Railway was the most profitable line on the planet. It was enlightened – the first pension scheme in Brazil was started by the SPR for its workforce – and entirely self-sufficient. Having raised most of their capital in London, and imported their management and rolling stock from Britain, the shareholders owed nothing to Brazil. When Brazilians demanded to know why the railway should be owned and run solely by foreigners, the British had a simple response: if Brazilians had been in charge, nothing would ever have been done. This wasn't intended as a joke, or even as deliberate provocation. The British honestly believed that nothing would ever get done in Brazil if they didn't do it. They looked around the country, and saw an indolent population, devoted to pleasure, barely capable of getting out of bed without assistance, and, worst of all, always late. For the British, punctuality is indistinguishable from morality. If a man is late for an appointment, you would not leave him alone in a room with your daughter. If Britain had managed to secure Brazil as a bona fide colony, perhaps the country's abysmal timekeeping could have been challenged. Promptitude would have been rewarded, and lateness punished. Unfortunately, the Portuguese rot had taken hold. Latin slackness flourished. When Peter Fleming visited São Paulo in the 1930s, nothing shocked him so much as the languid attitude of the natives towards time.

> Delay in Brazil is a climate. You live in it. You can't get away from it. There is nothing to be done about it. It should, I think, be a source of pride to Brazilians that they possess a national characteristic which it is absolutely impossible to ignore. No other people can make this boast. The English are a race of shopkeepers; but it is possible to live in England without being seriously inconvenienced by the process of barter which rages around you...A man in a hurry will be miserable in Brazil.

The British who owned the SPR refused to relinquish their monopoly, but they agreed to build a second line alongside the first, allowing twice as many trains to be run down to Santos. Work started in 1895. The same year, the SPR laid the foundations for a splendid new station in São Paulo, the third to have been built on the same site in thirty years, each one bigger and smarter than its predecessor. The first had been little more than a brick hut. When they knocked that down, they built a long covered platform and a two-storey building with the ticket office and the waiting rooms on the ground floor, the managers on the floor above. Now that had been demolished too, and the railwaymen were building themselves a huge new home. A ten-minute walk from Charles Dulley's estate, the new Luz station would be a monument to British skill and daring, a shining edifice of brick and steel, always filled with the roar of engines, the hiss of steam, the footsteps of hurrying passengers, the whistles of guards and the shouts of porters. Under its roof, shielded from the sun, you could forget your Brazilian surroundings, and imagine yourself in Exeter, Glasgow, Madras, Ontario, Auckland or any of the other places where the British ran their trains.

In their own small way, the British community in Brazil tried to impose their own values on the limp, lackadaisical natives. They laid tracks on the earth. They imposed timetables on the population. Their trains waited for no-one. In their design for the new Luz station, the engineers topped the building with a tall, slim tower that would rise above all the buildings in São Paulo. When it was finished, the clock at the top of the tower could be seen from almost any part of the city. The clock always told the right time, and its four faces looked down on the citizens like a disapproving father, ticking them off, reminding them that they were late for their next appointment.

If Trindade had possessed any political, economic or military significance, things might have been very different. If someone had found oil bubbling under the rocks, or the waves had carved a natural harbour where warships could refuel, then a war would probably have been fought to establish who owned the island. A British fleet would have sailed from Portsmouth to the South Atlantic. Brazilian soldiers would have waited in newly dug trenches, clutching their rifles, peering into the mist and praying. But neither country wished to lose money and shed blood over a lump of uninhabitable rock in the middle of the ocean. They let the issue rest for a few months. Once the attention of editors, backbenchers and students had fixed on some other topic, the two countries surreptitiously communicated through a Portuguese intermediary and reached terms. The Portuguese Foreign Minister brokered the deal, finding a compromise that allowed each country to achieve what they wanted in private but could not say in public.

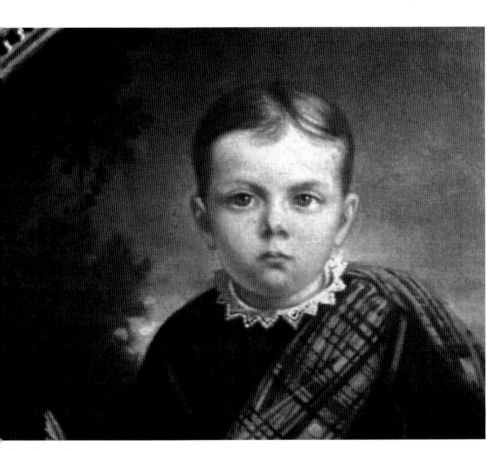

Charles Miller.

4 Corinthians visit to Southampton. Charles Miller is seated on the far left. The whole team is, from left to right, back row: Pickford, Nethercote, Dorkin, Reynolds, Stokes, Ward, Bencraft; middle row: Walker, Stewart, Denning, George, Miller; front: Ridges, Dawson.

5 The *Magdalena*.

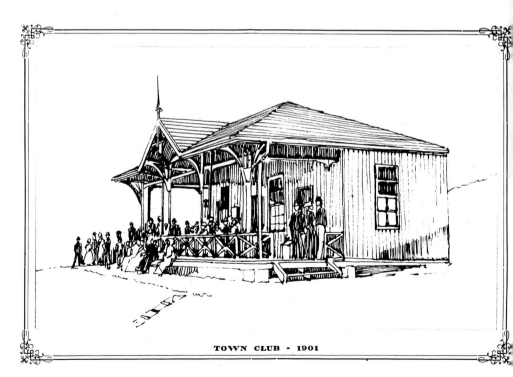

TOWN CLUB · 1901

6 The SPAC clubhouse.

7 Charles Miller's SPAC team.

10 The San Paulo Railway, looking down the Serra do Mar at the Grota Funda viaduct and one of the winding stations.

11 *Above left:* Hans Nobiling.

12 *Above right:* Charles Miller – captain of SPAC's championship-winning team.

17 The house on Rua México.

13
Pau

18 Charles, Antonietta and Helena.

19 Antonietta Rudge and Menotti del Picchia.

20 Sailing back to Britain, Charles Miller took the opportunity to practise his swing.

The *Barracouta* sailed from Montevideo to Rio, then headed into the Atlantic. Five days later, she moored alongside Trindade, and sent a few sailors ashore in a small boat. They removed the flag and the bottle. Although they left the eight-foot-high letters that had been painted on a rock, the wind and rain had already washed away most of the white-wash, and the rest wouldn't last much longer. In Brazil, newspapers carried long, boastful articles, describing the great triumph that their fledging republic had won against the bullying tactics of European imperialism. In Britain, a few small notices appeared in the foreign pages, noting that a trivial dispute over a distant lump of rock had been concluded to the satisfaction of Her Majesty's Government. Some months later, Queen Victoria invited the Portuguese Foreign Minister to Buckingham Palace, and presented him with a medal.

The only loser in the entire affair was a lonely, depressed American, confined to a squalid room in New York City. Newspapers had forgotten him. Foreign governments did not even acknowledge his letters. His wife had stomped off in a huff and fled to her father's mansion. In the surge of publicity following his initial announcement, Baron Harden-Hickey had been offered the throne of Honolulu, but he turned it down, wanting his own island. Trindade remained his obsession. He knew that the Brazilians would never organise an invasion, and probably wouldn't even notice if he set up his royal residence in the middle of the Atlantic. No, his enemy was Britain. Relying on his ancestry to gain friends and allies, he decided to invade England with an Irish army. He sent letters to nationalists in Dublin, offering support and suggesting routes for a possible invasion. They humoured him, hoping that he might be a crazy American millionaire, but turned their attention elsewhere when they realised he was just crazy.

Harden-Hickey left his apartment in New York, and headed south, carrying all his possessions in a suitcase. For several months, he wandered around Texas and Mexico, looking for good land, planning to buy himself a little farm and some healthy cattle. One night, he booked into the Peirson Hotel in El Paso. When the maid came to change his sheets in the morning, her knocking got no answer. The manager broke the door down. Baron Harden-Hickey was lying on the bed, an empty bottle of poison by his side. When they searched his suitcase, they found a few clothes, a couple of books and the crown of Trindade.

Ten

ugustus Farnham Shaw was twenty-nine years old and ablaze with missionary zeal. As a devout Presbyterian, he had made an early decision to devote his life to the Church. Born in Clayville, New York State, and educated at Yale, he became a teacher in Dobbs Ferry, a village just north of Manhattan, but felt frustrated by the lack of a true purpose to his life. He longed for a challenge, a mission that would allow him to prove himself. When he learnt of a Presbyterian school in Brazil, offering the opportunity to preach the true gospel to Catholics, he packed his bags and sailed for thirty days down the coast of the Americas, prepared to do battle with the misguided Latins. In his luggage, he carried the twin tools of his mission: a bible and a deflated leather ball.

When Shaw passed through customs at Santos on his way to Mackenzie College, both book and ball must have attracted some curious attention. As a Protestant, Shaw read his bible in English rather than Latin. As a loyal citizen of the USA, he played an American game – a game that had been created on North American soil and embodied North American virtues. When the officials let him pass, the first basketball arrived in Brazil.

Five years earlier, during the winter of 1891/92, the game had been invented by another devout Presbyterian. A teacher named James Naismith, who taught at the YMCA college in Massachusetts, had been set a task by his boss. You have fourteen days to invent a new sport. The college needed a game that could be played indoors by boisterous young Christians. During the freezing winters suffered by the residents of Springfield, Massachusetts, they could hardly be expected to play outside. Naismith not only met his deadline, he invented one of the most successful games of all time. He wrote thirteen rules, mingling snatches of football and lacrosse with a homemade game that he had played during his own childhood. The new game used two peach baskets, nailed to the wall at opposite ends of the gym, so Naismith called it basketball. With admirable modesty, Naismith rejected a friend's insistence that the game should be christened 'Naismith-ball'. To the inventor's amazement, the game swept across the United States within months, then vaulted international borders and conquered the world.

Despite the fact that Naismith was a Canadian born of Scottish parents, his game was claimed as authentically American, possessing no ugly links with Europe – and, most importantly, no taint of Englishness. Proud Americans refused to cringe before their old colonial rulers by playing English games with English rules. No true American would waste his time on soccer or cricket – not when he had baseball, American football and, best of all, brand-new, all-American, pure Presbyterian basketball. American missionaries poured out of the United States and into the world, carrying American values, American Bibles, American dollars, American know-how, American can-do and American basketballs. They were the first of many. Soon, they knew, America would be ruling the world. Soon, all the old powers would have to step aside, and leave things to be ruled by:

> the greatest country in the whole of God's Universe. We shall be giving the word for everything: industry, trade, law, journalism, art, politics, and religion, from Cape Horn clear over to Smith's Sound, and beyond, too, if anything worth taking turns up at the North Pole. And then we shall have the leisure to take in hand the outlying islands and continents of the earth. We shall run the world's business whether the world likes it or not. The world can't help it – and neither can we, I guess.

The American school in São Paulo had been started by some of the earliest of these missionaries to head south from the USA: a pair of enthusiastic Presbyterians, armed with little more than egalitarian ideals and evangelical fervour. They opened a small primary school in the town, shocking local residents with their radical ideas. Not only did they teach boys and girls in the same room, but they refused to segregate races or social groups. Everyone sat together. Locals would have liked to boycott the school, but the standard of teaching was simply too good, and the Presbyterians found their classes expanding every year. Soon, the headmaster could buy a plot of land and construct new premises. He even started a training college to ensure a constant stream of qualified teachers. By the beginning of the 1880s, the American School taught every age from kindergarten to graduate, and expanded yet again, building a boarding school for boys, a business college and a library.

Alice Humphrey visited the school in the 1890s. When she published her memoir of a journey to Brazil, she included a short biography of John Mackenzie. 'He travelled extensively in the Old World and his attention was constantly drawn to the ignorance, super-stition and poverty of the masses in Italy, and the lack of Christian culture in what should have been the most Christian of countries. This spectacle of a lapsed Christianity affected him deeply, and he deter-mined to honour his father's memory and satisfy his own convictions by establishing, somewhere, a College where the Bible should be the foundation of education. After at least one unsuccessful attempt to carry out his idea in Europe, he heard of the work that was being done by the Protestant Church at S. Paulo, Brazil, shortly after the fall of the Empire. A staunch American, his heart went out to the youngest of the American Republics, and he saw, at once, the value to the nascent Republic of having its youth grounded in a knowledge of God's Word.' Although Mackenzie had never visited Brazil, he changed his will, leaving a donation of $50,000 to the American School, asking only that the money should be spent on an institution that did two things: bore his name and inculcated its students with the virtues of the Protestant Bible.

The American School changed its name to Mackenzie College, and spent Mackenzie's money on an engineering faculty. And when it came to the final clause in Mackenzie's will, the teachers did what they could. They taught Protestant virtues, but their lessons rarely dented the beliefs of their pupils. The staff of Mackenzie may have been American and Presbyterian, but their students were mostly Brazilian, and thus Catholic. When Augustus Shaw arrived, brimming with Presbyterian enthusiasm, the school had almost 550 pupils, comprising 427 Catholics, 117 Protestants and two Jews. Shaw had no doubt that the proportions would soon be changing. Perhaps his fellow teachers warned him that the students might be a little intransigent, but Shaw took no notice. He knew how to instil honest Presbyterian beliefs in malleable young minds. He summoned his class, pumped air into his basketball and explained the thirteen rules. Then he took them down to the gymnasium, and played the first game of basketball on Brazilian soil. As Shaw stood on the sidelines, watching the game, his pride turned to astonishment and then disbelief. Were his students stupid? Mischievous? Or deliberately disobedient? For whatever reason, they ignored everything that he had said, and played by rules which had no resemblance to those that he had just taught them. Finally, Shaw could restrain himself no longer, and ran onto the court. 'No! No, no, no! Use your hands!' he yelled at them. 'Not your feet! Listen to me! Don't use your feet, use your hands!'

The students took no notice. They kicked the ball along the ground, dribbling from one end of the court to the other. To score, rather than lobbing the ball into the basket, they whacked it against the wall. To Shaw's fury, his pupils disdained the good, honest North American game that he had taught them, and insisted on imitating the ridiculous sport that unhinged Englishmen played on the other side of town.

A year later, one more young man arrived in São Paulo with a deflated leather ball in his luggage. His name was Hans Nobiling, and he had sailed from Hamburg. There, he had played for one of the first football teams to be founded in Germany, 'Sport-Club Germania von 1887'. An athletics club, Germania only started playing football when a quartet of new members joined the club in 1891. Named Hilton, Webb, Humphries and Cotterell, they were, of course, English. Most Germans recoiled from this deranged new sport, preferring to devote their attention to gymnastics, and football quickly acquired a new nickname: '*die englische Krankheit*': The English disease. The name had originally been used to describe rickets, but grew to encompass anything ugly, misshapen and English – such as football.

The connection between football and England would be broken by the outbreak of the war in 1914; until then, spectators in Hamburg shouted encouragement at their team in English, yelling 'Play up, Germania! Play up!' In 1919, Germania merged with two other local teams. Weakened by the war, none of them could summon enough fit young men to field a full team. Together, they united to form Hamburger Sportverein. Best known in Britain as the employers of

Kevin Keegan – and for losing the European Cup final to Nottingham Forest in 1980 – Hamburger SV were among the sixteen teams that founded the Bundesliga, which they won in 1979, 1982 and 1983.

Nobiling played for Sport-Club Germania alongside those four Englishmen, and learned his football from them. An intrepid young man, he decided to flee the old world and seek his fortune in the new. Bound for Brazil, Nobiling packed all his football gear: boots, balls and a book of rules published by Germania. He expected that his fellow Germans in Brazil would not yet have discovered the joys of football – and he was right – but he could hardly have anticipated their total lack of interest in the English game. As soon as he arrived in São Paulo, Nobiling started a team, but couldn't tempt a single German to join. They preferred gymnastics. Try the British, they told him. If you want to catch *die englische Krankheit*, go to the Dulley estate. Over there, near the railway station, you'll find some crazy Englishmen playing this ludicrous game that they like to call football.

Leaving his fellow countrymen to their wooden horses and parallel bars, Nobiling walked across town and sneaked through the gates of the Dulley estate. He arrived on a Saturday afternoon, and caught the English in the midst of a game. Nobiling watched from the sidelines and, to his delight, immediately saw some excellent players. Two in particular caught his eye – a forward, a small man in his mid-twenties, and a full-back, a much younger man who looked only sixteen or seventeen, but already had the strength and skill of a great footballer. At the end of the game, Nobiling approached those two, and introduced himself. Walter Jeffery was the young back, he discovered, and the forward was Charles Miller. Both of them were polite, shaking Nobiling's hand and inviting him for a cup of tea, but neither was particularly friendly. When Nobiling let them know that he had played with Germania in Hamburg, and implied that he might be a useful player for any team in São Paulo, his hints were pointedly ignored. SPAC was open only to the British. A Canadian would certainly be invited to join, as might a South African, an Australian or a New Zealander. Space could even be found for a man from New York or San Francisco. But if a German wanted to play football in São Paulo, he had better start his own team.

So he did. Lacking the support of any particular national community, Nobiling gathered a group of young men who had only one thing in common: they wanted to play football. Whatever their nationality –

German, English, Irish, American or Brazilian – they shared two common languages. Firstly, for general conversation, they used Portuguese, the language of the country that they inhabited. Secondly, for football, they used English. Within the rectangle of a football field, English words might be shouted in twenty-three different accents, but everyone understood them. Goal, foul, offside – even the people who couldn't speak a single sentence in English soon learned the meaning of those words. Just as French has always been the undisputed language of the military (reconnaissance, avant-garde, lieutenant) and Italian is always used for music (piano, allegro, fortissimo), so the language of football is English.

Now the city had three teams. Only one question remained. Which was the best?

For the British, this was a question that did not need to be asked. Just as the English Football Association refused to play in the first World Cup, knowing that they would win it too easily, so the British teams in São Paulo never bothered inviting anyone else to play against them. The humiliation might prove fatally embarrassing for those unfortunate Germans and Americans. But the Germans and Americans did not fear humiliation. Perhaps they even deluded themselves that they could win. At the beginning of 1899, a formal letter was delivered to Charles Miller, care of the São Paulo Athletic Club, inviting him to bring his best eleven to the grounds of Mackenzie College and play a game of football. Charlie was busy with other things – polishing off a satisfactory season of cricket fixtures, for instance – and took a couple of months to respond. Meanwhile, another club had stepped in, receiving and answering a similar letter, and a match had been arranged. On 5 March 1899, the Hans Nobiling Team entertained Mackenzie College, and they played the first football game between two clubs on Brazilian soil. All twenty-two players were young, male and wealthy, but neither team corresponded to a particular country or culture. Nobiling picked his players for their skills and enthusiasm, not their nationality, and his players yelled across the field in a bewildering babble of accents. The Mackenzie team were American only in the widest sense of the word: their coach came from New York via Yale; their education was Presbyterian; their nationality was mostly Brazilian.

The game between Augustus Shaw's Americans and Hans Nobiling's internationalists ended in a anti-climactic nil-nil draw, but energised

Charlie Miller into corresponding with his new rivals. He located the unanswered letters that had been lying around his office, and rattled off a couple of responses, inviting his opponents to take their chances against the British. A week later, Augustus Shaw and his best eleven from Mackenzie College crossed Rua Consolação and visited SPAC at their home ground. There, the Americans saw how football should be played, and were relieved to lose only 3-0.

Throughout the year, the three clubs continued playing one another. By July, Hans Nobiling's side managed to score their first goal against the British, but the smirks faded from their faces when the British responded by scoring four. Charlie Miller's team looked invincible, and so they remained for a long time. Another four years would pass before anyone managed to beat the British.

At the age of twenty-four, Charlie Miller had decided to strike out on his own. He left the comfort of his uncle's firm, and found a job for himself as a clerk at the London & Brazilian Bank. For the first few months, he did well. The manager's reports describe him as a courteous young man, usefully fluent in both English and Portuguese, and prophesied that he would make a valuable contribution to the firm. He earned an annual salary of £17. Even after four years of working, he was still earning less than he would have been paid as a professional footballer in England. At the beginning of the 1890s, English players earned between £2 and £4 per week. By the end of the decade, this had risen to £7 per week for the stars of the game, and half that for more ordinary players. Although this could not be described as a fortune, any decent player would earn as much as a skilled craftsman – and two or three times what Charlie was paid as a bank clerk in Brazil. Money went further in Brazil than Birmingham or Bond Street, of course, and the bank tempted him with the prospect of promotion. A junior manager earned £140 a year, and Charlie could easily rise to that level in a couple of years. He simply needed to endure the boredom and resist the temptation to daydream. But he couldn't. After only a year, he was already being criticised for carelessness in the manager's reports.

Given a little time, Charlie might have stopped daydreaming, learnt to concentrate on his ledgers and clambered slowly up the rungs of promotion, but the deaths of two women ruined his prospects of managing his own branch. The first to die was Lilian Lupton, the wife of Percy, and a well-loved figure in the British community. 'Of her kindness to sick and suffering friends, it is unnecessary to speak. She did good without ostentation, and as a simple matter of course. Her bright and engaging presence will be missed wherever British and American Paulistas are gathered together.' While Percy mourned, his compatriots debated a suitable memorial. Should a bed in the foreigners' hospital be christened in her honour? Or a fund established in her name? Eventually, they decided to place a stained-glass window in the British church and a simple stone engraved with a dedication. 'The above window representing the Christian Graces of Faith Hope and Charity is erected by friends of the late Lilian Lupton as a mark of regard for her memory and in recognition of her services to this church.'

Scarcely had the community unpinned the black drapes hanging from their windows when another woman died, and the drapes went up again. This time, every Briton in the city wore black, and many foreigners too, sympathetically expressing their respect for the nation's grief. They hung black banners from the Luz station, the offices of the London & Brazilian Bank and every other British business in the city. At the age of eighty-one, having ruled Britain and the Empire for all but eighteen of those years, Queen Victoria was dead. British residents met at the club to commiserate. As a mark of respect, Charlie cancelled all games. The community sent a telegram to London, expressing their sympathy and grief. Being practical people who did not like to wallow in their emotions, they set up a memorial fund, raising money to be donated to the widows of soldiers and sailors killed or disabled in the Boer War. The fund's largest donor was Percy Lupton, but he showed none of his usual zeal for organisation, letting other people take charge of arrangements. After the death of his wife, Lupton had lost his enthusiasm for colonial life. He began to dream of England, and even made tentative plans for retirement in Essex. The frost on the grass, pints of beer in village pubs, children playing on the village green. People advised him against it. When you go back to England, they said, you'll find that things aren't how you remembered them.

When you get there you find that nothing is the same, you're a misfit. During the time you've been away your friends have made new connections and they're no longer interested in you. You don't even think along the same lines as they do. You meet and they say: 'Why, hallo! When did you get back? How is Peru?' and you say: 'Peru? I was in Brazil!' and then they say, indignantly, mind you: 'Well, same thing, it's South America, isn't it?'

Lupton decided to visit England. When he had seen Essex, and supped a few pints in the local pub, he could decide whether to spend his dying days in the mellow mists of southern England or the fierce heat of southern Brazil. He had only one problem: if he was going to be gone for a few months, perhaps even a year, he needed to leave his office in the charge of a sensible chap, not one of the ninnies who currently slumbered there. He summoned his nephew, and made him an offer. Charlie resigned immediately from the bank, who let him leave without serving out his notice. Only eighteen months after breaking free of his family, Charlie Miller was back where he started.

News travelled quickly. People gossiped. Within weeks, everyone knew that three separate groups had started playing a bizarre new game called football. Young men and women wrangled invitations to SPAC, or stood on one another's shoulders to peer over the walls, and watched twenty-two men chasing a leather ball up and down a field. Unlike cricket, this was a game that other people actually wanted to play. No-one but the British could hear the romance in the crack of leather on willow. No-one but the British could see the thrill of three stumps and two bails shattered by a spinning ball. The British had been playing cricket in South America since 1806, but their efforts to inspire a love of the game in the local population had proved an embarrassing failure. The locals showed some willingness to stare at cricketers and laugh – the game nicely confirmed the British as lunatics – but refused to join in. Over the entire stretch of the nineteenth century, while the British knocked bat against ball every summer, not a single Uruguayan, Argentinean or Brazilian ever showed the slightest interest in imitating them. Football was different. As soon as the British set up a couple of goals and started kicking a ball around a field, spectators thronged to watch. Crowds formed. The walls of the British Club may have been high, but they weren't high enough to keep foreigners from football. The bug could not be isolated. The game spread, leaping out of SPAC, proliferating through the city, spreading across national, social and racial boundaries. However much the British might have wanted to keep the game to themselves, retaining its purity, insulating themselves from foreign influences, they had no choice. Some of them tut-tutted at the sight of black boys in the street, kicking a stone with their bare feet. Others bemoaned the enthusiasm of Germans, French, Swiss, Americans – and even Brazilians! – who wanted to learn the rules for this beguiling game. But not Charlie. Oh no, not him. He wouldn't try to isolate the virus. He had no fear that his game would be contaminated. Quite the opposite. He was thrilled by the prospect of more players, more teams, more games. He welcomed the competition.

The fourth club in São Paulo was founded by the same man as the third. After a disagreement with the other members of his original team, Hans Nobiling decided to abandon his internationalists and rely entirely on fellow Teutons. He managed to tempt ten men out of the gymnasium, and christened a team in homage to the Hamburgers who had taught him to play football. He called his new team Sport Club Germania. Meanwhile, Nobiling's old teammates continued playing without him, deciding to change their name to Sport Club Internacionale.

On the other side of town, yet another team started. A group of young Brazilians had been watching football and, disdaining the foreigners who ran SPAC and Germania, decided to start their own Brazilian team. They named themselves after their city: the Club Athletico Paulistano (the name abbreviated either to Paulistano or CAP). Through family connections, they received permission to use the Prado family's cycling ground, the Velódromo, as their pitch. The games soon became so popular that the cyclists had to move elsewhere, and the Prado family paid for stands to be constructed for spectators. As mayor of São Paulo, Antonio Prado must have been one of the first men in Brazil to see the potential political benefits of football, and encouraged the smart set to come and watch games on his land.

The city was changing. Roads streaked across the landscape. The hills disappeared under new suburbs. The Luz station opened. Around 1,500 mules lost their jobs when the trams were finally electrified. Attracted by the possibility of work, people poured into the city from Europe, North America and the poorer parts of Brazil. One day, people said, the city might overtake Rio de Janeiro in size, wealth and prestige. One day, the world would give them the respect that they deserved.

And what could be a better advertisement for the citizens of São Paulo than their prowess at the most modern, thrilling game on the planet?

A new generation of young, aggressive Paulistas were determined to mould their city into a modern, outward-looking place. One of them was the new captain of Internacionale. His name was Antonio Casimiro da Costa, and his entrepreneurial spirit welded São Paulo's five amateur-ish, haphazard teams into Brazil's first fully fledged league. Like many of the sons of the richest Brazilian families, da Costa had been sent to Europe for his education. When he returned from Switzerland, desperate to continue playing the new game that he had learned, da Costa was delighted to discover that his native city had been gripped by a lust for football. Being Brazilian, he didn't want to play for the British, Germans or Americans, so he joined Sport Club Internacionale. Within weeks, he was captaining the team, and enforcing a new regime of efficiency and discipline. He organised a series of fixtures, started youth teams and encouraged school children to play football rather than baseball or basketball. Irritated by the long wait for British footballs, which took a month to arrive by ship from Southampton, he carried a ball to a shoe-maker on the Rua Ipiranga and placed an order for the first Brazilian footballs. The shoemaker unstitched the ball, took it apart, cut leather swatches to the same pattern, sewed them together, and started a new line that soon proved much more profitable than uppers, soles or laces.

Miller, Shaw and Nobiling loved football, and wanted nothing more than the chance to play the game. Antonio Casimiro da Costa saw some-thing else: he realised that football offered unprecedented opportunities. Although he can never have guessed how completely football would come to be linked with Brazilian national pride, he sensed that the game could easily be used as a focus for disparate emotions and ideals. São Paulo was changing, swelling and thriving, but people still dismissed the city as a dull, dusty backwater rather than praising it as an emerging industrial powerhouse. Proud Paulistas like da Costa wanted their home to be noticed. Art is one easy way to earn the world's respect, and several of the coffee barons plunged their profits into building a municipal theatre, sponsoring opera and ballet, or filling art galleries with antique canvases in elaborate gilt frames. Sport is another straightforward way for the nouveaux riches to announce their presence. Buy a football club, build a team, win a competition and, although people might not forgive your accent or your manners, they will certainly remember you.

Rio de Janeiro remained the first city of Brazil in every way, and thus the first opponent of any challenger to the crown. From his Swiss schooling, Antonio Casimiro da Costa knew some posh Brazilians who played football and lived in Rio. He issued a challenge. Represent your city in the first match between Paulistas and Cariocas. In October 1901, a team took the train from Rio, arrived at the Luz station, and played two matches. The team that represented São Paulo had a strict balance of players, using at least one from each of the city's five clubs: W. Holland (Internacionale); Belforte Duarte (Mackenzie), Hans Nobiling (Germania); Vanorden (Internacionale), Walter Jeffery (SPAC), Muss (Germania); Ibanez (Paulistano), Herbert Boyes (SPAC), Antonio Casimiro da Costa (Internacionale), Charles Miller (SPAC), A. de Carvalho (Mackenzie).

Both games ended in draws, 1-1 on the first, 2-2 on the second. Large crowds watched the games, and local newspapers carried lengthy reports, using a curiously mangled Anglo-Portuguese to describe some unfamiliar footballing terms. At a celebratory banquet after the last game, toasts were drunk to the President of Brazil and the King of England. If the Germans or Americans wondered why their leaders did not deserve toasts, they kept such gripes to themselves.

At the end of that year, a couple of months after the matches against Rio, da Costa summoned São Paulo's five clubs to a meeting. The following year, he told them, they would play a league, each team playing every other team twice, home and away. The league would meet its costs by charging an admission fee to spectators. Half the ticket price would go to the two teams playing that particular game, and half would be taken by the league. When the meeting ended, da Costa lifted a large silver cup by its two spindly handles. Soon, he promised, he would be handing it to one of the men in the room. He had commissioned an exclusive French jeweller to sculpt this cup, which would be presented to the team that won the Liga Paulista.

One of the British in São Paulo spotted a leaflet posted to a wall.

INGLÊS
English and North America
It to learn by the professor P Louteiro
In three months
It is the time for to speak very well

Professor Louteiro probably had few pupils, not because he was a terrible teacher (as he surely must have been) but due to a lack of interest among Brazilians in learning English. Why bother? Everyday business was conducted in Portuguese, and even the most incompetent foreigners knew how to order a coffee or ask for directions. Smart Brazilians spoke French as their second language, and looked instinctively towards Paris, taking their cue from the French in fashion, music, art and every other sphere of life where style mattered more than money. Painters made pilgrimages to Paris. Poets wrote in French. Only businessmen had any need to learn English, and even they dealt mostly with British or American agents who spoke some Portuguese.

The Liga Paulista intended to earn a decent profit from its gates, but punters would never return to a game that they couldn't understand, so spectators needed to be given a little explanation. Sometimes players did too. The Liga printed programmes for each game, giving the names of the players, details of other games, an explanation of the rules and a dictionary of terms.

Explicação de alguns termos

HALF-TIME – é o tempo que dura o jogo até o intervalle.

FREE-KICK, Korner-hick, Goal-Kick – são os pontapés dados na bola nas diversas partes do campo, como penas.

PENALTY-KICK – é o pontapé dado na bola em frente ao goal como pena a uma falta commetida dentro da linha das 18 jardas.

OFF-SIDE – é quando um jogador fica momentaneamente impossibilitado de bater de bola.

CARRYING – é quando o goalkeeper anda mais de 2 passos com a bola nas mãos.

HANDLING – é quando o jogador toca propositalmente na bola com as mãos ou com os braços.

HOLDING – é segurar ou impedir ao adversario com as mãos.

HIPPING – é passar rasteira ou procurar derrubar ao adversario.

REFEREE – é o juiz da partida.

LINESMAN – é o juiz de cada partido que percorre as linhas para marcar o logar por onde a bola sahia do campo.

The Liga Paulista played its first fixture on 3 May 1902. Hans Nobiling took Germania to Mackenzie College. Antonio Casimiro da Costa refereed. The following morning, a newspaper printed a full report of the game.

'No primeiro half-time, o sr. Mario Eppinghaus fez um gol para o Mackenzie... Poucos minutos antes do half-time, o sr. Kirschner, center-forward do Germania, consequiu fazer um scap e dahi marcar o primeiro gol do Germania.'

They played forty-minute halves, and Mackenzie won 2-1.

Three days later, SPAC played Paulistano. The three British forwards, Herbert Boyes, Charlie Miller and Walter Jeffery, ran amok, scoring a goal apiece plus a second for Boyes. Charlie refereed the next game, when Germania defeated Internacionale, then scored for SPAC in a 3-0 demolition of Mackenzie. A couple of weeks later, after Mackenzie had drawn against both Internacionale and Paulistano, and SPAC beat Internacionale, the league looked finished before half the games had been played. Charlie Miller led the race for the golden boot, and his team sat comfortably on the top of the table. Then came disaster. After four years of invincibility, the British lost a game.

Their opponents were Paulistano, and the game's only goal was scored by Alvaro Rocha. No-one doubted the significance of this moment. At the end of the game, the crowd charged onto the pitch, cheering and whistling, surrounding the Brazilian players and hoisting them into the air. When the British insisted that the crowd remove themselves from the grass, which would have to serve as a cricket pitch later in the year, the revellers poured out of the gates and continued their celebrations on the surrounding streets, parading through the city, whooping, dancing, setting off fireworks. That night, during a dull performance at the Teatro Municipal, a group of fans started humming the Paulistano chant. People turned in their seats, shushing the hooligans, who responded by humming louder and louder. No-one could hear the actors on the stage. People shouted at the fans, ordering them to shut up. In response, they stood on their chairs and belted out the anthem at top volume. Finally, a policeman arrived. He threatened to take every single one of the fans into custody, until they told him why they were singing. Then he joined in.

The following day, newspapers hailed the event, and suggested that Paulistano should be the city's official team. Power had shifted. The pupils had thrashed their masters. Just like Australia winning the Ashes in 1878, or the All Blacks touring the Northern Hemisphere in 1905, when they lost only one match in thirty-five, or India finally defeating England at Lord's in 1971, Brazilians knew that the boundary had been breached. Nothing would ever be the same again. The defeat of SPAC by Paulistano sent a quiver of distress through the stiff upper lip of every Briton in São Paulo and added a surge of adrenaline to the blood of their Brazilian rivals, who sensed that their time had come. A few more games like that and, come October, the first season of the Liga Paulista would be won by Paulistano. The silver cup would be raised by Brazilian hands. Only one person could stop them. Only one man could salvage British pride. Charlie Miller rallied his troops. Were they going to succumb, as so many had done, to the climate and the customs and the culture of the lascivious country in which they lived? Would they slither into foreign ways? Or would they remain Britons abroad, defiant, tough, self-reliant, unbeatable? Remember Clive of India, he said. Remember Gordon of Khartoum. Will you wilt or fight? Will you surrender or work? The choice, said Charlie, is yours.

Charlie Miller might have been born in Brazil, but he learnt his game in England, just as he had learnt his manners and his ethics. He played football like an Englishman, and that was how he wanted his team to play. A hundred years ago, the English game was ferocious, physical and violent. Players were driven by the same forces which had propelled the Empire's expansion: strength and discipline. The rules gave them little protection from physical assault. From 1893, goalkeepers could only be charged when playing the ball or obstructing an opponent; before that, a common tactic saw one forward knocking the goalkeeper to the ground while another kicked the ball into the goal. Firm tackling, the shoulder charge and 'hacking' (kicking an opponent's shins) remained vital parts of the game. Like soldiers, they fought hard and worked as a team. No single person was more important than the group. Strength, discipline and team spirit – these were the great virtues of the British game.

As the first truly Brazilian football team, Paulistano had no need to imitate British, American or German styles of play. They had no colonial masters. They were independent and free. They were Brazilian. And they played in a Brazilian style.

The name Brazil has two etymological candidates, and no-one is quite sure which is correct. The first is prosaic. The Romans imported a red wood from the Far East which they called *brasilium*. When a similar wood was discovered in South America, the area was christened *terra de brasil*. The second explanation is more romantic. Celtic legends described an island far to the west, an ancient, fertile, mysterious, mystical paradise called Hy Breasil. The island lay close to the west coast of Ireland, but was rarely seen. A dense fog hung around the shores, shielding Hy Breasil from passing ships. Once every seven years, the fog lifted, exposing a mountainous island covered with fertile grasslands. In 1480, a ship left Bristol, and sailed around the south coast of Ireland, searching for the island of Hy Breasil. They hunted for nine months, criss-crossing the Atlantic, before giving up. The following year, two more ships set off on the same quest, but were equally unsuccessful. For the next decade, between two and seven ships set sail for Hy Breasil every year, convinced that the island would provide a useful staging post in the mid-Atlantic. When news arrived of Columbus and his extraordinary discoveries, sailors forgot Hy Breasil and concentrated their thoughts on larger prizes, but the island stayed on maps for several more centuries, making its last appearance on a chart published in 1865.

This is the country that Brazilians like to imagine themselves inhabiting: the Celtic paradise of Hy Breasil, a magical place, opposed in every way to the cold, dreary rationality of North America and Western Europe. There is a deep-rooted Brazilian distrust of logic, and a preference for intuition and creativity. When Brazilians watch a game of football, that's what the spectators are always hoping for. A moment of magic. An unpredictable instant of creativity which produces a goal from nowhere and changes the game.

In his autobiography, Peter Chapman describes playing a friendly match during the 1986 World Cup: Brazil *v.* The Rest of the World.

The Brazilian team arrived with only ten players, having forgotten – or not bothered – to bring a goalkeeper. Brazilian teams have a reputation for treating defence as an embarrassing duty. They'll do it, although they would rather not. The goalkeeper stands behind the team, forlorn and forgotten, abandoned by the other players as they charge up the field, looking for another amazing individual goal. In 1986, Chapman was volunteered by his own team, and ended up playing for the other side, a British goalkeeper behind ten Brazilian forwards.

As it is now, so has it always been. Even in the first games played by Brazilian teams, the crowd and players wanted to see excitement, speed and, more than anything, magical moments of individual skill and creativity. Players launched wild attempts towards the goal from twenty or thirty yards out, forgetting to pass to anyone else on their team, forgetting anyone or anything but themselves. The British played as eleven small parts of a larger unit, each man subsuming his own creative brilliance to the greater need of the team; the Brazilians played as eleven individuals, each of whom might have been alone on the pitch, caring for nothing except the ball at his feet and the blank mouth of the goal that awaited him.

The first season of the Liga Paulista finished on the last Saturday in October. After every team had played eight games, two of them found themselves drawn on twelve points apiece. Club Athletico Paulistano and the São Paulo Athletic Club, CAP and SPAC, the Brazilians and the British, tied at the top. Charlie Miller's men had a superior goal difference – but who would settle a football league on such a piffling technicality as goal difference? Luckily, the possibility of a tied league had already occurred to da Costa when he wrote the rules of the Liga Paulista, so everyone was prepared for what would happen next. That Sunday, one day after the league had ended, Paulistano and SPAC met to play a decider.

Both sides knew that they could win. During the league, each had beaten the other. The British had not only shed their invincibility by losing to Paulistano, but drawn their previous two games before the play-off, showing signs that their sprit was weakening. While SPAC sank, Paulistano were rising. Momentum favoured them. They had just beaten Internacionale and Mackenzie, and arrived at the final aflame with confidence, striding about the pitch like conquering heroes. The last battle had not yet been fought, but they knew who had won the war. Their time had arrived. That Sunday's final had the atmosphere of a symbolic occasion, dripping with historical significance. The British would be handing over their baton to the Brazilians. The father would be defeated by the son. Those supercilious Englishmen would have the swagger knocked from their steps, the grin wiped off their faces, the cup snatched from their greedy fingers.

Four thousand people assembled to watch the game. Men, women and children lined the pitch, cheering and screaming before the ball had even been kicked. The wooden stands trembled from the constant stamping of feet. On the pitch, the referee fiddled with his whistle, and the two teams waited, biting their lips, trying to ignore the noise that surrounded them. None of them had ever played in front of such a huge crowd.

CLUB ATHLETICO PAULISTANO

Jorge de Miranda Filho
Thiers, Rubião
Barros, Olavo, Renato
Cerqueira, Marques, Rocha, Ibanez, Marquez

Blacklock, Mondadon, Miller, Brough, Boyes
Heycock, Wucherer, Biddell
Kenworthy, Kenworthy
Jeffery

SÃO PAULO ATHLETIC CLUB

The referee blew his whistle. The game started. Almost immediately, Marques sprinted forward, tripped over the ball and fell to the ground. As players scrambled for the ball, a SPAC player trod on Marques, dislocating his shoulder. Marques had to be led from the pitch by a teammate, and could not continue. If the same thing happened today, we might assume that the Englishman had deliberately trodden on his opponent. At the time, everyone felt certain that he had stumbled accidentally. Whatever the truth, the removal of Marques certainly helped SPAC. Before half-time, Charlie Miller scored twice. After the ten-minute interval, Alvaro Rocha scored once for Paulistano. SPAC spent most of the second half defending. Walter Jeffery stopped shot after shot, and the game ended with victory for the British.

In a ceremony watched by the 4,000 silenced fans, and 100 grinning Britons, each member of the two teams was presented with a small bouquet of flowers. The players stepped aside, and Antonio Casimiro da Costa presented the silver cup to Charlie Miller. A bottle of champagne was opened. Da Costa poured the contents into the cup. Charlie took a sip, then passed it to the captain of Paulistano. When each team had been toasted, the cup was handed back to Charlie. He tipped it up and poured the rest of the champagne over the ball.

Eleven

Four years into the new century, the Banister Court school magazine published a lengthy letter from Charles Miller. Contact with old boys remained an important part of Christopher Ellaby's life, partly as a duty – their sons provided a valuable percentage of the school's intake – and partly out of sentiment. Three times a year, a bundle of school magazines was tied with string, loaded onto a steamer at Southampton docks and sent across the Atlantic to be distributed among alumni in Brazil, Uruguay and Argentina. Every issue carried a few notes from Old Banisterians, describing an honour won on the battlefield, a promotion in the Colonial Service or a sporting triumph on some distant pitch. The column regularly featured two cousins in southern Brazil. 'Charles Miller has played in some cricket matches at São Paulo,' readers learned. 'W. Fox Rule has just left England to go back to Brazil, after staying for a few months in England and Paris. He stayed at Banister for several days.' For the following issue, Charlie wrote to say that he had made 125 not out for SPAC while Willie Fox Rule made 17. At the end of the century, the magazine reported a parade of deaths, wounds and honours in the Boer War. 'The fighting in the Transvaal has shown that some of our old football players are not more afraid of bullets than they were of tumbles.' While the sportier Old Banisterians subdued savages, the arty boys had been putting on face paint. Maundy Gregory was studying to take Holy Orders at Oxford, but devoted most of his attention to amateur theatricals. Harold Davidson became an entertainer, touring masonic lodges in the provinces, reciting risqué poems and singing dirty ditties. Depressed by his lack of success, Davidson eventually gave up acting and followed his father into the Church.

For the 1904 issue, Charlie sent the magazine a more complete record of his life in the tropics. He enclosed a wad of postcards and wrote an evocative description of his Brazilian home, but devoted most of his attention to sport. 'You will be surprised to hear that football is the game here,' he wrote. 'We have no less than sixty or seventy clubs in S. Paul's city alone.' As the sport's foremost missionary, Charlie was now a famous figure in the city.

A week ago I was asked to referee in a match of small boys, twenty a side. I told them it was absurd them playing twenty a side; but no, they wanted it. I thought, of course, the whole thing would be a muddle, but I found I was very much mistaken. They played two half-hours, and I only had to give two hands. The youngsters hardly spoke a word during the game, kept their places and played well; even for this match about 1,500 people turned up. No less than 2,000 footballs have been sold here within the last twelve months; nearly every village has a club.

Charlie wrote his letter during the lengthy summer break between the 1903 and 1904 football seasons. Perhaps he was sitting on the beach at Santos or idling away a humid afternoon in the office. He looked back to the previous October when, for the second year in succession, SPAC and Paulistano had fought a one-off match for the cup. 'We always get two or three thousand people to a league match, but for the final we had 6,000. The Brazilians scored the first goal, and you never heard such a row as the spectators kicked up.'

Back in May, the second season of the Liga Paulista had opened with a match between SPAC and the students of Mackenzie College. Duff and Miller scored one apiece to take the points for the British. A fortnight later, they played a return match at Mackenzie's ground, and SPAC won 2-1. With maximum points from their first two games, the champions looked set to repeat their triumph, and perhaps this allowed complacency to trickle into their game. They played Paulistano in July, and lost 2-0. Knocking five goals past Internacionale helped to restore confidence, and the return game against Paulistano ended in a 4-0 victory. By the end of the season, SPAC had dropped only one more point. Paulistano and SPAC had won six, drawn one and lost one.

Echoing the previous year, they met for a decider on the last weekend in October.

Six thousand voices cheered the two teams onto the pitch. The crowd was well-dressed, elegant, sophisticated and extremely loud. The red and white of Paulistano could be seen everywhere – flags, badges, crests, caps – smothering the rare outposts of SPAC's blue and white stripes. In the first half, Alvaro Rocha scored for Paulistano, and the crowd went crazy. Finally, this year, the snooty English would be booted out, and there was no better man to deliver the boot to a British back-side than Alvaro Rocha. Young, fit and beautiful, he was a well-known figure in the city and a hero on the pitch. When he touched the ball, men cheered and women swooned. A tall man with curly locks, he always wore his shirt open to expose his bronzed chest. No more appro-priate player could have scored the goal that ended British dominance of Brazilian football, and began a new era of Latin power. Alvaro Rocha weaved through the British like a king among peasants – until they tapped the ball from his feet and left him sprawling in the dust. He brushed himself down, accepted the ball from one of his teammates and sprinted forwards – and the damned British tackled him again. They had no respect for his god-like status. Again and again, the British won back the ball and made onslaughts on the Brazilian goal, firing shot after shot after shot until, unable to withstand the pressure, Paulistano dealt themselves a cruel blow. A couple of minutes before half-time, one of their players knocked the ball into his own net. The crowd was silenced. A few English voices burst out, suddenly audible, yelling with joy. As the Brazilians left the field with their heads down, the British sensed the game swinging in their favour. Charlie Miller gathered his men, and whispered to them, reminding them that an historic victory was only minutes away. 'Play up! Play up! And play the game!' In the second half, SPAC scored a single goal. Paulistano failed to respond. The crowd wept, Charlie poured a second bottle of champagne over the ball, and the cup returned to the British clubhouse on Rua Consolação.

Percy Lupton returned from Essex to São Paulo, reorganised his various business enterprises and resumed his duties as vice-consul. After a few months, he was off again, sailing back to England, leaving Charlie Miller in control of his Brazilian affairs. Lupton wrote to the Foreign Office in London, requesting six months' leave and asking permission to appoint his reputable chief clerk as acting vice-consul.

As His Majesty's Consular Representative, Charlie had few duties. He helped the confused, drunk or lost Britons who arrived at his office. When the new organ purchased by the Anglican Church was impounded by customs, he despatched an angry letter, demanding its release. He received an urgent request to send some seeds to a British company in South Africa. He was instructed to interview the Minister of Agriculture, and discover whether the Brazilian government intended to lure British emigrants to work as low-paid agricultural labourers. Along with all the other consular officials in South America, he was asked to look out for Max Goldberg, who had fled Eastbourne with his underage lover, Gertrude. They were said to be bound for Buenos Aires, and might be travelling under assumed names. To the great excitement of the community, the illicit couple were spotted in Santos. Goldberg was arrested, charged with immorality and marched onto the next boat back to Britain.

Consular staff in Santos and São Paulo earned double wages as compensation for the dangerous living conditions. The climate rotted British bodies. The atmosphere of political chaos crazed British minds. No-one knew how long the republic would last. Regular revolutions popped politicians in and out of office. Anything might happen. Long-term residents like Charlie Miller had grown used to such chaos, and learned not to take it seriously, just as they knew never to believe a Brazilian when he said, 'I shall arrive at such-and-such a time.' Unfortunately for Charlie, he received his orders from the consul in Santos, a punctilious career diplomat who had recently arrived from Africa and showed no willingness to compromise with Brazilian habits. His name was Roger Casement. Appointed as consul for the states of São Paulo and Paraná, he had taken an immediate dislike to Brazil, Brazilians and, more than anything, the British who lived in Brazil. Their sloppy attitude appalled him. Half a century earlier, when Richard Burton came to Santos, he had discovered the consular documents in a state of chaos. Rather than files or folders, Burton found two wicker baskets stuffed with ripped-up sheets of paper. Seeing this, Burton had laughed. Confronted by a similarly chaotic office, Casement was furious. He pored over the files, and found a trail of idleness, incompetence and stupidity. Checking marriage certificates, he discovered that most of the ceremonies had been conducted with a worrying lack of respect for the law, thus placing any offspring in a most awkward position. He sent a stream of letters to his minions throughout southern Brazil, querying their decisions, correcting their protocol, demanding to know their precise justification for every judgement.

No surprise, then, that Percy Lupton preferred to stay in England. He found a house in Southminster, a quiet Essex village about fifty miles directly east of London, and settled down among the ancient pleasures of warm beer, church bells and girls in cotton dresses cycling across the village green. He transferred his business to Charlie Miller, who became the official representative of the Royal Mail Steam Packet Company on an annual salary of £700. The Foreign Office invited Charlie to continue as vice-consul until a permanent replacement could be found. Despite the burden of answering regular aggressive letters from Roger Casement, Charlie accepted. With his various salaries, his business interests and his official posts, Charlie found himself not only established at the heart of the British community in São Paulo, but a relatively wealthy man. Not bad for a chap who had devoted almost every hour of his existence to football, cricket and the odd spot of tennis.

His new position brought not only power and influence, but the opportunity to pay back a few of his debts to his extended family. Among the first to be reimbursed were the Prados. Martinho and Veridiana Prado had four sons. The eldest, Antonio, was an important political figure, serving for several years as a government minister. Another son, Caio, had married Charlie's cousin, Maria Sophia Rudge. The youngest, Eduardo, was a poet and critic whose incendiary political rhetoric made him many enemies. When a warrant was finally issued for his arrest, Eduardo fled to his mother, and begged for her help. She knew exactly whom to approach. Later that night, one of her servants hurried through the streets, carrying a message to the most discreet community in the city. The following day, inquisitive citizens noticed William Fox Rule walking through the city with an unusual companion: a priest, whose features were hidden by a hooded cape. Striding through the streets, they argued earnestly in French. Reaching the railway station, William and the priest took the train to Santos, where Charlie Miller awaited them. He had already reserved a private cabin on the next Royal Mail steamer heading for Southampton. Customs officials were persuaded to look the other way while Charlie and William sneaked Eduardo aboard the ship and confined him to his cabin. A few months later, when things had calmed down, Eduardo returned from his travels and resumed his career as a well-known poet and critic.

Back in São Paulo, while her foolish son was sailing towards Europe, Veridiana Prado summoned the two young Englishmen, and thanked them for saving one of the Prados from the horrors of public humiliation. She had a single question: how could she repay them? Charlie Miller and William Fox Rule glanced at one another, then looked at Dona Veridiana. Both started speaking at the same time. There was one thing that she could do...

SPAC was homeless. Charles Dulley had died. While the young Dulleys were sent to Europe and the USA to finish their education, lawyers divided the estate into lots and sold it off, leaving British sportsmen to find new homes. The golfers had already organised themselves, and bought a plot of land. Their nine-hole course immediately acquired a new nickname: the Morro dos Ingleses – the hill of the English. The footballers and cricketers had not been so efficient. The Prados had land to spare – they owned vast swathes of the city – and Dona Veridiana handed over several fields that lay between two of the city's most important roads, Rua Augusta and Rua Consolação. The British levelled the ground and created a pitch which could be used for cricket, rugby, baseball and football. Overlooking the pitch, carpenters constructed a neat little pavilion where the ladies could shelter from the sun, drink lemonade and applaud their gallant men.

For the 1905 season, the Liga admitted a sixth member. Football had become so popular that too many new players joined the Club Athletico Paulistano, and they couldn't all be fitted in a single team. Disdaining the suggestion that they should play as Paulistano's reserves, a group broke away and formed their own new team, calling themselves Associação Atlética das Palmeiras. With six competitors in the league, each team played ten games, but the season ended with its familiar climax: Paulistano and SPAC both occupied the top spot. They had eighteen points apiece, each having won eight games and drawn two. Internacionale came third, followed by Mackenzie and Germania. The new boys of Palmeiras lurked at the bottom, having won a single game and lost nine. On the last Sunday in October, Paulistano and SPAC met at the Velódromo on Rua Consolação. For the third year running, the rivals duelled for the top spot.

Antonio da Costa's silver trophy had squatted above the bar in the SPAC clubhouse for two consecutive years. That Sunday, Charlie Miller lifted down the cup, and carried it to the ground. Huge excitement greeted the game. Thousands of fans lined the field, and broke into frenzied cheering as the teams jogged onto the pitch, SPAC in their blue and white striped shirts, Paulistano in white shirts embroidered with a small red badge, the three letters C, A and P entwined in a neat logo. After this frenetic build-up, the game itself was an anticlimax. The two teams knew one another too well for any surprises. Nerves crippled their creativity. The first half was scoreless. In the second, Charlie Miller took advantage of a goalkeeping error, and scored the game's only goal.

Even as the British celebrated, the Brazilians started complaining. Paulistano lodged a series of grievances. The game had ended six minutes early, they said, and Jeffery had clearly handled the ball. The committee examined these complaints with great care, and decided that not one of them had any merit. The fact that Charles Miller chaired the committee did not help to pacify Paulistano, and they resigned from the Liga.

Less than a month later, Charlie celebrated his thirtieth birthday. Drinking in SPAC's clubhouse, he could glance up at the shelf above the bar, see the silver cup sitting there, and know that it would never move again. Having won the Liga Paulista three years running, he and his team would be allowed to keep the cup.

Over the Christmas break, Paulistano considered their position, and rejoined the league for the next season. But they made some changes. Having realised that they had only one way to break British supremacy, the Prado family reached for their chequebooks. They demolished the Velódromo stadium and started afresh, building tennis courts, a swimming pool, a new stadium and a clubhouse with all the most up-to-date facilities. None of the other teams in the Liga could compete with this level of investment. Even the British ground still belonged to the Prado family. Against this sudden influx of hard cash, SPAC would have to rely on the old virtues: guile, dexterity, discipline and team spirit.

The league kicked off in May. Antonio Casimiro da Costa persuaded a wealthy local industrialist to pay for a new cup, which was made in Paris and shipped to Brazil. SPAC won their first two matches, then narrowly lost the third. In July, they had a routine game against

Germania. As usual, Charlie played at centre forward, but his wizardry had deserted him. Three months short of his thirty-first birthday, he was made to look like an old man. The lithe Germans danced past him, left him sprawling in the dust, and scored goal after goal. Six times, SPAC had to pick the ball out of their own net, and didn't manage to repay the favour even once. Morale collapsed. Charlie's team fell to pieces. In their next four games, they lost to Paulistano, Palmeiras and Internacionale, then to Paulistano once more. At the end of the season, SPAC took fourth place in the Liga, having lost six and won only four. Paulistano had not lost a single game, winning eight and drawing two. The humiliation was complete.

Charlie didn't seem to care. He hardly even noticed. While his team slithered down the league, his eyes drifted from the ball and focused elsewhere. Not for the first time in his life, he had fallen in love, but his new passion was unlike any that had gone before. You could not have found her in the lists of any sporting almanac. She had no rules. Her name was Antonietta.

Back in 1895, the year after Charlie Miller sailed to Brazil, Christopher Ellaby had fulfilled the one ambition that he had desired for so long: his fellow players elected him as president of the Hampshire Football Association. 'An earnest and kindly headmaster of Banister Court School,' according to William Pickford, 'he filled the office with distinction.' His presidency lasted a year, then he lapsed back into the more familiar roles of referee and committee member. His ambition achieved, he allowed himself to turn away from the football field and devote his attention to other matters. In 1902, he married Gertrude Christine Gladys Gilman, the daughter of a clergyman in Southampton. With a married headmaster, Banister Court changed. When Charlie attended the school, the atmosphere had been overwhelmingly masculine. Other than Ellaby's mother and the occasional parlour maid, no women ventured into the building. Ellaby must have warned his boys to beware the wanton lasses who lurked in the streets, cooing to passers-by, fluttering their lashes and unbuttoning their blouses. Like all ports, Southampton supported a huge population of prostitutes. Walking to a football game, the boys passed a line of women loitering on street corners, dressed in ragged clothes, their pock-marked faces disguised by blusher and lipstick. One or two of the braver boys might have ducked into the shadows of an alleyway and surrendered their virginity for a few pennies, but most of them averted their eyes and concentrated on discussing Latin grammar or tactics for the forthcoming game. Their unspeakable urges found release in athleticism. The effect of this bizarre education can be seen in the unhappy sexual lives of Old Banisterians, many of whom found themselves in murky waters when they left the cloistered comfort of their school. Harold Davidson was a peeping tom who kept a notebook with a thousand names of skinny teenage girls. Maundy Gregory was arrested for poisoning his wife. Alongside them, Charlie Miller's marriage looks blissful.

Charlie would have been given only one piece of advice by his British chums in Brazil. Don't marry a local girl. British men chose wives from their own community. Young men would return to England to find a bride, and embarked on a six-week dash around obscure relatives and sisters of friends, rushing from teas to dances, chatting with suitable girls, hoping to find a woman who would be willing to spend her days in the tropics. Everyone understood the ludicrous nature of this desperate chase, but they had no choice. The only alternative would have been marrying a local girl, and they knew the dangers of that.

'Well, Grayton was a young chap who came out from England,' Hale started, 'and married a Brazilian girl. She was of a very good family, and her parents and grandparents seemed of good Portuguese stock. Grayton took his wife to England with him when he went on leave, and then they returned here. Shortly after they arrived back, she had a child, and nature, through the germ plasm, played a dirty trick on them, for the baby was as black as your boots. There must have been a nigger in the family somewhere at some time and it turned up then. A case in a thousand, of course, but there you are. He could never return home with the baby, so he's been out here ever since.'

This was the conventional British view of intermarriage. Of course, not everyone felt the same way. That quotation comes from *Brazilian Marriage*, a novel by George Royston, which eventually presents a more hopeful picture of cultural collision. By the end of the unexpectedly intimate and moving novel, we are left in no doubt that Hale and his cohorts are narrow-minded bigots, crippled by their own prejudices. The plot of *Brazilian Marriage* is straightforward. Basil Forbes flees London when his fiancée drops him for his best friend. Distraught, desperate to get away, Basil takes a ship to South America, intending to spend some time in Buenos Aires, but stops in Pernambuco, and decides to stay. He shares a house with some Britons, joins the British club, and falls in love with a Brazilian woman. Both his British friends and her Brazilian family try to separate the couple, but Basil refuses to be deterred. To his surprise, the woman feels just as passionately about him. When she gets pregnant, they marry. Grudgingly, her family accepts him. He takes over the family business – sugar – and builds himself a new life in Brazil. The novel ends with the arrival of Basil's best friend and ex-fiancée from London, giving him the opportunity to see whether he has made a terrible mistake. He realises that his new life in Brazil is better than anything he could have hoped for if he had stayed in Britain. Having forgiven his ex-fiancée and oldest friend, he tries to explain to them what he has discovered in Brazil, and why he will not be coming back to London.

> 'Everything here is a fight against something that you don't quite under-stand. It's hard to explain. It's as if you were conducting a chemical experiment and someone had changed all the labels on the bottles. In England you know, more or less, what sort of reaction you're going to get – but not here.'
>
> 'Because England is settled, you mean.'
>
> 'Exactly. You can depend on race, customs, traditions. Of course, there are customs and traditions here too, more than you can imagine, but there's so much new blood, seething, boiling, fermenting, and every day new material pouring in. And they all have to go through the pangs of rebirth. Many come out on top, some are deformed, others miscarry. But, innately, it's a wonderful country, Don, although it's a child, a precocious child, trying to grow up.'

If Charlie was advised to find a pristine girl with pure Anglo–Saxon blood running through her veins, he spurned the advice and courted a girl who was not quite British. She had an excellent Gloucestershire heritage on her father's side, but her mother's family was Portuguese, and the dangers of 'the germ plasm' lurked in her blood. Her name was

Antonietta Rudge. Like most of the people who played an important role in Charlie's life, she was one of his cousins. No-one knows why they married. No-one can tell if their relationship was based on love, friendship or a family arrangement. Charlie was ten years older than Antonietta. He had a secure job, good prospects and an excellent background. A good catch. Although her parents were wealthy, Antonietta was the fifth of their sixteen children, and cannot have hoped for a large settlement. Striking rather than beautiful, she had thin features, a gangly body and large hands. Quite apart from her unconventional looks, she was a difficult child, slightly peculiar, not the easiest girl for anxious parents to match with a suitable boy. She was, her parents confessed with a sigh, artistic. Nothing is more pleasing to proud bourgeois parents than a daughter who sings a little, or paints neat watercolours, or learns to play a few elegant snatches of Liszt or Chopin on the pianoforte, but no right-thinking parent wants a daughter who is artistic. What will become of her?

Antonietta Rudge was born in 1885. Like Charles Miller, she was a great-great-great-grandchild of John Rudge and Abiah Smythe, one-time residents of Stroud in Gloucestershire. Two of John and Abiah's sons had quit the Cotswolds for Brazil. Charlie traced his ancestry from the younger, and Antonietta from the elder, so their cousinly connections were sufficiently distant to permit marriage. Antonietta grew up in a large house in São Paulo, overrun with children and servants, violins and bicycles, books and tennis rackets, all the paraphernalia of a wealthy nineteenth-century home. The house had a piano, of course, and each of the daughters received some instruction – just enough to play for five minutes after dinner, and charm the visiting young men with their finger-work. Not long after learning to speak, Antonietta sat at the keys, and started tinkering. When her sister wanted to take their turn, she refused to move. She gave her first public concert at the age of seven, then spent her adolescence studying with the best teachers in Brazil.

Three weeks into 1906, Charlie married Antonietta. That season, SPAC suffered repeated disasters. They lost to Palmeiras, Germania, Internacionale and Paulistano, scraped a draw against Mackenzie, and then, playing Internacionale for the second time in the year, scored one goal and conceded nine. SPAC ended the season in last place, having won a single point. Appalled and ashamed, Charlie withdrew the team from the league and resigned from the committee. He had learnt a depressing lesson. Love cannot be divided.

Charlie could have neglected his wife for football. Many men do. Had he preferred the team to the woman, he might have won the league for the fourth year running, and even the fifth. But he had won thrice, and kept the cup, and that was enough for him. He unlaced his boots, deflated his football, handed over his responsibilities to other men, and devoted himself to his wife. Some husbands could not have made such a decision – particularly not with such a wife. Many men would have been terrified by her talent, unwilling to watch her walk to the centre of the stage while they stood in the wings. Not Charlie. He encouraged Antonietta to play, and devoted himself to her career. When she wanted to travel to Europe, he took six months' leave from his various duties, despite the personal and professional complications. Their first child, a boy, was born in February 1907, and christened Carlos Rudge Miller. To ensure that Carlos could claim British citizenship, Charlie registered his birth at the consulate in Santos. Six weeks later, the football season started. SPAC had rejoined the league, and the British were determined to regain their crown, but Charlie played only a couple of games before travelling down to the docks with Antonietta. They boarded the *Danube*, one of the Royal Mail's steamers, and sailed across the Atlantic.

The captains of the RMSP ships knew how to treat artists. Nijinsky travelled from Southampton to Buenos Aires on the *Avon*, and practised every day with the Diaghilev Company. Passengers crowded the decks to watch. During the three-week voyage, confined to the boat, Nijinsky fell for one of his dancers, and asked her to marry him. Refusing the captain's offer of a mid-Atlantic ceremony, Nijinsky and Romola de Pulszky married in Buenos Aires. On another voyage, the Polish pianist Paderewski travelled to South America on the *Asturias*, and allowed himself to be persuaded to play an impromptu concert for passengers. Perhaps Antonietta did too.

Landing in England at the beginning of August, the Millers headed straight for Banister Court. Charlie introduced Antonietta to Christopher Ellaby, who reported the visit in the school magazine. 'Miller was in England for some months this summer. He spent a week-end at the School, and a few minutes after he arrived he was playing in a match.' From Banister Court, the Millers travelled to

London, where Antonietta met agents. One offered to represent her, and organised a series of small concerts in Britain, Germany and France. Antonietta Rudge Miller made her London debut at the Bechstein Hall on Wigmore Street (a venue that still exists, although it is now named after the street rather than the German piano-makers whose wares were originally exhibited there). Antonietta played a programme of Grieg, Chopin, Mendelssohn, Ravel and Liszt. *The Times* printed a short, respectful review, applauding her crisp touch, praising her particularly for playing Greig's *Ballade* with exactly the right kind of simplicity. But if Antonietta had been hoping for the rapturous reception accorded her concerts in São Paulo, she was disappointed. In the same short column in *The Times*, the critic also reviewed Herr Buckhaus playing Bach, Liszt and Chopin, a Promenade Concert devoted to works by Beethoven, a Sunday afternoon concert by the London Symphony Orchestra and a performance of Tchaikovsky's Fifth Symphony at the Queen's Hall. At home, Antonietta Rudge Miller was a respected public figure, connected to the city's most important family, married to a well-known sportsman and acclaimed as one of the world's finest musicians. In London, she was a neat pianist with good technique and a funny little husband who never stopped talking about football.

After Christmas, they went home. If they had stayed a few more months, they could have seen another musical production on the London stage; not a serious concert, but a comic opera funded by two of Charlie's old school chums. The original production of *Dorothy* starred Marie Tempest, and became a huge hit due to one jaunty number, *Queen of My Heart*, which was the song on Londoners' lips for an entire year. Maundy Gregory revived the show. Harold Davidson raised most of the necessary capital by borrowing large sums from his friends in the clergy. If they worried that their savings might be better invested, Rev. Davidson could have assured them that he and Gregory had been educated together at the very reputable Banister Court, and nothing could possibly go wrong. After a few weeks, despite good houses, the show collapsed. Gregory had 'borrowed' most of the box office receipts. When he failed to pay the musicians, they refused to play. Years later, during Harold Davidson's trial, the jury learnt that he had serenaded prostitutes with jaunty renditions of 'You are the Queen of my Heart'.

Back in Brazil, Charlie and Antonietta had a second child, Helena. As a married couple, their interests may have been different, and their lives increasingly divergent, but they seem to have been happy. Antonietta devoted her evenings to smart conversation in São Paulo's largest drawing rooms, discussing artistic theories and the nature of Brazilian nationalism, poring over the latest magazines from Paris, examining new fashions in poetry, painting and frocks. She went to bed late, and got up late. Charlie did the opposite. He was a busy man, busier year by year. As Percy Lupton had taught him to do, Charlie spread his professional interests, working as a salesman and an agent for innumerable British companies, selling insurance and soap, wine and jewellery, coal and cricket bats. Issuing tickets for the Royal Mail boats, acting as an informal post office for their passenger's letters and offering an impromptu tourist office for all the Britons visiting São Paulo, he had a steady stream of new business. After work, he played tennis or practised for an hour in the cricket nets, stopped for a couple of drinks in the SPAC pavilion, then hurried home, kissed his sleeping kiddies on their foreheads, and went to bed early. While Antonietta dozed, Charlie sprang up at dawn, full of vim.

There was just one flaw in this idyllic life. Charlie found himself falling out of love with football. Heading into his mid-thirties, no longer the most skilful player of the field, left panting in the wake of younger runners, Charlie was increasingly alienated by a new feature of the sport: professionalism. Predictably, the richest club in São Paulo was the first to hire a professional. The Prado family demanded the best for the Club Athletico Paulistano, so they had chosen to ship someone over from London, paying a professional player to spend his summer holidays in Brazil. Jock Hamilton played for Fulham, who had just been admitted to the Football League, and he spent a few months with Paulistano, training the first team, teaching basic technique to the youth team, refereeing matches, and helping them to win the league. The investment had clearly been worthwhile – quite apart from the prestige of engraving their name on the silver cup, huge crowds brought hefty profits for successful teams – and other teams immediately followed Paulistano's lead. Cash flowed into the Liga Paulista, spent first on trainers, then on players. Only a decade after the first competitive game between Mackenzie and Germania, and fifteen years after Charlie brought his Corinthian football to Brazil, the elite status of the players, the crowd and the game had been swept aside by the power of money.

By 1911, the Liga Paulista itself was looking wobbly. SPAC managed to win the league, despite having come bottom in previous years, but their victory went unrecognised by other teams. Palmeiras, the previous winners, refused to hand over the trophy. Americano showed no remorse for paying a wage to two of their players. Some of the Liga's players refused to kick another ball unless they were paid too, while others boasted that they would boycott any match that featured professionals. It was chaos. No-one knew whether the league would be played, dissolved or split into two divisions, one for gentlemanly amateurs and another for professionals. Charlie took the only sensible course of action. He removed SPAC from the Liga Paulista, and left the Brazilians to squabble amongst themselves.

Twelve

Sixteen of them sail from Southampton. They have first-class cabins on the *Amazon*, one of the Royal Mail's finest. She ploughs across the Atlantic in less than three weeks, and arrives in Rio de Janeiro at the end of August. For them, the timing couldn't be more perfect. They leave Europe midway through their summer holidays, arrive in Brazil during the coolest part of the year, and will return to Oxford or Cambridge in time for the autumn term. On board the *Amazon*, the sixteen laze around. They don't bother training. In the hot sun, they play a little deck cricket, read light novels and flirt with the three pretty girls – one pale English rose who shelters under her parasol and two swarthy Portuguese beauties whose laughter echoes down the corridors.

In Rio, men line the quay, waving as the *Amazon* eases into the harbour, cheering as the sixteen men troop down the gangplank. Two days later, they play their first game. The squad consists of fifteen players, accompanied by the secretary of the English Amateur Football Association. A full house comes to watch Fluminense versus the Corinthians. It is not merely a contest between a Rio team and a group of English ex-public schoolboys, but Brazil versus Britain, the modern versus the ancient, the New World versus the Old World.

It's not even a contest. After less than a minute, the Corinthians concede a goal. Fluminense kick off, pass, pass, pass again, reach the box before an Englishman had made a single touch, and knock the ball through the posts. As the scorer throws his arms into the air, the crowd goes crazy. The Brazilian players whoop and yell and sprint across the pitch. What a triumph! The famous Corinthians – a goal down after one minute! The legendary Corinthians! They might have swaggered into Brazil, sneering and twiddling their moustaches as if they owned the game of football – but look at them now! Humbled! Humiliated! Taking lessons in football from a bunch of Brazilians!

It was 1910. Over the previous few years, English football had not been treating the Corinthians with much respect. In response to the challenges of professionalism, they had refused either to adapt or to fade gracefully into history. During the 1880s, when Blackburn Rovers couldn't stop winning the FA Cup, the Corinthians played them after every final, and always beat them. The following decade, the Corinthians supplied several players for each international played by England. But by the turn of the century, their prowess had collapsed. The England team contained only one amateur, and although he was given the captaincy, suiting his status, his gentlemanly conduct won him few friends. He sat in a different compartment on the train, ate at a separate table in the hotel and only spoke to his team when he was giving orders. Quizzed later by the press, the captain explained that he had travelled and eaten alone so the other players wouldn't feel inhibited by the presence of a gentleman.

You can get away with that when you're winning. As soon as you puff and pant, your legendary insouciance starts to look like priggish arrogance. Every year, the professionals were fitter, faster and more skilled. The Corinthians found themselves left further and further behind, isolated and redundant, unable to compete. They still toured to the grounds of the big teams, but their annual challenges were never taken seriously. Although they inflicted Manchester United's heaviest ever defeat (an 11-3 victory) the Mancunians had not bothered to field their best side, reserving their strength for more meaningful games. Unwanted at home, the Corinthians devoted themselves to missionary work, touring the world and preaching the gospel of gentlemanly football. They had varied success. In Holland, their codes of behaviour were instinctively understood, and a gang of gents created the Dutch Corinthians in homage to the British originals, hoping to preserve amateurism and stem the growth of professionalism. They flopped, managing to attract only incompetent players who couldn't get a game elsewhere. In Brazil, they inspired another new team, who also named themselves in homage to the British. But something must have been lost in translation. Whereas the British Corinthians opposed every aspect of democratisation and popularisation, harking back to an era when strong social divisions kept the classes apart, the founders of the Brazilian Corinthians were firemen and navvies, who embraced professionalism as quickly as possible.

In 1910, when the Corinthians sailed from Southampton to Rio, they travelled first class, stayed in the finest hotels, and played all their games against fellow gentlemen. Since their first tour, a trip to South Africa in 1897, they had travelled across Europe, back to Africa and across the Atlantic. They remained undefeated on foreign soil until 1906, when they were beaten in Boston. Always travelling in the summer holidays, when the chaps weren't burdened by school or university terms, they went to Hungary, Canada and the USA, before rolling down to Rio. They weren't the first British team to tour South America – Southampton had been to Buenos Aires as early as 1904 – but huge excitement greeted the news that they were coming. Their proud hosts laid on parties, dinners, receptions, trips to tourist spots, a game of cricket against the English cricket club and six games of football against Brazilian teams. Everyone understood that the Corinthians represented the British elite. Half of them had played for England, and one for Wales. Educated at Oxford and Cambridge, they had the poise and confidence of imperial masters. They were true gentlemen. And one minute into their first game on Brazilian soil, they were losing by a goal to nil.

But not for long. Like well-bred gentlemen, the Corinthians allowed their opponents to enjoy their fun, then took the ball back, and showed them what to do with it. The Englishmen kicked off from the spot, passed the ball languidly around the pitch, and knocked a goal past Fluminense. And then another. And another. And another, and another, and another. By half-time, the British led 7-1. By the end of the match, they had scored ten, while the Brazilians had failed to get a second.

The sixteen Corinthians stayed in Rio for six days, seeing the sights in the morning, playing football in the afternoon, enduring lengthy dinners every night and partying in the clubs till dawn. Even so, they managed to win their other games 8-1 and 5-2, then caught the overnight sleeper to São Paulo. Arriving at the Luz station early in the morning, they found a large crowd awaiting them. Hundreds of footballers from all the city's communities queued to shake their hands.

A line of cars, decorated with flowers, drove them in convoy to the Hotel Majestic. The following afternoon, they played their first game at the Velódromo, the ground owned by CAP and the Prado family. The large crowd was dressed in its Sunday best. Quickly, the Corinthians realised that the Paulistas made far tougher opponents than the easy-going Cariocas. A taut game ended in a 2-0 victory for the visitors. The tension proved too much for the crowd, who erupted into violence. A little boy sprinted onto the pitch, swung his bare foot and kicked one of the Corinthians on the bum. The Corinthian gave chase, but couldn't catch his attacker.

The following day's newspapers carried lengthy reports of the game, dissecting British methods and tactics, suggesting that Brazilian teams could learn two particular skills. Firstly, the Corinthians seemed to have an instinctive understanding of one another's intentions and, rather than concentrating selfishly on his own game, each player would be watching the others, anticipating their forward runs or running into space to meet a long ball. Secondly, the Corinthians never wasted their energy on speculative shots from a long way out. They passed the ball from one to the other, came as close as possible to the opponent's goal, then popped it over the line. A dull method, concluded reporters, but effective.

The Corinthians played two more games at the Velódromo, beating a mixed Paulista team 5-0, then playing a Foreigners XI assembled by Charlie Miller. It was the last competitive game of his life. He was thirty-six. From now on, he had decided, he would devote himself to more middle-aged pleasures: refereeing, sitting on committees and golf. For his final game, he gathered a group of Anglo-Brazilians, and lost heroically. The final score was 8-2. That night, the Liga Paulista threw a party at the Hotel Majestic, and lengthy speeches were made by the hosts and visitors, culminating in two toasts. One of the Paulistas thanked the British for their visit, and asked everyone in the room to sing a resounding chorus of *God Save the King*. Responding on behalf of the Crown, His Majesty's Consular Representative, Mr Charles Miller, invited the assembled guests to drink the health of the President of Brazil.

For several weeks afterwards, the cinemas of São Paulo played a film of the visit, showing clips of the matches. This film was seen by a group of navvies and firemen from the San Paulo Railway, who decided to name their newly formed team in homage to the English gentlemen. A month later, when the original Corinthians were back on the other side of the ocean, settling into their new rooms in the placid courts of Oxford and Cambridge, the Sport Club Corinthians Paulista played their first game.

Across the world, British prestige was showing signs of strain. Scott failed to reach the Pole. Oates was gone for some time. The unsinkable *Titanic* sank. In Brazil, things were no different. Year by year, the British were sidelined. In business, in politics and in football, their influence diminished. When Roger Casement went on leave, his replacement wrote a report on British interests in southern Brazil, and concluded that there was significant room for improvement. British shipping dominated the docks at Santos, but their control did not extend onto the mainland. Of the 300 factories in São Paulo, only three had British owners. Britannia ruled the waves, but not the shore. On the football field, although British referees and coaches remained coveted status symbols – the equivalent of British butlers in American mansions – few British players competed in the leagues, and even the touring British teams had lost some of their lustre. When the Corinthians returned in 1913, they could not even win their first match. They offered several excuses. The voyage out had been so full of excitement – a birth, a death, a wedding, a suicide and a mad cook – that they had lacked any time to practise. The game itself had been poorly managed, and they lost their first goal to a dodgy penalty. The second wasn't even scored by a Brazilian; the Rio team had recruited Harry Welfare, an Englishman who had played for Liverpool before getting a job at an Anglo-Brazilian boarding-school. The British consul, Ernest Hambloch, offered yet another excuse for the defeat: 'Brazilian hospitality is proverbially lavish, and the night-clubs of Rio in those days were full of attractions. But the Brazilian youngsters who were acting as hosts to the Corinthians in their nocturnal rambles were not the team that was playing.' The British team went to bed at dawn, then 'yawned and rubbed its eyes' through the game, paying penance for a night on the town.

In São Paulo, the Corinthians played three games, winning them all. Charlie Miller refereed. Perhaps he told them that their Brazilian namesakes had been prospering. That year, Sport Club Corinthians joined the Liga Paulista. The more aristocratic clubs fled, appalled by the stink of these jumped-up working-class newcomers, and started a separate league of their own, restricting entry to gentlemen and amateurs. Sport Club Corinthians didn't care. They won the jumped-up working-class newcomer-league in 1914, then again in 1916, and haven't looked back since.

In July 1914, the Corinthians embarked on their third and final tour of Brazil. Gavrilo Princip had recently fired five bullets across a street in Sarajevo, but no-one anticipated that his shots would have such rapid, cataclysmic results, and the young men thought of nothing but sport. Midway across the Atlantic, the ship's radio received a message that changed their minds. Austro-Hungary had declared war on Serbia. By the time they reached Rio, Germany had invaded Belgium. The Corinthians stepped ashore, walked along the quay, boarded the next boat, and returned to Southampton.

On the first day of fighting in the Somme, soldiers waited nervously for the signal to attack. They checked their guns, their shoes, their helmets. They wrote notes to their wives and burnt letters from their mistresses. Surrounded by mud and bullets, confronted by the enemy's guns, Captain Nevill of the East Surrey Regiment suddenly realised exactly how to inspire his men. He dug into his kitbag and pulled out a football. At school, Nevill had been captain of cricket and head boy of his house. He understood that war was just another game, which had to be played in the right spirit. Borrowing a pencil from one of his men, he scrawled a legend on the leather ball:

> The Great European Cup Tie Finals
> East Surreys v Bavarians.
> Kick-off at zero.

When the time came, Nevill hurled the football over the top of the trenches, yelled encouragement at his men, and launched himself onto the muddy pitch. Whooping and cheering, the troops followed him. Sprinting across No Man's Land, Captain Nevill and his men passed the ball across the mud like forwards heading for the opposition's goal, until every one of them had been killed by German bullets.

The masters, pupils and old boys of Banister Court showed similar determination. Three months into the war, sixty Old Banisterians had volunteered and two had died. Others won a Military Cross and a Distinguished Service Order. At the school, the boys drilled rather than playing cricket or football. Christopher Ellaby wrote regular reports for the school magazine, which began the war in a tone of cheery chest-beating, descended into gloom as the disaster's magnitude became apparent, and finished with an unconcealed sigh of despair. More and more old boys died every year, including some who had been called up directly from the school. Cecil Ellaby, Christopher's nephew, was blown up by a shell at Gallipoli. By 1917, the school dispensed with the prize-giving ceremony, spending their energy on Red Cross work instead. The boys kept pigs and goats on the football fields, and dug allotments to grow potatoes.

Ellaby did not report the antics of one old boy: Harold Davidson, serving as a chaplain with the Royal Navy, who not only earned the wrath of his superiors by holding regular ceremonies on the boat, always at the most inconvenient moments, but also managed to get arrested in an Egyptian brothel. He had gone there, he protested, to track down a diseased prostitute who had infected several of the ship's men. His visit coincided with a raid by the military police. Surprisingly, the MPs decided to believe him, and Davidson was released without charge.

In Brazil, the British and German residents found themselves caught in a situation which was almost as embarrassing. The young men sailed across the Atlantic to join their respective armies, leaving their families unsure how to behave. Should they cut one another in the street? Sabotage the opposition's business? Or act as if nothing had happened? This social conundrum was solved in 1917. After the sinking of a Brazilian merchant ship by a German U-boat, and directly following the USA's decision to join the war, Brazil severed all diplomatic relations with the German government, then declared war. Although no Brazilian troops crossed the Atlantic, the symbolic gesture was much appreciated by the British government, who were very conscious of the fact that no other South American countries showed any interest in the conflict.

Throughout the war, the blockade on Atlantic shipping had an increasingly harsh effect on daily life in Brazil. Charlie Miller suffered more than most. People stopped travelling, so Charlie lost his commission on ticket sales. More and more ships were requisitioned for military duty. The *Magdelena*, which had carried Charlie from Southampton in 1894, was used as a troopship from 1915 onwards, along with the majority of the RMSP's fleet.

Two of Charlie's staff joined the army. While they fought, the RMSP continued paying them a token salary (a tenth of their normal wages). Thirty-six members of SPAC sailed to Europe, and five died in the trenches. One of the dead men, C.P. Tomkins, had played in Charlie's triumphant triple-winning team. Charlie's nephew also volunteered. Gordon Fox Rule joined the fledgling air force, and trained as a pilot. Still only nineteen years old, he criss-crossed the skies, searching for German planes. In the last few months of the war, he managed to shoot down seven, and won both the Distinguished Flying Cross and the Croix de Guerre. The citation for his DFC reads: 'Whilst on a bombing raid this officer dived to 100 feet and obtained a direct hit on a bridge, completely destroying it. Seeing a body of the enemy on the bank of the river he attacked them, causing them to disperse in disorder. He was then attacked by five biplanes; these he drove off, though his observer had been hit twice, and he landed safely at a French aerodrome. In all, he has taken part in thirty bomb raids and ten photographic reconnaissances, invariably displaying a marked offensive spirit.'

Charlie's old boss at the consular office, Roger Casement, volunteered for the other side. He travelled to Berlin, persuaded the Germans to supply him with 20,000 guns, and sailed for Ireland in a submarine. Landing, he was captured immediately, tried for treason and sentenced to death by hanging. Lobbyists in London tried to have his sentence commuted. They drew attention to his valiant diplomatic work and his knighthood, awarded in 1911 for his investigations into forced labour in the Congo, Brazil and Peru. The fortuitous appearance of his diaries, which may or may not have been forged, turned these influential friends against him, and Casement was hanged in August 1916.

While Charlie's friends, relatives and colleagues played an active role in the hostilities, he could do little except wait and watch. Forty years old in the year that war was declared, his services were not required by his country. While his business collapsed, his income plummeted and his own government repaid him for years of service with a slap in the face, he showed his patriotism by never complaining, never arguing, never exhibiting any emotion except pride. For more than a decade, he had served Britain with selfless dedication, working as vice-consul, guiding lost tourists, quizzing Brazilian ministers and answering pernickety letters from pompous asses like Roger Casement. As a reward for his service, he had been paid in little more than prestige. After a decade, he could have expected nothing less than a mention in the honours list or a letter of thanks from Buckingham Palace. Instead, he got the sack.

To mark the burgeoning status and economic importance of São Paulo, the Foreign Office had decided to appoint a fully-fledged consul, replacing the part-time vice-consuls who had run British affairs in the city for the past couple of decades. They sent out a career diplomat, George Atlee, who had previously worked in the embassies in Paris, Sulina and Valparaiso. Arriving in Brazil, Atlee inspected the consular office, counted the flags and stamps, pored over the registers of births, marriages and deaths, and concluded that the whole place had gone to rot. He sent a series of letters to the Foreign Office, subtly giving the impression that the current vice-consul had slipped into native habits. Atlee's insinuations had their intended effect, and the Foreign Office gave him permission to fire Charlie Miller. Showing the flair for public relations that would later ensure his place in Brazilian history, Charlie contacted all the local newspapers. The following day, they printed reports that, due to the rapid expansion of the Royal Mail Steam Packet Company's business in São Paulo, Charles Miller found himself unable to devote sufficient time to his work as British Vice-Consul, and had resigned his post.

As the British flooded into Europe to commit collective suicide in the trenches, another nation arrived to take their place in Brazil, securing the lucrative contracts that would otherwise have gone unfulfilled. South America severed its traditional ties with Europe, and succumbed to North American energy, expertise and capital. In a survey of the continent published a year after the Armistice, W.H. Koebel wrote, 'notwithstanding the thousands of British who left South America to go to war, I never heard so much English spoken in the capitals of the southern half of the continent as in 1918.' However, Koebel was confident that the British would revive their fortunes in South America, once they returned from Flanders and diverted their attention from their second-favourite pursuit (war) to their favourite (trade). Koebel points to an obvious symbol of British dominance on the continent: football.

What would have been said twenty or thirty years ago of the fact of a crowd of Argentines in Buenos Aires burning down the pavilion in their hot indignation at the postponement of a match! No crowd in the Midlands could have been more bitterly disappointed, nor shown their annoyance in a more thoroughgoing fashion! Now here is a point which must appear far more insignificant on the surface than it is in reality. When the baseball ground begins to take its place beside the football field – as, of course, it has already done in the north of the continent – then, I think, will be the time to judge of the respective social influences of the two nations.

Not only does Koebel equate footballing enthusiasm with hooliganism – only a truly passionate fan, he suggests, will burn down a stadium – but he feels the need to stress that Argentinean football fans are no less passionate than those from Nottingham or Manchester. However, perhaps his analysis isn't entirely trustworthy; although no-one would suggest that baseball has overtaken football as the chosen sport of Brazilians, even in 1919 most observers could see that the British were willing to surrender their South American prestige to the USA. A perfect symbol for this switching allegiance was Brazil's decision to abandon railways in favour of roads. Brazilians might have chosen football over baseball, but they chose cars over trains, tarmac over rails, Henry Ford over Herbert Spencer.

In the first years of the twentieth century, very few cars could be seen in the streets of São Paulo. Due to the scarcity of good roads, these cars stayed in the centre of the city, driving up and down the Avenida Paulista. Status symbols rather than useful vehicles, all of them belonged to a small, elite group of wealthy families. The first Rolls-Royce in the city was bought by the Telles family – to whom Antonietta was related on her mother's side – who paid for the car to be shipped over from England. Although Rolls-Royce were delighted to export their cars to Brazil, they refused to hand over responsibility to any Brazilian garages, insisting on sending their own mechanic to service the engine. The mechanic spent three weeks on a boat to Santos, a day on the train to São Paulo and a few hours under the car, then wiped his hands on his overalls and headed back to England.

Antonio Prado Junior – owner of the Velódromo, financier of Paulistano – founded the first car club in São Paulo and enthused the public with his automotive exploits, hurtling through the city like Toad of Toad Hall. He insisted that the government must cover Brazil with roads, and founded lobby groups to put pressure on state officials and decision makers. New roads were opened with grand ceremonies – a procession of 327 cars christened the São Paulo–Campinas highway – and the state's president, Washington Luiz, donated a cup to be given in his name to the winner of the São Paulo–Ribeirão Preto rally. The US supported Brazilian drivers, road-builders and lobbyists with cash, expertise and lots of cars. Before the First World War, Brazilians imported three-quarters of their cars from France, Germany and Britain. During the war, when Atlantic trade shrivelled, the balance shifted. While wealthy drivers preferred luxury models from Europe, farmers and landowners switched their allegiance to straightforward, reliable North American models. A Rolls-Royce could venture hardly any further than the end of the Avenida Paulista, but sturdy American cars bounced cheerfully along pot-holed country roads – and if a part snapped, or the engine started gushing steam, any old mechanic could get it working again. There was no need to summon someone from England. The Brazilian market for cars grew so rapidly that Ford decided to open a assembly plant in São Paulo, where local workers put together cars from parts made in the US. Only the seats were made in Brazil. Inspired by Ford's success, General Motors opened an assembly plant in São Paulo in 1925. By that time, Ford had built factories in three other Brazilian cities, supplying 2,000 licensed garages around the country.

British manufacturers failed to compete. In São Paulo alone, car ownership leaped from 2,000 in 1917 to 60,000 in 1928, almost entirely supplied by Ford and General Motors. The automobile and its American manufacturer came to be seen as symbols of the future, adopted by forward-looking Brazilians who wished to escape their colonial past, shake off European influences, and forge a new identity for modern Brazil. Artists and poets revered Henry Ford as a symbol of the new century. Echoing the Futurists, Brazilian poets wrote pane-gyrics to industrial production, while Brazilian painters covered their canvases with thrilling pictures of roads and factories.

As roads prospered, railways faltered. In the state of São Paulo, the railways had been built specifically to carry coffee from the plantations to the coast, and would have needed significant investment to adapt to postwar economic diversity. The government chose to build roads instead. When Washington Luiz was governor of São Paulo state, he devoted huge resources to building a highway to Rio de Janeiro. Passengers usually did the 300-mile route by rail, while heavy cargo went by sea. When the first cars finally raced along the highway in 1928, they seemed to symbolise the end of one era and the beginning of another. A train still ran between the two cities, but that was reserved for the lackadaisical. If you were modern and dynamic, you went by car.

British residents in Brazil saw exactly what was happening, but found themselves unable to intervene. During the First World War, their businesses suffered because they could not reach their usual markets, and they lost any potential new trade to aggressive US traders. A bad situation was worsened by the brutal winter in 1918, when a bitter frost killed the buds on half the trees in the state, crippling what remained of the coffee industry. Even after the postwar reopening of European markets, the British found themselves unable to recapture their previous dominance. They felt increasingly isolated, and grew nervous. Their victorious government showed little interest in South America. When Britain sent a delegation to thank Brazil for supporting the Allies during the war, the five men chosen had a depressingly low profile. According to Ernest Hambloch, the delegation consisted of a diplomat, an admiral, a general, a businessman and a writer. During their brief visit, the diplomat gave speeches, the businessman made contacts, the writer gathered material for his next book, the general looked at women and the admiral looked at boats. None of them gave the impression that Britain cared much about Brazil. Slowly, reluctantly, Anglo-Brazilians came to the painful realisation that they had been deserted. Britain had more vital priorities. Fighting a vicious war had drained the country of its resources. The Empire was collapsing, and terrifying forces had been unleashed. Women wanted the vote, the working classes demanded a fairer share of the cash, and millions of His Majesty's imperial subjects no longer showed much willingness to be ruled from London.

The British in Brazil found themselves thrust back on their own resources. In São Paulo, they set up a branch of the British Chamber of Commerce. Charlie was a founder member, attending every meeting, and sitting on a sub-committee with responsibility for shipping. They donated a cash prize to be awarded for the best essays written by a

British pupil resident in the city. The subject was, of course, the glories of the British Empire. They gave money to the British church, held concerts, dances and tea parties, sang the national anthem, and discussed starting a British school so their children would not have to mingle with the natives.

It was a war that could not be won. The community was too small, too insignificant. The more perceptive Anglo-Brazilians realised that they had a simple choice. If they wanted to remain British, they would have to return to the Old Country or make their way to a new home that had more direct links with the Empire: Australia, New Zealand, Rhodesia, South Africa. If they wanted to stay in São Paulo, they would have to become Brazilian.

For Charlie, things were more complicated. Not only was he married to a woman who considered herself Brazilian rather than British, but his own national identity had always hovered somewhere in the middle of the Atlantic, not quite at home on either shore. Throughout his life, he had been pulled in opposite directions by two huge forces, Britain and Brazil. Every immigrant feels this same terrible wrench at the heart of their existence. Some of them, the lucky ones, find a synthesis between the culture that they have left behind and the country in which they have arrived. Others retreat into an imaginary recreation of their homeland, retaining old customs and habits, cocooning themselves in an unchanging version of Back Home. And a few, the most unfortunate, are destroyed.

Thirteen

A man walks onto the stage. He ignores the audience, staring at his feet as if he is walking along a quiet country lane, alone, unobserved, lost in thought. He walks to the centre of the stage, and stands there for a moment. Some of the people in the audience, the ones who know him, his friends and enemies, stop their conversations and watch. Others keep chatting. No-one knows how many people are here. No-one counted them as they came through the doors of the theatre. No-one issued tickets, and no-one checks names, but there must be several hundred in the building, perhaps even a thousand, milling in and out of the high glass doors, stopping to chat in the foyer, drinking coffee, smoking cigarettes, giggling, gossiping, arguing about art and love and sex and politics. Some of them sit in the seats, and others wander up and down the aisles, nodding to acquaintances. They are the city's elite. They buy their clothes from Paris, and take their ideas from French magazines, and their conversations are peppered with names like Picasso and Breton, Chagall and Leger, Apollinaire and Duchamp, Picabia and Tzara, but almost every one of them has been born here in Brazil.

Standing at the centre of the stage, the man still looks distracted, as if he imagines himself elsewhere, not standing before a large, packed auditorium. The mumbling of their conversations doesn't seem to concern him. He takes a sheet of notepaper from his pocket and unfolds it. He stares at the words for a minute or two, then starts reading them aloud. But there's something odd about the way that he reads. He doesn't use the low, reverential tones that people usually reserve for reciting poetry. He takes a deep breath before each line, then yells. He bellows. He hurls the words at the audience, barking every syllable.

I insult the bourgeois! The nickel bourgeois,
    the bourgeois-bourgeois!
The well-made digestion of São Paulo!
The bent man! The buttocked man!
The man who, being French, Brazilian, Italian,
is always a cautious little-by-little!

When they realise what he is saying, they go quiet for a minute, unable to believe his gall. Is he... Did he... Who is... What the hell? Does he think we're just going to sit here and listen to this? Someone yells back. Then another. They leap up, and wave their fists. They hiss, and shout, and toss his insults back at him. All around the theatre, people are gesturing and gurning. Someone hurls a half-eaten apple. Objects bounce onto the stage around the poet, and a scrunched-up programme hits his face. He takes no notice. All his attention is focused on the sheet of paper, and he reads in a loud, clear voice, as if he is standing on the edge of a ravine, shouting across to the other side.

Eat! Eat yourself, oh! amazing jelly!
Oh! purée of moral potatoes!
Oh! hair in the wind! oh! bald heads!
Hatred to the normal temperaments!
Hatred to the muscular watches! Death and infamy!
Hatred to them all! Hatred to the groceries!
Hatred to those without weaknesses or regrets,
    always the same conventionally!
With their hands on their backs! I mark their rhythm! There it goes!
Two by two! First position! March!
Everyone to the centre of my inebriating rancour!

Hatred and insult! Hatred and anger! Hatred and more hatred!
Hatred to the bourgeois on his knees
smelling of religion and who doesn't believe in God!
Red hatred! Fertile hatred! Cyclical hatred!
Fundamental hatred, with no pardon!

Out! Out with the good bourgeois!

By the time he reaches the end, the entire audience is on its feet. Half of them are applauding, throwing their hats in the air and screaming for an encore. The other half are booing, whistling and waving their fists or scuffling around on the floor and searching for some rubbish to throw at him. The poet folds up the sheet of paper and returns it to his pocket. Without even glancing at the audience, Mario de Andrade walks off the stage.

Over the course of Charlie Miller's life, São Paulo had changed from a tiny backwater into an industrial hub, and it was swelling all the time, smothering the fields with neat little suburban homes and smoke-gushing factories. When Charlie was a young man, he could not have gone to the theatre or walked in the park without bumping into a friend, an acquaintance, a cousin. By the time that he reached middle-age, the streets had filled with strangers. You could stand in the lobby of the Municipal Theatre, watching the audience file past, and recognise no-one. A village in the hills had been transformed into a vibrant, hard-working city, the equivalent of Leeds or Sheffield. As Peter Fleming quipped, 'São Paulo is like Reading, only much further away.' The rapidly growing population turned the city from a gossipy introverted community to a metropolis that faced outwards, determined to be involved with the wider world. Trade blossomed. In 1907, an industrial census of Brazil showed industry concentrated in three cities: Rio (40 per cent), São Paulo (16 per cent) and Rio Grande do Sul (15 per cent). By 1920, the positions of the two biggest cities had been reversed, and São Paulo was indisputably the country's industrial centre. Rio had the swish, the swank, the sweet talk, the sophistication of boulevards and beaches and old money. São Paulo had cash and hard graft and muscle. Rio was the girlfriend, but São Paulo was the wife, and the world wanted to marry her. The city's growth was not merely terrifying, uncontrolled and anarchic, but unstoppable. Speculators laid roads in every direction, filling the blocks with factories and mansions. The streets were engulfed in a permanent revolution of construction. Scaffolding crawled up every façade. Any building more than twenty years old faced the threat of demolition and replacement. Upturned cobblestones littered the streets. Residents started complaining about the traffic. Lines of carriages blocked the streets, competing for space with the first motor cars. Horse shit rotted in the hot sun and exhaust fumes filled the air; the stench of the past mingling with the stink of the future.

A group of businessmen decided to take advantage of the building boom, and create a large suburb in the heart of São Paulo, providing weary, wealthy residents with a haven of peace and serenity. Mostly British and North American, they drew their inspiration from Ebenezer Howard and the English Garden Cities. They formed a company, 'City of San Paulo Improvements and Freehold Land Company Limited' (stressing their roots by choosing San Paulo over São Paulo), and bought a large tract of extremely cheap land, punctured by ponds and swamps, presumed uninhabitable by any decent folk. Using plans sketched out by Barry Parker and Raymond Unwin, the two British architects who had been responsible for Letchworth Garden City and Hampstead Garden Suburb, the developers swept aside the few shacks on the site, drove away the grazing animals, drained the swamps, and built one of the most elegant suburbs in South America. They laid out wide streets, allowing every inhabitant to own a motor car. They planted thousands of trees. They allowed large plots for every house, so each well-heeled resident could live in a self-contained villa, surrounded by a private garden, guarded by walls and fences, giving the illusion of rural serenity right in the middle of the city. Britain had Welwyn, Letchworth and Hampstead; Brazil had the Jardins Europa and the Jardins America.

Charlie Miller had the nous, or the good contacts, to get in at the beginning, investing his own money in the project. Not only did he make an excellent return, but he got to pick himself a prime location for his own home. He built a large villa in the heart of the Jardins America, right on the corner of Rua Mexico and Rua Guatemala, surrounded by lawns and trees. There he lived with Antonietta and their two children. It was idyllic. Charlie continued working for the Royal Mail, and devoted his weekends to playing golf, watching cricket and refereeing football matches. Carlos was despatched to Magdalen College School in Oxford, where he learnt to become a proper gentleman like his father. Helena stayed in Brazil, devoting most of her attention to the piano, just like her mother. Thus their life should have continued, and would have done without the intervention of a tall, dark man with a pair of little round glasses perched on his long nose.

When Oswald de Andrade travelled to Paris and read Marinetti's Futurist Manifesto, he saw a vision that fitted his home town. Returning to Brazil, he brought back this new creed – the gospel of modernity – and spread it through São Paulo. He didn't manage to persuade Marinetti to visit the city until 1926, by which time people had learnt of the connection between futurism and fascism, and the futurist's public lecture was disrupted by protestors booing, jeering and throwing tomatoes. Marinetti didn't care: his creed had already been absorbed by the city, even if he hadn't been there to witness it.

Brazilian high culture had always looked to Europe for inspiration, and particularly to Paris. The Brazilian Academy of Letters imitated the Petit Trianon. The Municipal Theatre in Rio was a replica of the Paris Opera House. The entire centre of Rio had been rebuilt on the Haussmann model. Now, a new generation of Brazilians brought the latest Parisian fashions back to their homeland, and adapted their ideas into local practice. They came from the city's wealthiest families. They had grown up in large houses, pampered by servants, funded by the coffee trade. Many had been educated in Europe, and almost all had travelled to France, where they came into contact with Dadaism, surrealism, futurism and all the other swirling isms that tussled in the clear bright light of postwar Paris. They knew the work of Picasso and Picabia. The verses of Apollinaire and Mallarmé tripped off their tongues. Replete and enthused, they left Paris, armed with a hundred manifestos, wild shapes writhing around their imaginations, crazy sounds booming in their ears, and headed back to São Paulo, determined to turn the city upside-down.

The son of a wealthy coffee baron, Oswald de Andrade owned vast tracts of land in the city and the hills, but chose to devote his time to art rather than business. The great Brazilian writers of the previous century, Machado de Assis and Euclides da Cunha, had died, and no-one had yet stepped forward to take their place. Oswald de Andrade volunteered himself. Through his work, he was determined to create a distinctively Brazilian identity – artistic, linguistic, cultural, personal – making a definitive break with the colonial past. Every Brazilian had been enslaved, he said, declaring that 11 October should be a public holiday throughout the Americas. The day before Columbus landed – that was the last day that America had been free. Around him, Oswald de Andrade gathered a fierce new young generation of painters, poets, musicians and polemicists. Only one thing mattered to them – to be modern. In 1922, the Prado family paid for these young Paulista artists to take over the Municipal Theatre, and hold a festival of modern art.

For three days in February, they covered the walls with paintings, filled the auditorium with their friends, and gave a series of concerts, reciting poetry, chanting lyrics, acting out scenes and performing the latest works by thrilling young composers. The 'Semana da Arte Moderne de 1922' is remembered as a landmark in Brazilian history, and has been described as the most significant single moment in Brazilian art during the twentieth century.

Brazil had declared independence from Portugal in 1822. A hundred years later, the Brazilian modernists declared their independence from the past. Seeing the collapse of Europe, they prophesied a new world order focused on the Americas. Britain, France and Germany had worn themselves out like old bulls, crashing their heads against one another. Let them stagger aside, shouted the Brazilian modernists, and we shall take over the world. Equating the past with Brazil's miserable status as a colonial vassal, they searched for a new model of Brazilian identity. In their art and their lives, their poetry and their music, their politics and their sexuality, they would fuse a European original with Brazilian flair, and create a new Brazil.

The Semana da Arte Moderne featured a series of lectures and performances in the Municipal Theatre. In the lobby, local artists exhibited paintings and sculptures. Determined to express their outrage, the scandalised public formed long queues outside the theatre. Walking through the high doors, passing the gilded statues in the lobby and heading up the formal sweep of the staircases, they were suddenly confronted by the garish colours of paintings hanging on the walls and the wild shapes of sculptures lurking in the corridors. Some of the audience jeered, others cheered, and most shook their heads in horror. Inside the auditorium, the response was louder and more violent. Boos interrupted Mario de Andrade's readings of his poems. When Villa-Lobos hobbled onto the stage, he was greeted by rhythmic clapping and a storm of heckles, ridiculing his walk. Sores covered his feet, which were heavily bandaged, causing him to walk with a lopsided limp, but the audience thought he was just playing the fool. When Villa-Lobos conducted his own pieces, the music was drowned out by yells and whistles, and the performers pelted with tomatoes and bananas. Confronted by this tirade of abuse and fruit, the artists couldn't have been happier. The hostile response was absolute confirmation that they had managed to shock the bourgeoisie.

Although Antonietta Rudge Miller was not asked to play at the Semana da Arte Moderne, although she knew most of the participants – Oswald de Andrade, who organised the events, Paulo Prado, who funded the whole thing, Mario de Andrade, the wild-eyed writer, Heitor Villa-Lobos, the composer and Menotti del Picchia, the poet who had translated Marinetti's Futurist Manifesto into Portuguese. No-one kept any records of attendances, but Antonietta was probably in the theatre for all three nights, and would have seen every one of the lectures and performances. Charlie Miller was almost certainly elsewhere.

After the Semana da Arte Moderne, the artists splinter into various different groups. They call themselves the Dynamists, the Hallucinists, the Primitivists, the Nationalists, the Spiritualists. They argue over politics and aesthetics, and find themselves unable to agree about anything. They spew out hundreds of journals and manifestos, justifying themselves and denouncing everyone else. Oswald de Andrade writes his *Manifesto Antropófago*, claiming that Brazil is a cannibalistic culture, swallowing influences and ideas from everyone and everywhere, absorbing them, remaking them, forging them afresh in a clear bright light of Brazil. Mario de Andrade publishes *Macunaíma*. Villa-Lobos leaves Brazil and goes to live in Paris, where he can work in peace and build an international reputation. Menotti del Picchia writes a constant flow of newspaper articles, publishes books and poems, and exhibits his paintings and sculptures.

One night, Menotti and his wife attend a salon at the house of Olivia Penteado, a wealthy society hostess and patron of the arts. In the elegant rooms of her large house, the city's smart young poets and painters mingle with bankers and journalists, landowners and property developers. Without any ceremony, a slim woman seats herself at the grand piano, and starts playing. Around her, most of the guests continue chatting, so involved in their arguments that they hardly even hear the music, but the woman continues regardless, ignoring the chatter, as if she is playing for herself rather than them.

'So, what do you say to that? Eh? Eh? Nothing?'

Menotti looks at the red face opposite him, and realises that he must have been asked a question. He didn't hear it. The conversation has continued, leaving him behind. Now the other people in the group are staring at him, waiting to hear his response. He shakes his head, and apologises. As he walks away, he can hear them laughing at him – these poets, huh? – but he doesn't care. He finds an empty chair, sits down, and listens. When his wife comes to find him, Menotti jumps up and agrees that they should be leaving. He drives her home. Then he makes some excuse – a forgotten glove – and hurries back to the salon. In the music room, the pianist has just finished playing, but she is still sitting at the piano, shy and silent, resting her fingers on the keys, not wanting to join any of the frenetic conversations that surround her. Menotti goes over to the piano, and asks if she will play one more piece. Never in his life, he says, has he heard anyone play with such finesse.

Brazil remained an exceptionally conservative country, embedded in antique traditions which had gone unquestioned for decades, even centuries. Unless they were married, men and women would rarely walk together in the street. If a young couple were engaged, they might get away with holding hands, although at least one pair of parents would probably follow them, watching from a discreet distance. Divorce was illegal. Abortion was unthinkable. And yet, like good Catholics every-where, Paulistas understood that life could hardly be endured without some give and take. Sin today, confess tomorrow. Everyone accepted that men would visit prostitutes. People appreciated that married men had affairs. A little discreet hypocrisy hurt no-one.

That was what shocked people so much about Antonietta's behaviour. Not the fact that she had had an affair, but her insistence on telling everyone what she was doing. No-one could have expected her to leave her husband. No-one imagined that a respectable woman, born into one of the best families in São Paulo, would abandon her home and her children, and cross town to set up house with a poet. The scandal was thrilling. When the family of Helena Miller's fiancé heard what had happened to her mother, they ordered the young man to break off the engagement. He did, of course. The Rudges made no secret of their fury. Menotti was pointedly never invited to family events. Refusing to attend without her new lover, Antonietta stayed away too, leaving Charlie in the odd position of representing his estranged wife at celebrations organised by her own clan.

Menotti del Picchia had been born in São Paulo, but grew up in Itapira, a small town in the coffee-producing heartlands to the north of the city. There, he married his childhood sweetheart, who bore his seven children. Menotti lacked Antonietta's fierce honesty, and tried to find a compromise between the two women in his life, hanging on to both of them. While living in São Paulo with Antonietta, he kept his wife and children in a house outside the city, and divided his week between the two.

Like Charlie, Menotti had been born in Brazil of recent immigrants. His parents had emigrated from Pontedera, a small Tuscan town, best-known today as the headquarters of Piaggio and the birthplace of the Vespa. Like Charlie, Menotti was the son of parents who fled poverty and created themselves anew in a fresh country, devoting a large slice of their income to funding the education of their children. But unlike Charlie, Menotti had no nostalgia for Back Home. He spoke Italian, the language that his parents used in their own home, but made no effort to visit the Old Country. He embraced Brazil. In his twenties, he made his name with *Juca Mulato* (*Jack Mulatto*), the first major Brazilian narrative to feature a non-white hero, and devoted much of his artistic output to the puzzle of Brazilian identity. What is Brazil? Who are Brazilians? Where is the heart of this huge country? Who owns it? Who can unite it? How can Brazil forge an independent national and cultural identity, free of European and North American influences? While Charlie Miller lingered in the nineteenth century, harking back to an already half-forgotten world of chivalry and gentlemanly amateurism, Menotti del Picchia hurled himself into the twentieth, thriving on the energy and excitement of a booming city, profiting from burgeoning industrialisation, surrendering himself to the ecstasy of modernity. Opportunities opened everywhere, and Menotti grabbed them. Never cautious, never nostalgic, always peering forwards and trying to second-guess the future, he may not have produced any great lasting works of art, but he was thrillingly preco-cious and multi-talented, spreading himself over a range of disciplines, publishing poetry and novels, spurting out a constant surge of newspa-per articles, working as a politician, and even dabbling in the visual arts, filling his home with his own sketches, paintings and sculptures.

It is easy to see Charlie Miller and Menotti del Picchia as represen-tatives of opposite extremes, and Antonietta standing between them, having to make a choice between the two. Should she pledge herself to art or sport? The poet or the player? Love or duty? Passion or obedience? The new or the old? The future or the past? Britain or Brazil? Perhaps all these dichotomies are too neat, too perfect, too far removed from the everyday complexities of any marriage or love affair. Perhaps the simple answer is that Charlie and Antonietta could never have been happy together. She liked late nights. He liked early mornings. She wanted smoky rooms filled with anguished arguments about the role of the artist in modern society. He preferred fresh air and a good kickabout. They had few friends in common. Charlie rarely accompanied his wife to private views or first nights. Antonietta never watched her husband refereeing football matches, and stayed away when he was cheering SPAC from the sidelines. Despite these differences, and their apparent incompatibilities, he loved her. When she left, he plunged into a depression from which he never truly emerged. Once again, the solid, disciplined Briton had been eclipsed by a passionate, creative Brazilian. This time, he did not pick himself up off the grass, brush the dust off his knees, and chase after the ball. This time, he did not fight back.

Fourteen

The artistic revolution of 1922 meant nothing to most Brazilians. The Semana de Arte Moderna had been created by a tiny group of citizens, mostly posh poets, a well-heeled painter or two, the highly educated, well-travelled sons and daughters of rich coffee barons and powerful industrialists. It may have been one of the most important events in the history of Brazilian art, but almost no-one noticed. That could not be said of the next revolutions to buffet São Paulo. Shrapnel flew. Blood flowed. Bombs fell and masonry shuddered. Lines of soldiers stomped through the streets. Horses pulled artillery onto the hills and gun barrels glared at the citizens, searching for troublemakers. Throughout the 1920s and 1930s, São Paulo was besieged by a continuous barrage of rioting students and twitchy soldiers. Confronted by this torrent of violence, the British barricaded their doors, hammered boards over their windows, and prayed for a quick resolution. Business requires stability. During a coup, the railway wouldn't run on time, the ports closed, shops and restaurants lost custom, crops went unpicked and profits plummeted. Predictably, this refusal to take sides satisfied no-one. Travelling through a small town just north of São Paulo, one British resident found himself in a sticky situation.

I was stopped by a half-breed armed with a Winchester rifle. His only insignia was a full cartridge bandolier. Then the following absurd conversation passed between us.

'You cannot pass.'

'Why not?'

'Orders.'

'Whose orders?'

'Our general.'

'Who is your general?'

'I don't know.'

'What! You don't know him, and yet you obey him?'

'What has that to do with it?'

'So if I tried to get to the station you would stop me?'

'It is my duty.'

'How would you do that?' He stroked the butt of his old rifle. 'You mean you would shoot me? A man who has done no harm either to you or your general?'

'It's general's orders. I would be obliged to, unless of course you are one of us.'

'No; I am neutral.'

'What's that?'

'Neutral means neither for nor against.'

'Never heard of such a thing! There can't be any such people.'

Neutrality was a concept that Charlie Miller understood only too well. As the city embraced chaos, and the British community faded into insignificance, he withdrew from the world, resigning from committees, curtailing his duties, devoting himself to simple pleasures that had no connection with the wider world.

A few weeks after her seventieth birthday, Charlotte Miller had died. Charlie buried her in the Protestant Cemetery, and placed a large plaque on the family tomb. 'In loving memory of my dear mother.' Throughout the 1920s, he must have felt that they were all deserting him – his mother, his wife, his children, and even the greatest love of his life. Football had surrendered to the twin evils of politics and money. In Britain, the game had been corrupted by professionalism, and men played for cash rather than love. In Brazil, football had been turned into *futebol*, co-opted by the government, bought out by financiers, used as a political tool, torn up from its roots. Bereft and lonely, Charlie did what any man will do when he needs a lover who will return his affection without contempt or betrayal. He bought a dog.

His son had gone to school in Oxford, then returned to São Paulo, married and started a family. His daughter kept a room in the house on Rua México, but spent most of her time with Antonietta and Menotti, mingling with their friends, dabbling in bohemia, playing the piano and falling in love with artists. Alone in the big house, Charlie devoted himself to his garden. He built a kennel for his new dog. He planted fruit trees, and cultivated orchids, and tended the springy turf with regular mowing. There he stood on the long, humid evenings, upright in the middle of the lawn, practising his golf swing. For company, he had the dog and a glass of whisky. He still went to SPAC almost every weekend, watching the games and stopping in the bar afterwards for a quick snifter. Everyone knew him. Like all the other old buffers, he resembled a figure from another era, wearing a stiff-collared shirt, a dark suit, a handkerchief in his top pocket. 'Good shot, old man,' he called from his deckchair beside the pavilion. 'Damn good shot, sir!' The crack of leather against willow, the gentle applause as a young batsman reaches his first fifty, the swallows swooping across the grass – the old men can dream that they are back in the England of their youth. For them, the past really is another country. When they return to the real England, they feel a little lost, as if they are walking into a house where they once used to live. New owners have knocked down a wall or two, repainted every room, and replaced some of the windows. The furniture has been changed, and even the air smells different. They can find their way around, but they have a permanent sense that something is missing, something has been forgotten.

Their England may have been stolen from them, but this didn't prevent them from longing for Back Home, a place that no longer existed outside their imaginations. They refused to surrender to the present. To the end of their lives, they would wear double-breasted suits in the tropical sunshine, drink gin and tonics rather than caipirinhas, check the cricket score in week-old copies of *The Times* and slap one another on the back with a cry of 'What's your poison, old chap?' They stressed their British identity so strongly that they become self-parodic, stuck in their own version of England and Englishness. When its symbols arrived in São Paulo, they could barely contain themselves. Rudyard Kipling persuaded a newspaper to send him on a gentle cruise across the Atlantic in exchange for a few waggish articles. Having ridden the SPR up the hill from Santos, he visited São Paulo, taking cocktails in the club. The joyous British members crowded around him, pledging their devotion and quoting their favourite passages from *The Jungle Book*.

And after Kipling, the Prince of Wales. On his tour of Brazil, the future Edward VIII stopped in São Paulo. He inspected the local branch of the British Legion, cast his eye over the Boy Scouts and the Girl Guides, then spent an evening in SPAC, where he was received with an almost deranged enthusiasm, more suitable for a saint than a playboy prince. Ernest Hambloch noticed one of the SPAC members seizing the Prince's discarded cocktail glass and wrapping it reverentially in a clean handkerchief. 'This I shall keep for ever: the glass from which the Prince drank!' A few days later, when the Prince had left São Paulo, Hambloch visited one of the houses belonging to a SPAC member, and noticed a long white glove lying on the mantelpiece, enclosed in a glass case. When he asked his hostess for an explanation, she told him that the glove was hers.

'I wore it at the ball to the Prince of Wales, and I touched him with it.'

'But you didn't dance with him,' I said. 'He danced with only two ladies, the wife of the Consul and the wife of the Chairman of the Chamber. And then he left.'

'That's true,' said the lady. 'But as he was dancing with Mrs Evans I stretched out my arm and managed to touch his back with that glove on my hand. Now it is sacred.'

Heitor Villa-Lobos had returned from Paris and chosen to live in Rio, but he visited São Paulo often. Through Menotti, Antonietta befriended the great composer. When Villa-Lobos assembled a small orchestra to tour the state of São Paulo, he asked Antonietta to be his pianist. They gave fifty-four concerts in villages and rural towns, taking contemporary music to new audiences. The Excursão Artística played a mixed program of Prokofiev, Chopin, Scarlatti, Beethoven and the immortal Villa-Lobos. Despite the difficulty of some of this work, the concerts always attracted large crowds, unless they happened to coincide with a football match. When that happened, just about everyone chose the stadium over the concert hall. The inhabitants of little towns and villages might have been delighted that a internationally renowned avant-garde composer had decided to visit them with a group of famous musicians, but if the local team happened to be playing on the same night, what were they supposed to do? Miss the football? Infuriated, Villa-Lobos gave a series of speeches in which he tried to persuade the Brazilian population that their priorities had grown dangerously muddled. The arts have permanent value, he reminded them, whereas kicking a leather ball around a field is a tragic waste of energy and time. 'Football will extract brains from the head and move them to the feet!' He often left the stage pursued by a hail of eggs and potatoes. Once, his lecture caused so much fury that he and his musicians had to check out of their hotel and flee to the next town on their schedule.

Villa-Lobos was a pragmatist, and soon decided to alter his views. He realised that art, football and politics had become inextricably linked in Brazil. If he wanted to be successful as an artist, he would have to be a cunning politician and an avowed lover of *futebol*. When the new Vargas government invited him to hold concerts in football stadiums, he composed a series of simple choral works that could be sung by vast crowds. Villa-Lobos stood on the field, conducting tens of thousands of singers in a perfect fusion of art, sport and politics.

Football had become a national obsession. Year by year, Brazilian footballers created a style of playing which was claimed as distinctively Brazilian, favouring short passes and individual dribbling, taking inspiration from samba and *capoeira*, treating the game as a dance rather than a discipline. At the same time, Brazilian football finally began to shed its apartheid roots, and reflect the country's racial diversity. The progress of black players was initially blocked or disguised – playing for Fluminense, Carlos Alberto smothered his black skin with white rice powder, which is still commemorated in the white powder thrown from the stands by modern fans – until simple pragmatism persuaded the clubs to embrace equality. When Vasco de Gama won the 1923 Rio state championship with a team of working-class players, both black and white, beating the students and businessmen who played for the other teams, they effectively began an era of professionalism that could not afford to impose colour bars. The five big Rio teams initially tried to resist, creating a new amateur league without inviting Vasco to join, but supporters and spectators refused to follow them. Over in São Paulo, Paulistano made one last lurch against professionalism by starting an amateur league. It folded in 1929, and Paulistano withdrew from competitive matches, leaving football to the professionals. Brazil's new president, Getúlio Vargas, encouraged the popularity of football, deciding that only bread and circuses could unite his vast nation. He invested money and energy into the Brazilian game, turning it into the mirror in which the country saw itself. Other leaders might have invented a good war; Vargas used football. By 1930, when the first World Cup was held in Uruguay, the Brazilian side had become a focus for national pride and prestige.

Charles Miller had played in the first international on Brazilian soil. A South African team arrived in São Paulo in 1902, and Charlie quickly arranged a game, summoning a few local players. Charlie's team consisted of a mixture of Britons, Germans and Brazilians. Perhaps they were incompatible; the game ended in an embarrassingly easy 6-0 victory to the South Africans. Twelve years later, Exeter City toured Brazil, playing three games in Rio, beating 'Ingleses do Rio' 3-0 and 'Rio de Janeiro' 5-3, then losing 2-0 to 'Brasileiros' at Fluminense Football Club. That game, played on 21 July 1912, was the first time that the Brazilian green and yellow was worn during a competitive match, and it is usually remembered as the first game played by the Brazilian national team. The first official Brazilian national side played their first formal game seven months later, defeating Argentina 1-0.

Only four European teams attended the first World Cup Finals in 1930 – France, Belgium, Romania and Yugoslavia – the others refusing to make the long sea voyage, despite the fact that Uruguay offered to pay the travelling and accommodation costs of every team that attended. Perhaps the other Europeans worried that the three-week sea voyage would be followed immediately by humiliation: Uruguay had won gold in 1924 Olympics, causing a sensation by beating the fancied European teams, and creating a sudden passion for South American football. Paulistano were the first Brazilian team to take advantage; led by Antonio Prado Junior, they toured Switzerland and France, playing an informal French national side before a crowd of 25,000 in Paris. Proving that their success had not been a fluke, Uruguay won gold again in 1928, beating Argentina in the final. That match convinced Jules Rimet to hand the first World Cup to South America. Uruguay built a magnificent new stadium for the tournament. After losing to Yugoslavia and drawing with Bolivia, Brazil was knocked out in the first round. In the semis, Uruguay beat Yugoslavia 6-1, and Argentina beat the USA 6-1. Uruguay won the final 4-2.

Four years later, Brazil and Argentina travelled to the second World Cup Finals in Italy, and were both knocked out in the first round after playing only a single match each. Uruguay hadn't even bothered making the trip. Boosted by playing at home, Italy went on to win. In 1938, the South American sides protested that the finals should have reverted back to their side of the Atlantic, but FIFA ignored their pleas, choosing France instead. Uruguay and Argentina agreed to boycott the tournament. In Brazil, Getúlio Vargas had no such scruples. He sponsored the national side, paying its expenses and sending his daughter to support the team. In the first round, Brazil and Poland were level at 4-4 after ninety minutes. In extra time, Brazil scored twice more, and Poland only once. Leônidas scored four of the goals, including the winner, which he shot barefoot when his boot came off. In the quarter-finals, the game between Brazil and Czechoslovakia exploded into a brawl; two Brazilian players were sent off and one Czech, five were badly injured, and two ended up in hospital, suffering a broken leg and a broken arm. The game ended in a draw. Brazil won the replay, then lost to Italy in the semi-finals. Italy went on to win the tournament, and Brazil beat Sweden in a play-off to take third place. Leônidas was the tournament's top scorer. The world's newspapers feted the Brazilian team. Enthusiasm swept through the country, uniting rich and poor, north and south, bankers and peasants, sweeping aside all thought of everyday misery and injustice. Vargas saw a magnificent return on his investment.

FIFA promised Vargas the next World Cup Finals in 1942, but war intervened, and the event was postponed until 1950. Vargas had dabbled with both sides throughout most of the war, pledging allegiance to the USA while sending congratulatory birthday telegrams to Hitler, before finally joining the Allies when he saw who was going to win. A nominal force of Brazilian troops fought in Italy. However, a military coup despatched Vargas in 1945, and he was not ruling Brazil when the world's footballers arrived in 1950. The Maracana, the biggest football stadium on the planet, had been built in Rio, and was almost finished in time for the tournament. Two hundred thousand spectators filled the stadium to witness the greatest tragedy in Brazilian history: losing 2-1 to Uruguay in the final game of the tournament. Stunned by the result, the Brazilian officials could not bring themselves to hand over the trophy. Jules Rimet had to go down onto the pitch, fetch the cup himself and present it to the Uruguayan team. Despite this loss, the wave of excitement in Brazil seems to have helped Vargas, and he regained the presidency through a public vote at the end of the year.

In 1927, Banister Court School closed for the summer holidays, and never reopened. In the final edition of the school magazine, Christopher Ellaby ended his editorial on a tragic note. 'I have lost the chief things that gave me work and happiness, and all the efforts of my past life appear vain and fruitless, but God's ways are not ours.' The school merged with another in Southampton. Arthur Denning continued as second master, having spent his entire working life at the school. Banister Court itself was bought by the newly formed Southampton Greyhound Racing Company Ltd, which knocked down the buildings, filled in the ponds and constructed a stadium. They held their first race in the late summer of 1928, and continued weekly for almost four decades, alternating dogs with speedway. When public tastes changed, the stadium was replaced by an ice rink, then a housing estate. Today, the site of Christopher Ellaby's school is occupied by meandering cul-de-sacs of squat ordinary homes.

News of Old Banisterians continued to filter through to Charlie. Many of his schoolmates had ended up in South America. Hodges was a bishop in Buenos Aires. Bryan owned a tea plantation in Paraguay. Eddy ran the most successful railway in Argentina. But none of them could compete with Harold Davidson, who featured on the front page of every newspaper in Britain. On one particular day, Davidson's trial was the only British news reported in the USA, and the coverage extended from the most tawdry provincial rag to the *New York Times*. During his weekly trips to London, the vicar of Stiffkey had befriended hundreds of prostitutes in the West End, and he found himself accused of impropriety, immorality and recruiting girls for the white slave trade. During the trial, Davidson claimed to have picked up between 150 and 200 girls a year, bought them a meal and given them nothing more than some sound moral advice. When asked by the Bishop of Norwich why he only helped pretty girls, Davidson explained that plain ones could look after themselves. The jury found him guilty on five counts of immoral conduct, but Harold Davidson escaped prison. Stripped of his religious duties, he planned to open a nudist camp for his parishioners in Norfolk, but could only find work as a performer at fairgrounds, replacing 'The Starving Woman of

Hasingden' in Blackpool. From there, he moved to Skegness, performing as a lion tamer. One of his fellow entertainers was Mahatma Gandhi's cousin, who sat for hours on a bed of nails. Davidson shared a cage with a docile lioness named Toto. In 1937, he made the mistake of adding a second lion to his act, and it killed him.

As trade declined, the Royal Mail slimmed down their overseas offices, cutting wages, reducing commissions, and encouraging their employees to start their own travel agencies. With Edward Goddard, an ambitious young man who had trained in Pernambuco before transferring to the São Paulo office, Charlie rented a swanky office in Praça da República, right in the heart of the city, and started selling tickets. They called themselves Miller Goddard. When the business grew, Charlie hired Carlos. Later, Carlos's daughter Therezina worked there too, and three generations of the Millers worked side by side.

While Carlos worked in the family firm, Helena remained elusive. Melancholy fizzes through Charlie's letters to her. 'There is going to be a big dance here on Saturday at the Terminus Hotel for King George's birthday (which is a Monday), I [am] looking forward to taking you to it, but shall be disappointed as no doubt you will not be there.' Helena's response has not survived, but she probably didn't return to celebrate the king's birthday. She was having much more fun with Antonietta and Menotti. Helena never married, although she had a famous affair with Victor Brecheret, the greatest Brazilian sculptor of his generation and a friend of Menotti's.

As for Charlie – well, he would have been much too discreet to leave any trace of his love affairs, but he seems to have had room for only one woman in his life. Once or twice a year, Antonietta came to lunch at the house on Rua México. Charlie would skip work and spend the morning at home, fretting over the menu and worrying what to wear. Like a nervous girl on a first date, he changed his shirt, his tie, the handkerchief in his top pocket, trying to find the perfect outfit. When Antonietta arrived, he greeted her with a curt smile, and started an earnest conversation about the weather.

In 1939, Helena and Charlie went on holiday together, sailing to England on one of the Royal Mail's steamers. When they arrived in Southampton, Helena went shopping and Charlie bought a ticket at The Dell. He even managed to see some of the men whom he played alongside fifty years earlier.

I was sitting in the stand, watching a game. So I asked some of the people around me if they could point out someone who had played in 1893 and 1894. While an elderly man was replying, I suddenly recognised two others who were there. I turned round and said: 'Hello, George! Hello, Alf!' The two men, a bit dazed, looked at me from head to foot and replied in unison: 'Hello, Nipper!' You can't imagine our joy!

He did not see the Corinthians. The First World War had not only massacred many of the members, but caused a rupture that could never be healed. The club tottered through the 1920s and 1930s, achieving little success even against the reserve squads that professional teams sent out to face them. In 1937, the Corinthians had made their final FA Cup appearance, beaten in the first round by Southend United. After that humiliation, they decided to amalgamate with another team of ex-public schoolboys, and formed the Corinthian Casuals. Gilbert Oswald Smith disapproved of the merger. If the Corinthians could not find sufficient support to continue, he suggested, they should accept the decision of history and disband.

São Paulo never stopped growing. Having climbed every hillside and covered every plain, builders had only one direction left in which they could go. Up. In 1928, work started on the city's first tower block, the Edificio Martinelli, a glorious, glamorous three-pronged leap at the sky. People shuddered at the thought of working at the top of those towers, so far from the earth, so close to the clouds. Today, the Edificio Martinelli is one of the few distinguished elderly buildings in São Paulo, and its three stubby towers look like saplings in a forest of mature trees. Over the course of Charlie Miller's lifetime, the city expanded a hundredfold. The population grew from twenty thousand to two million. Amid this astonishing growth, the British community stayed roughly the same size. A few hundred wealthy and well-connected individuals, working as bankers, merchants or engineers, their influence necessarily dwindled as the city grew. Throughout the 1930s and 1940s, one humiliation followed another, and the British lost their influence both literally and symbolically. In 1937, the Companhia Sorocabana opened an alternative line from São Paulo to the coast, breaking the SPR's monopoly, severing the British grasp on the state's economy. Then, following a strident nationalist agenda, the Vargas government forced all foreign companies and clubs to change their names into Portuguese. SPAC stopped being the São Paulo Athletic Club and became the Clube Atlético São Paulo. For the first time in the history of the São Paulo Golf Club, the minutes of its monthly meetings were written in Portuguese rather than English. St Paul's, the British school in São Paulo, even started holding its classes in Portuguese, although just about all the pupils were British or American. Finally, after the end of the war, the remnants of British influence were brushed aside in one brutal emblematic act: the SPR was nationalised, and the Brazilian government took responsibility for running the trains on time. To no-one's surprise, they failed. The trains went slower and slower, then stopped. A new motorway zigzagged down the Serra do Mar, and anyone wishing to travel between São Paulo and Santos went by car.

When Carlos Miller's wife died, he and his three children moved into Charlie's house on Rua México. Charlie was a frail man in his late seventies, who had grown used to the company of his orchids and his German Shepherd, but he welcomed this unexpected arrival of youth. So did Bobby, the dog, who suddenly had three teenagers clamouring to take him for walks.

Every evening, Charlie and his granddaughters had a battle that might have started seriously but developed into a jokey routine. The girls would be playing dance records at top volume, practising their moves. Charlie banged his stick on the floorboards and demanded silence. Keep the noise down, he shouted. The BBC news was just about to begin, and he wanted to know what had been happening in the world. Precisely as the broadcast started, the girls switched off their gramophone, and Charlie settled back in his armchair to listen to the announcer's leisurely tones. Like millions of others around the world, he had grown into the habit of listening every evening throughout the Second World War, and continued the routine into peacetime.

At the beginning of June 1953, Charlie heard the BBC's newsreader announce an extraordinary piece of news. In a few hours, Her Royal Highness the Princess Elizabeth would be crowned queen, but everyone already knew that. What they hadn't known was that the coronation would be prefaced by an unexpected British triumph. Edmund Hilary and Tenzing Norgay had reached the summit of Everest, and stayed there for fifteen minutes. In his armchair, sitting beside the radio, listening to the voice from London, Charlie must have been transported back to his youth. Once again, a woman would be ruling the empire. Once again, Britain stood on top of the world.

Four weeks later, Therezina went into her grandfather's bedroom, and found him lying on the floor, breathing but unconscious. He was taken to hospital, where he died on the last day of June. The following afternoon, as the funeral cortège walked past the Pacaembu Stadium, the referee blew his whistle and halted the game. Fans and players stood in silence until the hearse had passed. In the Protestant Cemetery, Charles Miller was buried in the family plot alongside his mother, his sister and his two brothers.

Fifteen

If Charlie Miller had lived a little longer, someone would have made a documentary about him. A small crew would have come round to his house, strung up a couple of bright lights, pointed a camera at his face and dangled a microphone above his head. An earnest interviewer would have nodded, smiled, and asked him to disgorge his memories. Charlie died too young for that, but they did it to Menotti del Picchia.

Antonietta outlived Charlie by a couple of decades, and died in 1974. After her death, Menotti continued living in their house, tending the garden, poring over editions of his books, awaiting visits from his grandchildren. A film crew came to capture his memories. In the documentary, Menotti is lucid and confident, enjoying the camera's attention, speaking in long sentences like the teacher and politician that he had been. At the end of the documentary, the camera waits for a moment outside the house, staring at the sunlit façade. The front door opens. Menotti emerges. He looks older and frailer than he did during the interview. Now he is walking rather than sitting, and he's not using a stick. Perhaps he is unwilling to show weakness. Perhaps he is conscious that biographers and historians will watch this film, years from now, and he has no wish to be remembered as a man who relied on a walking stick. He hobbles down the path that runs through the shady garden, and opens the gate. Leaving the white wooden gate ajar, allowing the camera crew to follow him, he walks along the pavement of the Avenida Brasil. Today, this is one of the city's main roads, packed with a continuous eight-lane torrent of traffic. Even at the end of the 1970s, when the film was shot, cars are bulleting past, but Menotti strolls across the road with an air of complete confidence, certain that no-one would have the gall to knock him down. Curious drivers glance at the old man, wondering what he has done to deserve the attention of a film crew.

Menotti reaches the traffic island. In the middle, surrounded by trees and grass, a bronze bust of a head sits on a marble plinth. Menotti stands before it. The head is a little higher than his own. He crosses his arms and gazes into the sightless eyes. By now, its unmoving lines must be as familiar to him as the real soft shape of her face, if not more so. The camera moves around him, viewing the scene from different angles, but Menotti never glances at the lens, never lets his eyes wander from the statue. He seems to have forgotten that he is not alone.

Every afternoon, the narrator tells us, Menotti makes this journey. He strolls out of his house, crosses the road to the traffic island and stands opposite the statue, paying a daily homage to Antonietta. Decades ago, he sculpted her face himself, trying to capture the expression that filled her features when she played the piano – her ecstasy, her abandon, the way that she forgot everything but the music. Then, moulding the shape of the sculpture, he hadn't imagined that it would be placed in the city's streets. He had simply wanted a reminder of her face, something that would stay in the house while she was travelling, teaching or giving concerts.

In the years after the film was shot, Menotti continued taking his walk to the statue and paying daily homage to Antonietta. One afternoon, he was crossing the road to reach the traffic island and a truck knocked him down. He broke a couple of bones. That was the end of his visits. From then on, he rarely left the house, retaining contact with the outside world through newspapers and visits from his grandchildren. There, surrounded by his books, his sculptures, his pictures and his sinuous Siamese cats, he died in 1988. His heirs could have buried him with Antonietta, but they chose to place his body in the family tomb alongside his wife.

One night, not long after Menotti's death, some thieves stopped on the traffic island. Using chisels or a crowbar, they wrenched Antonietta's statue from the plinth. In those days there was a craze for stealing statues. People melted them down, and sold the metal. Whether that was Antonietta's fate, or she is sitting in someone's front room in a suburb of São Paulo, anonymous and unguarded, the statue has never been recovered. The empty plinth still stands there, squatting in the middle of the traffic island, surrounded by balding grass and overlooked by shiny tower blocks. Day and night, the island is wreathed in a mist of fumes. This junction is always busy. When the lights turn red, men hurry along the lines of cars, waving their wares at the impatient drivers, offering water and Coke, chewing gum and chocolate, bananas and slices of watermelon. When the lights change back to green, the beggars and hawkers leap onto the pavement, and the traffic flows on.

Sixteen

'Just as only a painter could do full justice to Rio de Janeiro, so could a proper description of São Paulo be made only by a statistician or an economist. He would have to compile numbers and figures, compare them with one another, copy charts, and try to describe growth in words, because it is neither its past nor its present which makes São Paulo fascinating, but its almost visible growth and development, the speed of its transformation.'

São Paulo exhausted Stefan Zweig, who eventually concluded that the city 'would best be described by a film, especially one which goes faster and faster every hour'. When he stayed in the immense metropolis, bewildered by its size and pace, the population had recently passed one million. Today, no-one is quite sure how many people live in the city, but it's many times that number. Eighteen million, say some. Sixteen, say others, or twenty, or just twelve. Geographers cannot decide whether this is the third largest city on the planet, or the fourth, or even the fifth. But everyone is agreed that São Paulo is big, and getting bigger. The transformation continues. The film is still running faster and faster, and the reel shows no sign of reaching an end. Every day, trucks and buses bring more migrant workers from the poverty-stricken northern states of Brazil, coming south to make their fortunes. Every month, the *favelas* grow another layer of tumbledown shacks. A decade from now, the number of inhabitants may increase to twenty-five million, even thirty. São Paulo might soon be the biggest city on the planet.

On the day that Charles Miller was born, 130 years ago, São Paulo was a tiny town. Twenty thousand people lived here, their small houses and dusty roads encircled by bare hills. You couldn't walk through the streets without meeting a familiar face. When Charlie travelled to Southampton in 1884, he moved from a sleepy village to a frenetic metropolis. Today, a hundred Southamptons could be crammed into São Paulo, or three Londons, or twelve Manhattans. São Paulo and Southampton are moving in opposite directions, just as Brazil and Britain are too. One grows, the other shrinks. One is young, and the other is old. One gazes towards the future, and the other looks mournfully into the past, remembering better times, old glories.

Much of Southampton has hardly changed in the past century. Banister Court may have gone, but Charlie Miller would recognise most of the streets and many of the houses that he wandered past as a schoolboy. His São Paulo has gone. Every home in which he lived has been demolished, and so have the offices where he worked. The city thrives on continual regeneration, knocking down old buildings, abolishing the past, thrusting towards the future, leaping at the sky. Not a trace remains of Companhia Lupton. A single door still stands from the offices of Miller Goddard, but it opens into an establishment which trades in beer and chips rather than tickets for transatlantic travel. The Royal Mail Steam Packet Company has been sold, sold again, then dismantled. The railway down to Santos hasn't been used for decades; the tracks have been scrapped, the tunnels have collapsed, and jungle has smothered the route. Henry Ford has triumphed here. Everyone travels by car or plane. Just about the only passengers who now use Brazilian railways are steam enthusiasts, who polish engines throughout the week and chug along the old lines on Sundays, carrying tourists on an antique train from the Luz station to Paranapiacaba, a tiny village in the hills. There, forty miles from the centre of São Paulo, barely beyond the outer rim of the suburbs, you can walk down Avenida William Speers, and stare at the old furniture in the Casa Fox, and poke around the railway workers' cottages which have somehow survived a century of neglect. When the mist sweeps over the hills, blotting out the trees, you can try to imagine that the palms are beeches or pines, just as Daniel Fox might have done, and pretend to yourself that you have returned to the valleys of Wales or Scotland.

Back in the centre of São Paulo, the Luz station is being restored as a national monument, but still hasn't been reclaimed from its most recent occupants: prostitutes in skimpy skirts and high heels, pushing out their boobs and butts at passing cars. If the stationmaster could see his platforms now, covered in gob and condoms, he would have a fit. The clock tower still gazes over the surrounding streets, but thousands of other buildings have sprung up and grabbed the skyline, drowning the Luz, and Paulistas no longer glance at the tower when they need to know the time. A new symbol of British prestige has replaced the Luz's clock tower: ceremonially opened by Tony Blair in 2001, the British Centre – also known as o Centro Brasileiro Britânico – is a gleaming modern building on a dusty, undistinguished street in Pinheiros. Shiny sculptures hang from the high ceiling. There is an ever-changing exhibition of dowdy watercolours and misshapen pots, showing off the delights of modern British art. The complex houses a restaurant with regular theme nights – cheap Guinness on St Patrick's Day, a night of Australian wines – along with the consulate, the British Council, the British Chamber of Commerce, the British and Commonwealth Community Council and a language school, which funded the whole enterprise. Most Paulistas want to learn English. Although only the least pragmatic students prefer a British bark to a Californian drawl, language schools have been one of the few areas in which the British have retained a firm grasp on the city's economy.

Other remnants of the British have adapted to modern Brazil in different ways. St Paul's School, which was founded to 'provide a sound education for the sons and daughters of British parents', is now one of the most expensive and exclusive schools in South America, catering for rich kids of all nationalities. Lessons are taught in English and Portuguese, and pupils can choose which syllabus to follow: British, American, Brazilian or the International Baccalaureate. Out in the distant suburbs, the Anglicans still have a church. It is a bizarre 1960s structure, punctuated by concrete pillars and round windows, topped with a sweeping roof. The vicar offers weddings, funerals, weekly services and Sunday School for English-speaking residents. The memorials to Lilian Lupton and Daniel Fox have been transported from the old church, and glued to the new walls. A couple of miles away, the British community has built a residential home for their retirees. Sixteen elderly residents live in Stacey House, speaking English to one another and Portuguese to the nurses. Having spent their lives in South America, the pensioners would be completely foxed by repatriation, but they remain defiantly British, taking tea at four, drinking Earl Grey and eating cucumber sandwiches, discussing the cricket and Ruth Rendell's latest novel.

And then there is one more remnant of the British. In the old part of town, down a little alleyway off the Rua Consolação, past the piles of cardboard boxes and the tramp counting change in his grubby palm, you come to the Clube Atlético São Paulo, better known as SPAC, still on the same patch of ground that it has occupied since the 1890s. The surrounding fields have been smothered under tarmac and concrete. High-rise blocks peer down on the tennis courts and bowling green. Few people know that the club even exists, and taxi drivers don't recognise the name of the street. The club has tall steel gates, guarded by four bulky men in blue uniforms. They speak no English. The name of everyone who enters is written in a large ledger, along with the licence plate of every car. This is a private space, serene and secluded, a haven from the noise and fear of the city's streets. As I walk up to the gates, the guards interrogate me, check my passport photo against my face, write down my name, then let me in. I hear the thwack of tennis ball against racket, the click of bowls, the splashes of swimmers. It is two o'clock on a Saturday afternoon. The tennis players shout to one another in Portuguese, and there are no English voices to be heard, but the notices posted to the swinging doors of each tennis court are written in both languages: 'Good courtsmanship and tennis ethics are expected to be practised by all players, independently of age.' On the bowling green, players in immaculate whites are following a solemn ritual, marking their scores on a card, watching in silence as the hefty balls roll across the grass. This might be the finest lawn in southern Brazil. The original turf was imported from Scotland, and its lush colour is evidence of daily sprinkling, snipping and pricking.

A stroll along the gravel driveway brings me to the front of the club. Inside, a wide wooden staircase leads up to the bar and the restaurant. None of this has changed for decades. Faded pictures of the Royal Family hang on the wall, alongside ancient photographs of the SPAC cricket teams that toured Argentina 100 years ago. There is a library of English books, and a memorial to the members who died in two world wars. All this Britishness is decorative, and doesn't reflect the national-ity of the people who actually eat, drink and play here. Nine-tenths of the members are wealthy Brazilians. For the administrators of the club, its British connections are a marketing ploy as much as than anything.

Paulistas are attracted not just by the tennis courts and swimming pool, but the hint of class suggested by the club's Englishness. Wealthy Brazilians like to wear Barbours, walk Cocker Spaniels in the park, eat from Harrods hampers, and play tennis on British courts.

Upstairs, a fire is burning in the hearth. Leather armchairs, faded photographs and glasses of Guinness glow in the flicker of the flames. Wooden panelling lines the walls, and a large photo of the late Queen Mother hangs in the centre of the room. Outside, the sun is shining, and the temperature would be described as pleasantly summery in England. Beside the crackling fire, a middle-aged woman sits alone, reading one of Joanna Trollope's novels. At another table, a group of four men chat in a mixture of English and Portuguese, all of them speaking both languages interchangeably. The oldest of them, a shrunken old chap with a heavily tanned face, has a strong Scottish accent. He describes his delight at a scene that he recently witnessed in the restaurant, when the waiter reprimanded a group of Brazilian businessmen for removing their jackets.

The leather-bound menu is Brazilian, but offers a few English dishes for anyone feeling homesick. There are different *sugestões Ingleses* for each day of the week. You can have shepherd's pie on Tuesdays, steak and kidney pudding on Wednesdays, chicken curry with rice on Thursdays, or fish and chips on Fridays. Looking around at the other diners, I can't see anyone eating the *sugestões Ingleses*. There's no reason that they should be. Almost everyone in the restaurant is Brazilian, and all of them are speaking Portuguese.

Chicken curry on a Thursday in the São Paulo Athletic Club. Could anyone find a more evocative, melancholy symbol for the collapse of Britain's imperial ambitions and the bizarre legacy that they have left behind? Unfortunately, today is Saturday. At the weekends, there are no *sugestões Ingleses*. I order cod and a glass of white wine.

Of the other teams that played in the first season of the Liga Paulista, none has become professional. Mackenzie College is now a large university, retaining its Presbyterian roots only in a couple of scholarships. Occupying a large plot in the leafy Jardins, Club Athletico Paulistano is still a private sports club, serving the same community as 100 years ago, providing exclusive facilities to a narrow band of extremely wealthy residents. Black nannies guide fair-skinned boys and girls through the turnstiles. High walls and armed guards prevent the hoi polloi from gaining entrance to the five pools, the raucous bars, the innumerable tennis courts. A few miles across town, Germania has evolved into Esporte Clube Pinheiros, another exclusive club for wealthy Paulistas, who can cruise the restaurants and bars, squash courts and swimming pools, never needing to worry that their bags will be snatched or their children threatened by junkies with knives. Not much seems to have changed in the past 100 years. Posh white boys are still playing football, and they are still watched by elegant women in long dresses, and they are still served orange juice at half-time by black servants.

For Corinthians, everything has changed. While the British version of the club has faded into insignificance, merging with another team of public-school old boys and struggling in a minor suburban league, Corinthians of São Paulo has evolved into one of the world's great clubs. Socrates, Rivelino, Gilmar, Rivaldo, Dida, Edilson – you could make a long list of all the famous names who have played for Corinthians. In 2000, the inaugural FIFA World Club Championship was held in Brazil. Supposedly a competition between the best clubs on the planet, the Championship featured teams from Mexico, Morocco, Saudi Arabia and Australia, plus Real Madrid, Manchester United and two Brazilian teams. Corinthians won.

One of the cheering supporters was Luiz Inacio Lula da Silva, better known as Lula, who has never made any secret about his preference for Corinthians over any of the other teams in Brazil. When his party took government in 2003, and Lula became president of Brazil, he filled the highest offices of state with Corinthians fans – men and women who, like himself, had worked and lived for years in the smoky industrial suburbs of São Paulo, and spent their leisure hours watching Corinthians on TV in a bar or from the stands of Pacaembu.

Here, if nowhere else in São Paulo, Charlie Miller is remembered. Even if they can't recall exactly who he was or what he did, every Corinthians supporter knows his name. The square outside their stadium has been christened to commemorate him. Anyone making the trek into Estadio Pacaembu will pass through the Praça Charles Miller. During the week, this is a large car park. On match days, the tarmac is covered with burger vans and men selling black and white striped shirts, scarves, hats and flags. When you have bought your ticket, and passed the line of police, who pat down every spectator, checking for weapons, you walk under a concrete arch. A line of plaques and statues commemorates the competitions won by Corinthians. Among them, there is a small brass plate engraved with Charles Miller's name and dates. No-one stops to look at it. They hurry past, emerge in the stadium, and head for the stands. The game will start in a few minutes. The twenty-two players are already on the pitch. Noise cascades from every side. Catcalls and boos from one half of the stadium, chants from the other. Up and down the aisles, flags are waving, people are singing. On the field, the referee fingers his whistle. Players stop dreaming about a move to Serie A or the Premiership, and start thinking about the next forty-five minutes. Two of them stand over the ball. The referee lifts the whistle to his lips. A roar of noise from the crowd drowns out the sound. And the game starts.

One man kicks a ball to another man. From the simplest of actions, everything else follows. The five World Cups that Brazil has won, the barefoot kids in favelas kicking a can against a wall, the multi-millionaires who play in the biggest European clubs, the packed hordes of fans screaming at TV screens – none of this means anything without one man kicking a ball to another man. None of it means anything without Charlie Miller filling the ball with air, and placing it on the dust at his feet. He glances at the men who have gathered around him. Play up, he says. His voice echoes around the field, across the decades and all over the country, from the dusty north of Brazil to the damp south, from the city to the village, from the jungle to the beach. Play up! Play up! And play the game.

Seventeen

There is a Bar Charles Miller in Salvador, the city that used to be a town called Bahia, a thousand miles up the coast from Santos, three hours in a plane from São Paulo. We stopped there for a beer. According to local gossip, the bar is part-owned by a businessman who also has a stake in one of the city's football teams. Football memorabilia covers every scrap of wall in the bar – banners, badges, flags, balls, stickers, tickets, posters, photographs – but there is only one small picture of Charles Miller himself, photocopied from a book, and no-one in the bar knows much about him. The waiters shrug their shoulders. The manager tells us to come back at midnight if we want to meet the owner, then ignores our other questions and scurries back into the kitchen.

Leaving the bar, and heading back into the centre of town, we ask the taxi driver if he knows anything about our man. Has he ever heard of Charles Miller? And does he know why that bar has been named after him?

'Yes, yes,' he replies. 'Charles Miller – he invented football.'

Notes

This is not an academic work. I have not provided footnotes or an index. I have borrowed, stolen and absorbed ideas from a large variety of sources and, while I have tried to acknowledge these, I should apologise in advance for anyone whom I have forgotten or neglected. Please contact me directly (josh@joshlacey.com) or via the publishers with any corrections or omissions, and they will be added to future editions.

Two biographical studies of Charles Miller have already been written, although both books feature his life only as one part of wider stories. Aidan Hamilton describes all the British players, managers and coaches who have had a vital (and unexpected) place in the history of Brazilian football (*An Entirely Different Game: The British Influence on Brazilian Football*, Aidan Hamilton, 1998). John Mills, the official historian of the Clube Atlético São Paulo, interweaves his biography with a full history of the club's first hundred years (*Charles William Miller 1894-1994 – Centenary Memoriam SPAC*, John R. Mills, 1994).

The following bibliographies are extremely useful: *Brazil in British and Irish Archives* by Oliver Marshall (2002) and *Brazil by British and Irish Authors* by Leslie Bethell (2003), both published by the Centre for Brazilian Studies in Oxford. Bethell gives full bibliographical details for many of the books that I have quoted, along with short biographies of the authors.

There are wonderful photos, accompanied by some useful text, in both *A presença britânica no Brasil*, published by Paubrasil (1987) and *Os Britânicos no Brasil/The British in Brazil*, the catalogue of an exhibition held at the Centro Brasileiro Britânico, São Paulo, in 2001.

English-speaking readers wishing to know more about Brazilian football should track down the following fascinating article and books: *Sport and Society: the case of Brazilian Futebol*, Robert M. Levine, Luso-Brazilian Review 17 (1980); *Passion of the People? Football in South American*, Tony Mason (1994); *Soccer Madness*, Janet Lever (1995); *The Beautiful Game*, Chris Taylor (1998); *Futebol: The Brazilian Way of Life*, Alex Bellos (2002). For up-to-date information, have a look at the excellent website run by Alex Bellos: http://www.futebolthebrazilianwayoflife.com/.

INTRODUCTION

AC Milan was formed by a gang of Englishmen who preferred their own spelling of the city's name, and Dynamo's original strip was donated by a Lancashire manufacturer, who copied the colours of his local team. Similar stories can be found in the histories of football teams throughout the world.

'There were tastes...' – Jan Morris, *Pax Britannica* (1968).

CHAPTER ONE

At the beginning of this chapter, as elsewhere in the text, I have allowed my imagination to add details that cannot be found in the sources. I have tried to confine myself to writing in the present tense for these more imaginative passages, while writing in the past tense whenever the material is based securely on written or verbal sources. I should also stress that, throughout the book, all the information that I have read, seen or heard has been chosen, shaped and interpreted by me.

I have not been able to establish any connection between Henry Fox and Daniel Fox beyond the coincidence of their surname. However, one friend of the family, now in her nineties, is convinced that the two were brothers. If so, Charles Miller was Daniel Fox's great-nephew.

A Bibliography of Brazilian Railway History by Paul E. Waters (1984) has most of the relevant material on the SPR. See also *Public Policy and Private Initiative: Railway Building in São Paulo 1860-1889*, Colin M. Lewis (1991) and *Britain and the Onset of Modernization in Brazil 1850-1914* by Richard Graham (1972). *A Very British Railway* by Paul Catchpole (2003) is a collection of photographs of the SPR, mostly from the 1920s.

'I well remember...' – Jacare Assu, *Brazilian Colonization from a British Point of View* (1873).

CHAPTER TWO

Information about the Millers can be found in the Glasgow Sheriff Court, the Glasgow University Library and the Watts Library in Greenock. I am indebted to Ada Mobbs and the residents of Fairlie, especially John Cunningham.

CHAPTER FOUR

'Southampton is a beautiful place' is adapted from W.H. Hudson's first view of the city in 1874 on his arrival from South America.

The Banister Court School magazines are now in the Local History Department of Southampton Library, along with the *Early History of Banister Court School* by Christopher Ellaby (undated). For Cheltenham College, see *Reminiscences of Cheltenham College* by an Old Cheltonian (1868) and *Then & Now: An Anniversary Celebration of Cheltenham College 1841-1991* by Tim Pearce (1991).

I found the following useful: *Our Public Schools*, Anonymous (1881); *Our Public Schools: Their Influence on English History*, J.G. Cotton Minchin (1901); *Memoirs of Archbishop Temple by Seven Friends*, E.G. Sandford (1906); *The Public Schools and the Empire*, Herbert Branston Gray (1913); *Character and Sportsmanship*, Sir Theodore Cook (1927); *Public Schools and British Opinion since 1860*, Edward C. Mack (1941); *Tom Brown's Universe*, John Honey (1979).

Tom Cullen has written biographies of Harold Davidson and J. Maundy Gregory, *The Prostitutes' Padre: The Story of the Notorious Rector of Stiffkey* (1975) and *Maundy Gregory, Purveyor of Honours* (1974).

'My father was one day...' – E.G. Sandford, *Memoirs of Archbishop Temple by Seven Friends* (1906).

CHAPTER FIVE

For the history of Southampton Football Club, see *Full Time at The Dell* by Dave Juson and David Bull (2001) and *Saints: A Complete Record of Southampton Football Club, 1885-1987* by Gary Chalk and Duncan Holley (1987). The minutes of the Hampshire FA, and other records, are held in the office of the Hampshire FA in Southampton.

For the Corinthians, see *Association Football and the Men Who Made It* by Alfred Gibson and William Pickford (1906); *Football* by G.O. Smith (in *Football*, edited by Montague Shearman, 1899); *Corinthians and Cricketers* by Edward Grayson (1955); *A History of the Corinthian Football Club* by F.N.S. Creek (1933); Ian Wilton's biography of C.B. Fry (2002) and Fry's own autobiography, *Life Worth Living* (1939). Wilton gives a much more balanced description of Fry than my brief mention, explaining his achievements and unpicking the fascinating contradictions in his character.

See also *Athleticism in the Victorian and Edwardian Public School*, J.A. Mangan (1981); *Land of Sport and Glory: Sport and British Society 1897-1910*, Derek Birley (1995); *The Games Ethic and Imperialism: Aspects of the Diffusion of an Ideal*, J.A. Mangan (1998).

For Henry Watmough, see *From China to Peru* by Ethel Vincent (1894).

CHAPTER SIX

The shipping records that show Charles Miller's passage from Britain to Brazil are in the Public Records Office in London. For detailed descriptions of the shipping lines, I recommend *MacQueen's Legacy: A History of the Royal Mail Line*, Stuart Nicol (2001); *South American Packets: the British Packet Service to Brazil, the River Plate, the West Coast (via the Straits of Magellan) and the Falkland Islands, 1808-80*, J.N.T. Howat (1984); *South Atlantic Seaway: An Illustrated History of the Passenger Lines and Liners from Europe to Brazil, Uruguay and Argentina*, N.R.P. Bonsor (1983). Contemporary descriptions of the voyage can be found in several of the books in Bethell's bibliography; *All Aboard* by W.H. Koebel (1923) and *A Winter Cruise in Summer Seas* by Charles C. Atchison (1891) are particularly good.

The translation from *O Imparcial* is Aidan Hamilton's. For the Johnstons, see *150 Years of Coffee*, Edmar Bacha and Robert Greenhill (1992).

CHAPTER EIGHT

For the Jesuits who visited Harrow, see *Visão do Jogo* by José Moraes dos Santos Neto (2002).

CHAPTER NINE

Ross G. Forman drew my attention to *The English in Brazil* by J.F.K. da Costa Rubim. The translation that I have quoted comes from his 'Harbouring Discontent: British imperialism through Brazilian eyes in the Christie Affair' in *An Age of Equipoise?* edited by Martin Hewitt (2000).

The Foreign Office files relating to Trindade are in the Public Records Office in London. The island is described in *The Cruise of the 'Alerte'* by E.F. Knight (1890) and *The Naval Officer, or Scenes and Adventures in the Life of Frank Mildmay* by Frederick Marryat (1829). *Real Soldiers of Fortune* by Richard Davis (1910) includes a chapter on Baron Harden-Hickey.

See also *Coffee and Society in São Paulo 1886-1934* by Thomas Holloway (1980); *Business Interest Groups in Nineteenth Century Brazil* by Eugene Ridings (1994).

'Delay in Brazil...' – Peter Fleming, *Brazilian Adventure* (1933).

CHAPTER TEN

The history of Mackenzie College is told in the memorial volume, *Mackenzie: 126 Years of Education* (1997) and *A Summer Journey to Brazil* by Alice R. Humphrey (1900). 'The greatest country in the whole of God's Universe...' is spoken by the American industrialist in Conrad's *Nostromo* (1904). 'When you get there you find that nothing is the same...' comes from *Brazilian Marriage* by George Royston (1936). The 'explicação de alguns termos' is taken from a Fluminense programme; the idiosyncratic spellings appear exactly as they do in the original text. Peter Chapman's autobiography is *The Goalkeeper's History of Britain* (1999).

For full details of the Liga Paulista, see *História do Foot-Ball em S. Paulo*, Antônio Figueieredo (1918); *História do Futebol no Brasil*, Thomaz Mazzoni (1950); *A História do Campeonato Paulista*, Valmir Storti & André Fontenelle (1997); *O Caminho da Bola*, Rubens Ribeiro (2000).

For Hy Brasil, see *Brazil and the Legendary Islands of the West Atlantic*, T.J. Westropp (1912); *Legendary Island of the Atlantic: A Study in Medieval Geography*, William H. Babcock (1922); *Phantom Islands of the Atlantic – the Legend of Seven Lands that Never Were*, Donald Johnson (1996); *Origins of Brazil: A Search for the Origins of the Name Brazil*, Angus Mitchell & Geraldo Cantario (2000).

CHAPTER ELEVEN

Antonio Casimiro da Costa's cup had an eventful life, being stolen from the clubhouse and disappearing for several years. Finally, it was retrieved from a pawn shop after an anonymous tip-off, then kept in a safe. In the 1980s, the cup was taken to SPAC's clubhouse in Santa Amaro, where it now sits safely and proudly in a cabinet above the door to the bar.

'Well, Grayton was a young chap...' comes from *Brazilian Marriage* by George Royston (1936). Documents detailing Charles Miller's work as a vice-consul are held in the Public Records Office in London. A CD of Antonietta Rudge playing Villa-Lobos, Beethoven, Chopin, etc., is available in the Grandes Pianistas Brasileiros series. Curiously, another famous musician of the period shared Antonietta's surname. However Olga and Antonietta Rudge were not related. Olga Rudge, a violinist, is now mostly remembered for her association with Ezra Pound.

CHAPTER TWELVE

The Great South Land, W.H. Koebel (1919). 'Autos over Rails: How US business Supplanted the British in Brazil, 1910-1928', Richard Downes in the *Journal of Latin American Studies* (vol. 24 part 3 October 1992). *British Pre-eminence in Brazil: Its Rise and Decline*, Alan K. Manchester (1972). *Britain and Latin America in the Nineteenth and Twentieth Centuries*, Rory Miller (1993).

CHAPTER THIRTEEN

'Ode to the Bourgeois' is a poem by Mario de Andrade, published in *Paulicéia Desvairada* (São Paulo Hallucinations). I have quoted the translation by John Milton, published in *Modern Poetry in Translation*, issue 6 (1994).

CHAPTER FOURTEEN

'I was stopped by a half-breed' is from *Brazilian Paradise* by Guy Walmisley-Dresser (1960). The Excursão Artística is described by David P. Appleby in *Heitor Villa-Lobos: A Life* (2002). Ernest Hambloch, *Here and There: A Medley of Memories* (1968). Charles Miller's description of his visit to Southampton is taken from an interview in the *Gazeta Esportiva*; the translation is by Aidan Hamilton, who tentatively identifies the two Southampton players as George Carter and Ralph Ruffell.

In Southampton, on the site of the old Hampshire CCC ground, there is now a block of flats called Charles Miller Court.

CHAPTER FIFTEEN

The documentary is 'Menotti del Picchia' in the *Grandes Escritores Brasileiros* series, produced by Zita Bressani for TV Cultura.

CHAPTER SIXTEEN

Stefan Zweig, *Brazil: Land of the Future* (1941).

CHAPTER SEVENTEEN

The bar in Salvador isn't the only one in Brazil with a connection to Charles Miller. Fifteen years ago, Barbara Siebert bought a door. A German living in São Paulo, she collects oddments: sculptures, mirrors, pots, chairs, bizarre machinery, industrial ephemera, photographs of forgotten people, all the bits and pieces of history that the city's forward-looking citizens leave in their wake. Having bought a neat old door from a dismantled office, she stored it in her back yard, hardly even bothering to read the logo engraved on the glass. Some time later, she and her husband decided to start a bar. Searching for a name, they remembered the door. It appealed to them. They built the door into the entrance of their new business, and christened the bar after the name on the glass: Miller Goddard & Cia Ltd.

A few days after the bar opened, a woman pushed open the door, and stood in the entrance, blinking, staring into the darkness. Barbara asked if she could help. Not really, said the woman. She just wanted to have a look around. Years ago, she had worked in her grandfather's travel agency, and opened that door ten times a day. Until then, Barbara and her husband had never even suspected that the door might have belonged to Charles Miller.

Miller Goddard & Cia Ltd is at Avenida Morumbi 8163, São Paulo (tel. 5535 5007).

PHOTOGRAPHIC ACKNOWLEDGEMENTS

Plates 1, 2, 17, 18, 20
From the collection of the Miller family, courtesy of Therezina Miller O'May Burt.

Plates 3, 4
From the collection of the Hampshire Football Association.

Plate 5
From J. & C. McCutcheon.

Plates 6, 7, 8, 12
From the collection of the Clube Atlético São Paulo.

Plates 9, 10
From the collection of D.T. Rowe, courtesy of Locomotives International.

Plate 11
From the collection of the Centro Pro Memoria Hans Nobiling.

Plates 13, 14, 15, 16
From the collection of the Centro Pro Memoria do Club Athletico Paulistano.

Plate 19
From the Casa de Menotti del Picchia in Itapira, Brazil.

If you are interested in purchasing other books published by Tempus, or in case you have difficulty finding any Tempus books in your local bookshop, you can also place orders directly through our website

www.tempus-publishing.com